Sex
Is the Least of It

Surrogate Partners
Discuss
Love, Life and Intimacy

By Tova Feder, Ph. D.

Note to the Reader

There is sexual and explicit content in this book and it is not suitable for minors.

Copyright 2014 – The Intimacy Press

ISBN-13: 978-0692288597
ISBN-10: 0692288597

Cover Design – Nikki Leigh

United States of America

Table of Contents

Dedication

May future generations of men and women
grow up in a sex-positive society
where they are nurtured as unique individuals,
their varied expressions of sexuality are
accepted and honored,
and they are encouraged to love with abandon.

"If sex and creativity are often seen by
dictators as subversive activities,
it's because they lead to the knowledge
that you own your own body
(and with it your own voice),
and that's the most
revolutionary insight of all."
Erica Jong, author

Foreword

Imagine a man or a woman who does not have access to a sexual partner, either because of being a late-life virgin, shyness, poor body image issues, lack of confidence in being a good lover, fear of being sexually dysfunctional, or embarrassed by a lack of experience in lovemaking. If these patterns are too strong, a psychotherapist may feel at a loss to help their client reach out to a potential partner.

What about the person with a disability, such as a severe brain injury, or spinal cord injury, or a person born with a developmental disability from birth or without full use of their body? According to the World Association for Sexual Health (WAS), all people have a human right to "sexual pleasure," "to emotional sexual expression," "to sexually associate freely," and "to establish responsible sexual associations" whether married or not. They declare that all persons also have "a right to sexual health care, which should be available for the prevention and treatment of all sexual concerns, problems and disorders." (Declaration of Universal Sexual Rights adopted during the General Assembly of the World Association for Sexual Health on August 26th, 1999, in Hong Kong.)

Dr. David Satcher, former Surgeon General of the United States, in his groundbreaking *Call to Action to Promote Sexual Health and Responsible Sexual Behavior* (2001) made a plea to combat the sexual ills of our society, which included recognizing problem areas such as sexual dysfunction and unhealthy sexual behavior and relationships. He called for a more mature and thoughtful discussion about sexuality across the life or ability spectrum. This book presents a comprehensive overview of surrogate partner therapy, a treatment modality for sexual health that has often been perceived as an immoral practice condemned by professional organizations. It is time that the stories of the many brave and committed practitioners be told and framed as truly promoting a path to sexual health and responsible sexual loving through sexual surrogacy.

In the early 1980s, a workshop was held for sex therapists from the Greater Philadelphia area. The program featured a sexual surrogate from New York City, who came and explained her work with clients and therapists. Sexual surrogacy was a subject that I, a sex therapist, had not heard about. The workshop turned out to be one of the most enlightening I had ever attended. The sexual surrogate asked if one of the attendees would be a client so she could demonstrate the "hands-on" part of her work. After she talked about the majority of her time with a client being spent on a socialization process, she gave us a demonstration of her work on teaching lovemaking skills, using sensate focus exercises. The person who volunteered to be a client and all those who watched the demonstration had a profound experience. We thought it would be advantageous for all sex therapists to have this experience.

After the workshop, many single clients who would have benefited from this type of surrogate partner therapy came to mind. Within a week, I called that surrogate about a particular client whose story sounded like a perfect match for this type of therapeutic intervention. He was a middle-aged man, so shy he had never dated, and was still a virgin. The client agreed to work with the surrogate. It was arranged for him to go to New York for a weekend intensive. The day after he returned from that intensive weekend experience, I could see that a transformation had taken place in four days. Before leaving New York, the surrogate told him that he was "truly a great lover." From then on, I was a convert to this type of intervention with appropriate clients.

The major question raised by both laypeople and professionals is how this form of therapy differs from ordinary prostitution. There is a dramatic difference, which will be highlighted in this book. Rather than speak to that significant difference here, I will let the reader make up his or her own mind after reading this work. On the following pages, you will read many stories of those who have gone into this work as trainer, therapist, or surrogate partner. You will read the wonderful stories of those who have trained and/or worked with surrogate partner therapy and the overwhelming effect it had on them personally and professionally.

You will also read the stories of those who became surrogate partners and the transformative effect this work had on their lives. These men and women tell about their upbringing, their surrogate partner work, their satisfaction in helping clients, and what their various experiences taught them about themselves and their understanding of the sexuality of their clients—their anxieties, fears, and hopes for meaningful sexual and emotional relationships. Reading each person's different story is an exciting adventure into this little known health-inducing practice. You may find that you will identify with some of the personal stories bringing about important reflections of your own life and story.

Finally, it is hoped that you will agree with many of us in the field that surrogate partner therapy is an important adjunct to sex therapy and that it is a special therapeutic modality that will not get lost in a society that is based on sex-negative attitudes and moral value systems that inhibit growth in sexually healthy relationships. As a sex therapist, I long for the day when our children can grow up in a sex-positive and sexually healthy environment that is based on authentic education to promote sexual health and responsible sexual behavior.

William R. Stayton, M.Div., Th.D., Ph.D.

Professor Emeritus / Scholar in Residence

Center for Human Sexuality Studies

Widener University, Chester, PA 19013

wmstayton@cs.com

December 2013

Introduction

"Often the hands will solve a mystery that the intellect has struggled with in vain." —*Carl G. Jung*

A Perspective of Surrogate Partner Therapy:

Interviews with 25 Current and Former Surrogate Partners

The concept of surrogate partners grew out of the work of Masters and Johnson in the mid-1960s. Their initial research centered on understanding and improving the sex lives of married couples. Eventually their work addressed the issue of helping un-partnered individuals treat their sexual dysfunction. As necessity is the mother of invention, they recruited an untrained group of women to aid these single individuals in resolving their sexual problems. Masters and Johnson created a mechanical approach to sexuality, devoid of emotional intimacy.

This book seeks to present the human face of a profession that has been shrouded in myths, misconceptions, and negative judgments. Rather than hearing the words of sexual robots, the participants reflect competence, intelligence (please see paragraph below), compassion, and wisdom. It is a profession that requires the ability to think and feel; to analyze and participate; to become emotionally involved yet maintain professional boundaries.

Over the past four decades, surrogate partner therapy has grown to combine social therapeutic modalities in addition to sexual therapeutic techniques. This book utilizes, in part, the approach of interviewing 25 current and former surrogate partners to examine, compare, and contrast their experiences. It seeks to present the skills of surrogates as opposed to the sexual sensationalism which clouds objective evaluation of the subject. In addition to the interviews there are several relevant articles, being used with permission, exploring the work of other surrogates.

Participants were chosen without regard to organizational affiliation, seniority in the field, or media prominence. Characteristics of interview participants are as follows:

- Range in age from 30 to 85

- Both male and female

- All are Caucasian

- All are heterosexual

- Represent American, Israeli, and Dutch nationalities

- 6 earned Ph.D. degrees

- 1 earned a D.H.S. degree

- 6 earned Master's degrees

- 7 earned Bachelor's degrees

A total of 22 of the 25 participants have college degrees, reflecting an impressive 88% of the interview population, a figure dramatically higher than the national average.

The purpose of the study this book is based on is threefold:

1. To present the degree of success of clients who worked with the interview participants as self-reported by clients and surrogates.

2. To describe the efficacy of surrogate partner therapy in resolving a client's problems, in some cases, more effectively than traditional verbal therapy.

3. To demonstrate how surrogacy has expanded its original mechanical model to become a behavioral modality, a tool for psychological reframing, and a therapeutic developmental method.

In addition, this book will detail the role and responsibilities of sex therapists who use the SPT (surrogate partner therapy) triadic model; specific training programs provided to train surrogates incorporating SARs (*Sexual Attitude Reassessment*); and a compilation of efficacy studies and related research documenting the effectiveness of surrogate partner therapy.

Practicing Surrogates

Larry Villarin, B.A.

Photo by Lisa Annette

"Love is always open arms. If you close your arms about love you will find that you are left holding only yourself."—Leo Buscaglia

Larry Villarin has studied human sexuality, psychology, and postural integration (the generic form of Rolfing), and has worked in anatomic pathology for almost thirty years. He has also been a drug and crisis counselor, EMT, and CPR instructor. Besides seeing surrogate clients, he is currently an artist residing in Long Beach, California. He trained as a surrogate at the International Professional Surrogates Association (IPSA) in Los Angeles.

Tova: How did you first hear about surrogacy?

Larry: I was training at the Los Angeles Free Clinic to be a sex counselor. During the training, they covered a lot of topics about human sexuality and we got into different modes of therapy. That's when I first learned of surrogacy.

Tova: What drew you into becoming a sex counselor?

Larry: Oh, just from being a sexual person. I was looking at the *LA Times* or the *LA Weekly* for volunteer opportunities. I've volunteered for most of my adult life. The LA Free Clinic announced it was looking for volunteers. I thought "Oh, this is perfect."

Tova: You learned about surrogacy while you were there?

Larry: Yes. A sex surrogate and a sex therapist gave a presentation. That's when I first learned about it. It was 1985.

Tova: Why did you feel surrogacy would be appropriate for you?

Larry: It made sense to me immediately. I'm a sexual person and I'm a natural teacher. And so it just felt right. I had been a drug counselor and a crisis counselor, so I knew how to help people. I knew how to listen. Growing up in school, I was always the one my friends came to when they felt bad because they could tell me anything. I'm a natural listener, so this was a great fit.

Tova: When you were training, did they tell you that there might not be too many opportunities for male surrogates?

Larry: No, they didn't tell me there were few opportunities and I didn't care. I had a job already, so making a lot of money, or even any money from surrogacy was not that important. I just wanted to do the work and help people.

Tova: What was most outstanding for you about your training?

Larry: Surprisingly, they taught no sexual techniques. We learned listening skills, how to touch, how to grow intimacy, how to evolve in an intimate relationship. I guess the most important element I learned would be how to slow down. I learned that you don't do two new things in one day. For instance, you don't touch and touch sexually. Also, we wouldn't get naked and touch on the same day. So it's one new thing at a time. That is still important to me to this day.

Tova: That's a wonderful lesson. So you take things step-by-step?

Larry: I like to build the intimacy and trust. Too often people just dive headlong into sex. On a first date, they're already having intercourse. That's the accepted way of doing things. I did it. It's exactly what a therapy client must *not* do! People think that's normal, but whether it's healthy is a different issue.

Tova: Why did the women that you work with seek out a male surrogate? What are the major reasons that they come to you?

Larry: They finally wanted to "do something about" whatever their problem was. They often had tried other avenues that just didn't work for them. Two major issues I see are late virginity and not being able to have orgasm with a partner. Clients have said, "You're my last resort," as far as losing their virginity. After all, they can't just meet some guy at the bar or walking his dog and start doing sex therapy! Also, they want to have what other women have: general sexual experience. I believe that some issues become more prominent for women around certain magical ages, like 30, or 40. They're 39 and they don't want to be a virgin when they're 40. Time passes and then they're 50.

Tova: They're landmarks in our lives.

Larry: And men are more apt to do something about a problem; men want to fix things. Women tend more to feelings so they'll hold on longer, whereas a man wants to get it done. Men don't like to hold onto feelings about something; they act on it and finish it. And you can see it in sex. Men are about resolution: coming, having orgasm, ejaculating. Women love to build the turn-on.

Tova: Why do you think you felt so comfortable with your body and your sexuality?

Larry: It was just something within me. It was innate. I really have no real analytical answer for that. I didn't necessarily have something happen early in my life that told me, "I'm a sexual person." I just knew it. When I was little, I would touch myself and tickle my skin lightly all over my arms and my belly and my chest. I discovered that when I was five or six. It felt so good. I think that helped me to be good at touching and to understand surrogate work right away, because I could do these light tickles intuitively. They were light touches to awaken the skin.

Tova: When and where did you get your initial training?

Larry: I was trained in 1988 in Los Angeles by the International Professional Surrogates Association. In those days they were training several couples at a time, so at the end of twelve weeks they'd have six or eight new surrogates. When I applied they didn't have any other applicants, so I waited and waited. One requirement was that applicants shall have been in therapy, so during that waiting time I began seeing a therapist. After a year, there still weren't other applicants so they decided for the first time to train someone alone. I had all these great teachers come in, and every week I had a new teacher, a new surrogate, or a new therapist. I had very special custom training.

Tova: What are the qualities that you possess that make you such a good surrogate?

Larry: I'm a sexual person, I like to help people and I'm a natural teacher. This leads to the making of a good surrogate partner. I'm a good listener. I accept people. Being raised codependent was big in that regard because I liked to rush in and help people. In fact, while I was a drug counselor, I was doing triage at rock concerts. Within a year, I realized the person I wanted to rescue was me, so I went into more therapeutic venues.

Tova: You used the term "codependent." Can you explain that?

Larry: Well, codependents like to take care of people. They just don't know how to take care of themselves. I was great at anticipating what others might want; that was my role. Roles are safe because they keep you from finding out who you really are or how you feel about something. The way I grew up, in a codependent household, you didn't really say what you wanted or what you needed because that was too revealing. You skirted the issues and learned to talk around it. I got used to that shorthand and to reading between the lines, so I knew what people were really saying. Codependents thrive in times of chaos because they're helpers. They're the ones who remain calm in turmoil.

It took me until I was a drug counselor to really know that I had feelings. Codependents don't have their own feelings because they fix other people's pain instead. When I trained to become a drug counselor at age 19, I found out that I had feelings. Alcoholics and drug abusers want to be numb to remove themselves from their bad feelings. At that time, I discovered I had feelings and it's taken the rest of my adult life to find out what those feelings are.

Tova: What were your two or three most memorable client experiences?

Larry: I was working with a thirty-five-year-old virginal client who was disabled at age sixteen. She was disfigured and she couldn't see very well. I would go to her house in the evening. She didn't want to alert the neighbors that she had what they would think was a boyfriend, so I didn't knock; I would just open the door and let myself in. It was the holiday season, so the tree was lit and the house lights were dimmed. And there she sat, beautiful, expectant, radiant, sitting on the side of the couch with her feet drawn up, and it was just a great scene. It was very romantic, very nice. And I saw that she had turned a corner in her life. She had never had a boyfriend or any intimacy—none of the stuff that most of us take for granted. We've all had boyfriends, girlfriends, or spouses. It was probably the first time in her life when she could claim some confidence in her own intimate affairs. I remember that whole night.

Tova: She was also claiming her femininity, something that I'm sure she experienced because of working with you.

Larry: Oh yes. It was beautiful. She was growing in her own ability and in her capacity to have intimacy, and for the first time in her life, a boyfriend. You know, a surrogate relationship is like a boyfriend or a girlfriend because it's a real relationship. It's intimate, and although it's contrived in a way, it's a genuine intimate relationship. And so I could see that this is the first time she'd ever had that. That's one memory that I'll never forget.

If you work long enough and you see enough clients, there are some quirky memories. I remember a woman who, when it was time to be naked for the first time, put a bed sheet over her head and disrobed underneath it. There was no hole cut in it; she was just standing under this bed sheet. I was naked and did my body image exercise in front of a mirror, but she would not, could not do it.

Tova: She stayed under her tent throughout your body image?

Larry: Eventually she lowered it and wrapped it around her, so it took a couple of weeks of sessions until she finally was naked. It was funny how she disrobed under the sheet and then wore it like a robe.

Tova: I'm sure your openness and patience in allowing her to move at her own pace encouraged her to finally be able to be naked.

Larry: As a surrogate, you have to let the client do that. During my internship and the first half dozen clients, I used to have my training manual at the ready. I knew that in session four we'd do this, and then next week we'd do that. But that's only if they're ready. Their hesitancy disrupted my sense of security. I learned to let them go at their own pace. It meant I had to throw away the schedule.

Tova: Anyone else who stands out?

Larry: Yes, there was a very interesting seventy-year-old woman who was grieving over her son's death. He had died of AIDS and now she was leaving her husband. Her life was just so sad and lonely. And for some brilliant but unknown reason, her therapist thought she might get something out of surrogate work. This woman was amazing. She had run away from home at age fourteen. She stole a lot of cash from her father's safe, jumped in a car heading to California and began her new life. She started working immediately because she was very smart; her I.Q. turned out to be 185. So she grew up, traveled the world, made a million dollars on her own, raised a family and had five master's degrees. And now her son's death tore her apart and her husband was of no help.

Her body was frozen from jaw to pelvis. And I do mean frozen. So we worked for several years just thawing her out, getting some expressive movement. She eventually had her first orgasm and felt love for the first time. It was interesting that she was still afraid of her demon of a father, who was long dead. In fact, she made up a new name when she got to California and never told me her real name in case her father's henchmen were still looking for her.

Tova: You were a change-agent for her. That was powerful in her life.

Larry: Yes, but at the same time I don't take advantage of or abuse that power. I feel that I need to take my ego out of it because it's about her, not me. It's always about the client. I don't get macho ego strokes from the experience; instead, I hide my light under a bushel. I don't claim, "I did that, I did this, I gave her an orgasm, blah-blah-blah." You can never give someone an orgasm anyway.

A footnote about acting ethically: I didn't know until much later that she was a millionaire. She would offer pricey gifts and cruises, and suites at five-star hotels, but I declined them. I also asked that she not put me in her will. I said, "No, no. Don't do that." She told me later she'd planned on it. But it didn't fit with my sense of ethics or propriety. I knew she loved me and that I could take great advantage of her, but it's not something I would do.

When therapy has finished, it's customary to not have contact with each other for six months so the client can integrate the learning and go out into the world. They have their dates, they enjoy sex. Well, one minute after midnight, after the six months had passed, she called me. She said she had been thinking about me the whole time, but she followed the rules. She was very obedient— she learned that from her father—to obey. She didn't know what she felt, but she would do anything you asked of her. Obedience was ingrained in her. I never got her to stop being obedient, but I think I helped her. I think she was able to shed the habit to some degree.

Tova: You said she left her husband, meaning that she was divorcing him?

Larry: Yes, she'd already moved out and his health was going downhill. In fact, he died during the course of therapy. And she felt absolutely nothing; no loss, nothing. That was how cold and bleak their marriage was. He died alone in that house.

Tova: Through your surrogate experiences, what did you learn about yourself?

Larry: That I'm not perfect and that I can't hide my mistakes. I learned that I'm not done learning. Someone once said, "We're never a finished product." I liked that and never forgot that. You're never a finished product unless you're an enlightened being. Other than that, surrogate work is Work with a capital W. For the most part, clients are not people I would meet in my personal life, so all my "normal" patterns of behavior will not work. What I mean is that she's not there for me, but I have to be there for her. From doing this work, I learned to throw away my timetable as far as growth. I have an ability to change and to grow very fast. I have insights and I can act on them. Surrogate work showed me that other people can't do that. I also learned that we all carry wounds from early in our life, and I found out what my wound was in my own therapy. I also learned that sex is not between the legs; that's gender. Sex is between the ears.

Contact information:

Email: larry@artlab.me

Adrienne Kirk, B.A. Psychology

Photo from istock

"Hands are the heart's landscape."

—Pope John Paul II

Tova: How did you first hear about surrogacy?

Adrienne: I had an undergraduate degree in psychology when I started doing some acting. I saw an ad for actors on the back page of an underground newspaper asking for volunteers to go to Nova University Medical School to serve as surrogate patients. I answered that ad and was a surrogate patient for third-year medical students doing gynecological exams.

Tova: What does it mean to be a surrogate patient?

Adrienne: I would go into an examination room, and there would be five students and a facilitator who was a doctor. He or she would go through the steps that the students needed to take to do a normal gynecological exam on me. Since I'd already had three children in teaching hospitals, I was quite comfortable doing that and it made me feel fulfilled that I could help teach them. I did that part-time for two years. And then I knew I wanted to get out there and do something. I didn't even know there was a field of surrogate partner therapy, but when I expressed interest in working in the field, a friend of mine introduced me to Dr. Marilyn Volker and she told me about the work of surrogate partners. I was fascinated and became very interested.

Tova: What were the early messages about sexuality that you received as you were growing up?

Adrienne: Basically, I didn't get any. I was just told by my single mother that sex was bad and not go near boys. Then I got pregnant at sixteen and was married, in that order, and had three children. My husband was the captain of the football team and he basically indoctrinated me into sex, and that was all I knew at that point.

Tova: So you became sexual with virtually no sex information.

Adrienne: Exactly.

Tova: What prompted you to become involved in surrogacy? Was it from your ability to give?

Adrienne: Yes, and to teach. My husband passed away in 1980, and after his death I had several different partners. I started noticing a pattern in which, years or months after I would break up with a partner, he'd either send me a message or call and say, "You were the best thing that ever happened to me; you helped me in so many ways." I never really understood what that meant, but I thought I had something to contribute.

Tova: When did you receive your training?

Adrienne: In 1999.

Tova: What was your previous profession?

Adrienne: I was in aviation. I was always in service-related fields and serving in some way.

Tova: In the home where you grew up, if there were no messages about sex, why do you think you felt so comfortable with your body and your sexuality? Where did that come from?

Adrienne: I've thought about that and I really don't know. I think it was just innate. I've never been able to explain it.

Tova: What kinds of clients have you worked with over the years?

Adrienne: Generally, I've worked with people who have had negative sexual experiences throughout their lives and they've come to a point where they realize they really need help but don't know where to turn. So they go to a sex therapist and the therapist refers them to me.

Tova: What physical conditions have you worked with?

Adrienne: I've worked with a quadriplegic and with men who had erectile dysfunction or premature ejaculation. I've treated men who had body dysmorphia, which is a distorted view of their bodies; they believe that they are too thin, too large, too small—the kinds of things that get into their psyches and they feel they're not good enough.

Tova: I'm inferring from this that some of them had issues about their penis size, their adequacy?

Sex Is the Least of It

Adrienne: In fact, for the majority of the men I have worked with who thought that they had a small penis, it turned out that it wasn't the case at all. They were measuring themselves against porn, which is very common. Watching porn is a significant factor for some men who have body dysmorphia issues. It's really very sad that many men view porn as sex education rather than as entertainment.

Tova: What qualities do you feel you have that make you such a good surrogate?

Adrienne: From what I've been told, I have a friendly face and a friendly, easily approachable demeanor. I can connect with all walks of life, be it a janitor or a CEO. I have empathy for every human being, no matter their walk of life. I think that's a big plus in this field, to be able to empathize with an individual and really put yourself in their position. I connect with people very easily and I really listen to them.

Tova: What are your most memorable client experiences?

Adrienne: The one that always comes to mind was a twenty-eight-year-old man who became a quadriplegic after an accident on the football field. He was sent to a nursing home by his caregiver and he became very frustrated there. Dr. Marilyn Volker was called in on the case to see if there was anything that could be done to alleviate his frustration. It turned out that primarily it was sexual frustration, because the limbic system takes over, even in quadriplegics, and they're able to have erections. Because of his condition, he couldn't even move his arm to touch himself. So he was lashing out, moving his body. He could move his shoulders and his head, and he had partial use of one of his arms; he would hit the nurses and he was really starting to get angry. Dr. Volker spoke to me about this young man and asked me if I would be willing to work with him in a step-by-step process. I went in and I met him, and gave him erotic massages. It got to a point where he was so happy that he looked forward to my visits. I saw him every other week for about a year. In time, he found another caretaker who got him in a big wheelchair and took him to the beach. He went to social events with other quads and was actually able to have a lot of fun. And then he got a prosthesis, which enabled him to touch himself.

Tova: So was he able to masturbate and ejaculate?

Adrienne: Yes, he was. When I was with him, he ejaculated two to three times within the hour. It was amazing.

Tova: So you must've had a great sense of fulfillment from working with that client.

Adrienne: Absolutely. I still think about him with fondness and it brings tears to my eyes.

Tova: Are there any other special client experiences?

Adrienne: The other one that was particularly memorable was a man who had been raised in a strict religious home and whose mother used to beat him for touching himself. And she would not allow him to be nude in front of her or anybody else. He never had a girlfriend, and one time his uncle actually hired a prostitute for him. When the prostitute came to his hotel, she was very cold and told him he needed to take a shower. He said that he had already taken one, and he had on aftershave and he was all primped up for her. She insisted that he go take a shower, and then he was not able to do anything after that. Later he joined the Merchant Marines so that he could detach himself from women. His mother passed away a few years later, and that's when he decided to seek treatment. He went to see a sex therapist and she referred him to me. At that point he was drinking and smoking; his hair was disheveled, and his fingernails were dirty. I saw him for the first time in the therapist's office and we had a little chat about grooming.

Adrienne: His therapist explained that he was not permitted to be under the influence of any alcohol and he couldn't smoke in my home. We had about six sessions. And when we came to the sensuous shower exercise, he had a breakthrough and started to cry. He was very afraid of the feelings that were coming up for him, feelings he had never experienced before. That was his moment, which he still talks about with Dr. Volker.

Tova: Do you have another client experience that stands out for you?

Adrienne: Yes, I do. There was a newspaper reporter who came to me, and he happened to be Jewish. Because Dade County, where I live, has a large Jewish population, it was not surprising that about 80% of my clients are Jewish. This reporter had never been married; he hadn't even had more than a first date because he was so fearful of having to be intimate with a woman. He didn't know if he had a normal-size penis; he didn't know if he had a nice body; and he didn't know if a woman would like him. He did finally go to see a sex therapist.

Tova: How old was he at that time?

Adrienne: He was thirty-five and he just wanted to have a fulfilling relationship with a woman. I saw him for about thirteen months and it took nine of those months for him to take his shirt off. That's how shy he was. But he did it, and when we got into nudity, he absolutely blossomed. To this day, he writes me thank you notes every few months, and this happened maybe ten years ago. Now he's married and has two children, and he's very happy.

Tova: You helped him change his life.

Adrienne: It's wonderful work. Now I'm working with a client who is a former surgeon in his seventies. He's Jewish and he's basically chosen the wrong women all his life—real emasculating types. He's a charming and wonderful man, and he's making great progress; I see no reason that he can't be successful. We're only in the beginning stages, but he's such a wonderful, sweet man. He was able to have erections on his own and could masturbate on his own. But when he's with a woman, he's an ultimate pleaser, and he does everything. About his previous relationship, he said,

"She'd just lie there." In other words, nothing was reciprocated to him at all. So he didn't even know what it would be like to have someone be intimate with him and touch him in a sexual way. Imagine that, at his age. Because he's such a pleaser, for him it's always been about the woman. And because he presents himself as such a pleaser, that's the kind of women he attracts.

Tova: So he's never had the experience of a woman expressing her desire or her affection.

Adrienne: That's right. It's always been about "What can you do for me?" It really turns my stomach.

Tova: When he's with a woman, is he able to have an erection and penetrate?

Adrienne: He loses the erection because his partner isn't reciprocating. She doesn't move, she doesn't hold him, she doesn't touch him. And he already had had her climax many times prior to that. The message was, "Well, I've got mine, and I'm happy, and that's all that needs to happen."

Tova: Anyone else that you would like to talk about?

Adrienne: I did have one more that illustrates a very rare situation in this profession. One client had gone through anger management and was supposedly okay. He'd of course been screened by the time he went to a psychologist and a sex therapist and was then referred to me. The screening process was usually very thorough, but this one slipped through the cracks. I had three sessions with him, and in the third session, he was on the massage table and started cursing about his ex-wife, saying, "That bitch, she deserves to be killed, and I swear to God I'm going to tear this house up." He was just so angry that I had to tell him to leave. He went back to the therapist and I refused to see him again, so she referred him out at that point. But that kind of experience is very unusual.

Tova: Is there another experience you wanted to share?

Adrienne: Yes. He was a doctor and he could only have sexual experiences through porn. He never sought out prostitutes and he never married, but he had a child from a previous affair. He sought therapy in his late forties, and during our session, everything was going fine. He was lying on the massage table, on his stomach, fully clothed. I was rubbing his back, and a startling memory arose from his subconscious about a time when he was seven years old and living in a brownstone in New York City. He would go to the basement to "play with the janitor." And he remembered at this particular moment, when I was touching his back, an incident when the janitor bent him over a table and masturbated on his back. He started sobbing uncontrollably; he then processed this experience with the sex therapist. We had therapy for about nine months, and then he was able to go out on his own. His whole objective was to be intimate with a woman, penetrate a woman, have an orgasm, bring a woman to orgasm, all without needing to have those porn visuals. And he accomplished that.

Tova: Through your surrogate experience, what did you learn about yourself?

Adrienne: The first thing I learned was that I was shy about nudity in front of other people. I remembered being in the eighth grade when I was in gym class, being nude in front of the other girls, and I was so embarrassed that I started to cry because I was flat chested and small. I realized that everybody goes through embarrassing experiences. And I learned through my surrogate training that I have feelings, and that my feelings are genuine and valid. So when I'm with a client, I show my feelings. It's a real relationship, albeit one that is time-limited.

Andrew Heartman, B.A. in Computer Science

Photo Courtesy of Andrew Heartman

"To remain intimate with textures of this present moment and feel everything completely, rather than wall yourself off from it, is a major step toward true spiritual practice in any moment."

—David Deida

Tova: As you were growing up sexually, what were the messages you heard in your home?

Andrew: My parents didn't speak negatively or positively about sex. And so there was no conversation about it. I had no clue; I didn't even have an orgasm until I was about twenty. I had heard other people talking about masturbation, but never knew anything about it. And so I didn't have an orgasm until I was in college; I was just kind of making out with a girlfriend and something happened, and I went, "Whoa!"

Tova: I'm interested in your thoughts about how surrogacy helps people and why do they need it? Why do people come to you?

Andrew: I heard a really great explanation from a well-known therapist about why it helps people. He says clients come to him, usually couples, who have problems with their sex life and want to talk about sex. He begins by asking them: "If you're watching TV, who has the remote control? If you go out to dinner, who decides where you should go? And if he wants Chinese and she wants Mexican, how do you work that out?" Sometimes the couples complain, saying, "We came here to talk about sex, and you want us to talk about communication and power, and all these other issues." And I agree with that approach, because there is so much that goes on both in and out of the bedroom that creates a foundation for how we interact with each other sexually. Even though a person may come to surrogate therapy for a sexual issue, there are always many other factors that need to be looked at and explored.

They may have unrealistic expectations about relationships; or they may have fear of intimacy or abandonment, or a fear of being vulnerable. Others have been hurt or abused, or have had other bad experiences that make them hesitant to enter into intimate personal relationships. And so they withdraw socially because they don't want to repeat them.

Tova: So very often, a sexual problem is not a sexual problem.

Andrew: Yes, exactly. I have gone through a change in the way that I view surrogate partner therapy (SPT). I originally thought that, if you compared surrogate partner therapy to any of the verbal therapies, what makes SPT different is that it's experiential. And that's really important, because there are certain things that you just can't learn by talking about them, or reading, or watching videos. I think everyone would agree that you can't learn to ride a bike by reading about it. Yet, when you look at the process of riding a bike, it's not just experiential. So I view "experiential" as the result of having an experience, and there is a benefit in that. But it won't necessarily transform your life.

I view surrogate partner therapy as a different class entirely. It is developmental therapy. Let me give you an example: I know how to juggle, and when I juggle now, I do it completely naturally. I might even be juggling right now while I'm talking to you and you wouldn't even know it. But when I first learned how to juggle, I had to break it down into small details and focus on each individual task. I had to pay close attention to how I held the ball in my hand, and what part of my arm moved as I threw it, and how high the ball went, and where it landed on my hand as I caught it. And I had to practice all of that repeatedly, until I got proficient. Then I duplicated that process with the other hand, until eventually, I could juggle from one hand to the other. So it was a different learning process and I made a lot of mistakes. It takes a lot of repetition, so it's something that requires both mental understanding and muscle learning. For me, developmental learning is made up of three components: repetition, experience, and a willingness to make mistakes. I view surrogate partner therapy as a way that people can develop the skills they need.

Tova: When people don't have an encouraging environment in which to feel at ease and to develop their skills, they'll never get past the point where things feel familiar and easy.

Andrew: Right. If there's someone sitting next to you saying, "You're not doing that right!" you'll probably freeze and feel uncomfortable. And that's going to interfere with your ability to gain a new skill.

Sex Is the Least of It

Tova: So, in a sense, if you're driving a car and the other person with you is supportive, you have someone who will provide encouragement and gentle guidance, as opposed to criticism. It's the same with surrogate partners.

Andrew: I think the word *supportive* is the key, because one of the most important qualities of a surrogate is to be accepting. For many clients, a learning process may feel embarrassing. And it's hard for them to face the awkwardness and discomfort of learning a new skill, because nobody likes to make mistakes. But in order to master one of these developmental skills, we need to accept that mistakes are part of it and take the risk. So the most important thing that surrogates can do is to create an environment of safety and acceptance. That allows the client to be willing to try and to make those mistakes, and to know that they are still whole, no matter what happens. I think the biggest fear we all have is: "If I show people who I really am, then they won't like me or they'll go away." Whereas, with support, we may feel: "If I can take the risks to show people who I really am, I may be very surprised by their reactions. They may like me even more."

Tova: Most people tend to think of surrogates as being female. What are some of the specific reasons that a woman might seek out a male surrogate?

Andrew: Just as with men, when a woman initially presents with a sexual issue, like the inability to have orgasms, or challenges with penetrative sex, or pain during intercourse, there's usually underlying emotional stuff going on, too.

Tova: Yes. I agree with that. I've heard that many men come to surrogacy with what I call the mechanical mindset: that is, if you fix my penis, then everything else will be wonderful, so just fix my parts. This means that the challenge for the female surrogate is to work with a male client to help him understand the need to cultivate emotional intimacy in order to resolve the physical concern. But I had envisioned that women came in with a different mindset.

Andrew: You mean a different mindset from fixing the parts?

Tova: Yes. More like, "I'm having trouble with relationships, with getting close to a man; or, I'm really uncomfortable with my sexuality." Do women have a greater recognition that it's not just a mechanical issue?

Andrew: Yes. Women generally have more self-awareness rather than focusing strictly on the mechanical aspects. Also, many women have been the victim of some kind of trauma or abuse, so those kinds of experiences undermine their ability to trust. That makes relearning the ability to trust an important part of the process between a female client and a male surrogate. What we do in SPT is create positive experiences to balance out the negatives so the client can see she has the potential to create healthy and meaningful relationships.

Tova: What prompted you to become a surrogate?

Andrew: When I was in my twenties, I had a good friend who was in the process of going through a divorce. She wanted to understand how she went from being an idealistic nineteen-year-old, expecting to be marrying for life, to being on the verge of divorce at twenty-four. Her idealism about marriage had been shattered. She was reading a lot of books about relationships and she asked me to read them, too, so that I could be her ally, and we would be able to discuss them together. And so I did and we read many books about relationships and intimacy. That's really what started me on this path of seeing relationships as a profound tool for personal growth and transformation. And it's probably what led me, years later, to take a workshop sponsored by the Human Awareness Institute (HAI), which offers workshops in love, intimacy, and sexuality. I took one of these workshops in December of 1999 and it completely transformed all of my relationships. Not just my relationships with a significant other, but my relationships with other men, with my family, and even with myself. It was in one of these workshops that a friend of mine told me she was planning on becoming a surrogate. I didn't know what that meant, but it always stayed in the back of my mind.

A few years later, I had gotten to know a woman who had been a victim of sexual abuse; she had been raped only a couple months before I met her. As we got to know each other and started becoming intimately involved, I learned that I needed to have great patience and compassion because of what had happened to her. I knew that if I pushed my own agenda, like wanting to get something from her, she would be resistant and neither of us would have a very happy or healthy relationship. So I just accepted her as she moved forward at her own pace. And there's another piece of that relationship that was very important to me. One night we went out to dinner with friends, and although I didn't know it at the time, during the dinner she started to get upset with me. Afterwards, when we went off by ourselves, she began to gently let me know that she was upset. I didn't get defensive but just listened; I encouraged her to express what she was feeling and she told me that she was angry with me. I didn't take it personally; I just wanted to support her in expressing herself. And that was truly significant for both of us. She learned that she could express whatever she was feeling and still be loved. And I learned that I had the capacity to be with someone, even if they're angry with me or saying things I don't want to hear. I got to experience that two people can be totally honest and still support each other.

Tova: How do you think the qualities that you cultivated in yourself have served you as a surrogate?

Andrew: The essence of the work is for someone to be willing to take the risk of showing a part of themselves that they judge or criticize. We are often taught to put our best foot forward, and many people feel that if they show who they are on the inside, there will be some kind of negative consequences. So what can happen is that if I'm feeling insecure and I pretend to act confident, there's disharmony between who I am on the inside and who I am on the outside. Surrogate partner therapy is really about helping clients to have an awareness of, a greater comfort with, and a greater ability to express who they are on the inside. And so for me, as a surrogate, I am able to allow a client to be herself, not just intellectually, but through experiences with me. It means clients can express those hidden parts of themselves and know that they're not going to be abandoned, judged, or criticized. With female clients especially, this is very important because they are socialized to not express anger. I have found that with my clients, there's always some component about being able to express anger or negative feelings. People often do not express anger well. It can be hurtful, full of rage, and demeaning. And we've all been hurt by inappropriate expressions of anger. So I show my clients how to express anger and how to handle it when anger is aimed at them.

Tova: I believe that what still lingers and has real dissonance for accomplished, successful women is the sense that they need to protect a man's ego. When it comes to sex, if a man doesn't have an erection or he has ejaculatory problems or other issues, a woman's energy shifts away from herself to supporting the man's ego, rather than retaining her own sense of self. It would be preferable for her to think, "Okay he's had this experience, and he's responsible for his sexuality just as I'm responsible for mine. We will navigate this situation together." Have you noticed this in your SPT work?

Andrew: Yes, what is beneath that shift in focus is taking care of the man to the exclusion of the woman's own experience. A lot of women tend to be people-pleasers. And if the man is happy and satisfied, they feel safer. That's why the sensate focus exercises that surrogates teach are so important. The essence of sensate focus is for a woman to develop a greater capacity to experience what she is feeling in the present moment as I am touching her. It's all about her, and not about me.

Tova: Would you describe sensate focus touching?

Andrew: Sensate focus is a touching exercise shared by two people. They touch each other at different times. There's an active role (the toucher, but note that I think initiation is a different action altogether and this confuses the issue) and there's a receptive role (the receiver). The active partner is touching the other person within prearranged boundaries, such as length of time and what part of the body is to be touched. The intention of this kind of touching is very important. I encourage my clients to pay attention to how it feels for them when they are touching me, as well as when I am touching them. They focus on how it feels: the sensations and the feelings. They are instructed not to pay attention to how the other person is responding to the touch; because if I share what I really like, then the client may adapt her touching to please me. Afterwards we talk about it, and I encourage my clients to talk about what they liked and what they didn't like. Some people view touching in terms of fairness. For example, I might say, "Well, I've been touching her for a long time now, so I think it's time for her to touch me." Or, "She's been touching me so much that I really should return the favor." This leads to a "touch-trading" mentality: if you do this for me, I'll do that for you. But if I'm touching for my own pleasure, if I'm doing what feels good to me, and I trust my partner to be touching for her own pleasure, then no indebtedness is created because the experience is mutually pleasurable in the moment.

Tova: That's one of the great existential paradoxes about sensate focus: the more you focus on yourself, the more your partner will experience because they are not burdened by reciprocity. If my partner is really trying to make me feel good, I can feel it. And that doesn't feel like pleasure; it feels like work. The problem is that in our society, we are told that if we're going to be a good lover, we must focus on our partner and on eliciting a particular response. Unfortunately, that's a setup that can create a host of problems. And that's the paradox: you're not going to focus on your partner, but you're there in a compassionate and loving way, so your partner will feel more comfortable and experience greater pleasure. This approach prompts you to look at yourself, your behavior, and what the act of giving really means.

Andrew: Yes, whenever the primary intention is to create a specific response from your partner, it creates pressure and actually makes it more difficult for sexuality to build naturally. If each person knows how to please themselves by interacting with the other person, then not only is there no performance anxiety, but there's also no resentment.

Tova: What have been some of your most memorable client experiences?

Andrew: With female clients, often there is some kind of body image issue involved because women are surrounded by perfect body-types on the covers of magazines. If they don't look like that image, they feel that there is something wrong with them; they feel bad and ashamed. So there comes a time in surrogate therapy, after many sessions of getting comfortable with touch, building trust, and a mutual relationship, when we start to do some body image work.

The intention of body image work is to look objectively at our own bodies. One way we do this is the mirror exercise, where we each stand in front of a full-length mirror and look at our bodies. As part of it, we may describe specific parts of our bodies, not just what they look like, but perhaps memories related to that. I worked with a client who became aware of her own vaginal scent when she was young, and she thought, "Oh, this must be bad or abnormal." From that time on, she always felt self-conscious because no one ever talked to her about it. In our body image session, she told me this story and how embarrassed she had become about her genitals.

At that point we had been seeing each other for a couple of months and we had a strong rapport. Because I knew she trusted me, I said, "May I smell you?" She knew I was asking to smell between her legs, the area about which she was most afraid of judgment. She looked at me with this horrified expression and said, "Why would you want to do that?" I said, "Because it's a natural part of you. There's nothing wrong with it and I want to appreciate and honor that part of your femininity."

I didn't have a shirt on and I noticed that I had a little bit of underarm odor, so I took advantage of that fact to make a point, "Oh, no, I forgot to wear deodorant this morning. I'm noticing some underarm odor. You must think that's really repulsive." But she said, "No, of course not. Why would I think that? It's just a natural body odor." Later in that session, she agreed to let me smell her and she saw that I wasn't repulsed and didn't run away. Two things were going on: First she took the risk of exposing herself in a way she felt she would be judged and then saw the actual opposite results. Second, I created an example that made obvious the double standard in body odors.

Tova: You gave her permission by acknowledging your own body odor to accept her own odors.

Andrew: Right and that's called normalizing. I could have said to her "I'm sure you smell fine," "It's a natural smell," and so on over and over, but that wouldn't have had the same effect as creating a situation that gives her the *direct experience* of that.

Tova: What have you learned about yourself through your surrogate experiences?

Andrew: I found out that I have the capacity to see a lot of good in people. One of the primary reasons people become engaged in surrogate partner therapy is because the relationships they've created in the past have not worked well. So if people have ingrained habits of how they interact in relationships, then these habits come out in SPT. A client reproduces their relational behaviors with the surrogate, and that's great. Because it gives us the opportunity to look at unconscious relationship habits and become more aware of them. Becoming more conscious of what's going on will allow the client to make other, better choices. And that's empowering because it gives a client the ability to consciously create healthier relationships, rather than behave in a habitual, maladaptive way. In this process, resistance and anger can come up, and it may be directed at me as the surrogate. When it does, I remember that they're just responding in ways that they have learned over time. It's all just a cry for love.

Contact information:

Email: andrew@surrogatepartner.us

Website: www.surrogatepartner.us

Jennifer Gedrick, Associate's Degree

Photo courtesy of Jennifer Gedrick

"Without the body, the wisdom of the larger self cannot be known."

—John Conger

Ms. Gedrick has an Associate's degree in educational consulting. Like many members of her family, she has an entrepreneurial spirit and has been self-employed for most of her working life. Her background includes professional experience in education consulting, conflict resolution, mediation and negotiation, real estate appraisal, property management, life insurance, Web design, cosmetic medical tattooing, and even a twelve-year vocation as a UPS driver!

Tova: How did you first hear about surrogacy?

Jennifer: I found out about sexual surrogates while researching terms on the Internet, such as "sex coach" and "sex educator," which led me to the associated topic of surrogacy. My interest in researching sex education was born out of my rebellion against societal sexual repression, as well as my interest in pursuing a career helping myself and others with sexual dysfunction. I was increasingly frustrated with the ethics of allowing people to watch excessively violent movies, while censoring the beauty and raw eroticism of films portraying explicit sexual acts that were not deemed tame enough for mature audiences. This made sexual surrogacy a perfect platform for me to find social catharsis.

Sex Is the Least of It

Tova: When you came across the term "sex surrogacy," did that resonate with you?

Jennifer: From there, some things popped up alluding to "sex coach," and then once I found that, it led to sex surrogacy. Then I became fascinated because, I felt a lot more at home with that concept. It seemed to fit what I wanted to do and who I was.

Tova: Growing up, what were the messages about sexuality in your household?

Jennifer: I have a really nice story about that, and I have my mother and father to thank for it. I was the youngest of four siblings and was raised in a family where sexuality was not repressed or shameful. It wasn't so much that my mother and father were condoning our sexual expression, but they never hindered or shamed it either. I remember coming home in the first grade and asking my mother what the word masturbation meant. She calmly asked me where I heard the word, and I told her that a classmate of mine used it in a conversation. My mother simply responded by telling me that masturbation is something that a person does to give themselves pleasure over their genitals, and then she asked me if I masturbated. I shyly said "yes," and the message she gave me was that masturbation was a wonderful and private moment to have to myself.

Tova: You were approximately how old then?

Jennifer: I was about six. There was no shame, or no guilt, or any drama in it. Truth be told, I started masturbating as far back as I can remember, which is at age two in my crib. I remember that, because I used to watch through the crack in my door for when my mother was going to look in and pick me up out of my crib or come and wake me up from my nap; I always made sure, at that age, that I was done masturbating so that she wouldn't see me doing that. It was a private moment, but it's not that I thought she would shame me. I just didn't want her to see me doing it.

Tova: Children can be uncanny.

Jennifer: Yes.

Tova: At two years of age, are children pre-verbal, or starting to become verbal?

Jennifer: I had some verbalization at that age, I know that. The child development courses I took state that children are pre-verbal at age two. And in classes I took at the Institute for Advanced Study of Human Sexuality, we studied child sexuality, sexology, and the sociology of human sexuality from birth to old age.

Tova: You were sexual at an extremely young age.

Jennifer: I was. I don't know how I found myself, maybe just accidentally, but I did find it. I went with a feeling. I was arranging all sorts of interludes with other kids in my neighborhood who were my age and never got involved with older or younger kids. I stayed within my own peer group and played with boys and girls. I started orchestrating those events when I was probably about nine, ten, or eleven. My compatriots, if you want to call them that, were involved. Everyone was willing; it didn't involve a twisting of an arm. If I had sensed any of that, I would've backed off. It stopped after that.

Tova: You mentioned that you became involved with surrogacy out of an interest in helping people with sexual dysfunction, and you referred to helping yourself, too. Did I hear that correctly?

Jennifer: I had suffered a breast augmentation gone wrong. This surgery left me with total desensitization of my nipple areas, a highly prized erogenous zone that was now gone, and left me at a loss for how to tap into much of my bodily sexual arousal response.

Tova: How did you adapt?

Jennifer: I adapted by trying to learn about sexuality and taking courses at the Institute for Advanced Study of Human Sexuality. I earned two certifications: one in Clinical Sexology and another in Sex Education. I took as many sex education classes as I could and I volunteered for the San Francisco Sex Information Hotline, which was another way that I augmented my education. I also took a Conflict Resolution, Mediation, and Negotiation course at Sonoma State University to help me understand better how to talk about things in a calm way and negotiate my way around a delicate conversation.

Tova: What did you do to transition away from an erotic pathway you had known for so many years, that worked so dependably?

Jennifer: First I went to see a sex therapist, but that wasn't very much help. What I realized was that I needed to find a way to help myself through more experiential relearning. I was fortunate to have a boyfriend during that time who was highly experimental, and although he wasn't into tantra, *per se*, he was willing to practice lots of sensate body touch. I told him that I needed certain tactile stimulation and to just explore each other's bodies, so I was very fortunate to have him be a part of that and to experiment with me. During that short six-month period of time, I became convinced that perhaps experiential relearning of how to body map was a way to go for me to adapt, rather than through psychotherapy.

Tova: Some things you learn by doing, rather than by talking.

Jennifer: Yes, I'm a big believer of that.

Tova: So you were able to create a new design for yourself that has worked to your satisfaction orgasmically.

Jennifer: Yes, I was. Today they call it orgasmic meditation, but I didn't know that at the time. It was a form of focusing just on bodily awareness and finding partners who I loved and had

25

reverence for, and who loved and had reverence for me, and who wanted to practice what is now called "slow sex." Slow sex is just the slowing down of the whole process of sex. I didn't know that's what it was called, but what I was asking for from my partners was to segue into sex very slowly, and not rush my body into having to give a command performance for a response. I needed to relearn how to have a response, something I was able to do quickly when I had nipple sensation; but having lost that, I needed to find a new way to communicate to my partners about how and what I needed to become aroused.

Tova: Do you think having that kind of actual experience yourself helped make surrogacy resonate for you?

Jennifer: Absolutely. My experience convinced me that if I can make it back from something like this, which I considered a disability, something so devastating that I wasn't able to talk to anybody about it because I didn't feel that anyone would take it seriously; it convinced me that I needed to translate for other people that same cognitive process that had worked for me, because it might work for them, too.

Tova: Where did your surrogate training take place?

Jennifer: You have to keep in mind that, at the time, when I initially sought out training, there weren't many organizations around doing this work. Eventually I happened to find the International Professional Surrogates Association. I applied to the organization and took the training in San Diego. It was either a seven-day or a ten-day training course. But it was new and very different for me. It was for training with only two, four, or six individuals. One of these students didn't have their partner accompanying them, so the senior trainer partnered with a student she knew. It was a traumatic experience, not because of the content I was learning, but because of the way the class was led. Because the trainer was partnering with someone she already knew, it affected her ability to be objective during the training. That meant there wasn't any room for the opinions of the rest of us. I was much more traumatized by the way I felt I was treated than by anything I learned during the training.

Tova: Did you learn about Masters and Johnson and other areas of sexology from this training?

Jennifer: Yes, it augmented what I had learned. But most of what I knew, I learned at the Institute for Advanced Study of Human Sexuality, which was a much more in-depth, immersive-type education. I still have all of the DVDs to look back on. It was great, great education.

Tova: What qualities do you think make you a good surrogate?

Jennifer: That would go back to the question that you asked "Through your surrogate experience, what did you learn about yourself?" I would say I've had confirmation about my reservoir of compassion, empathy, and acceptance for the people who see me, and the healing work that we do together. I am happy to know that my intuitive nature has become one of my best personal attributes because I didn't know that until I became a surrogate. It started to emerge as I was beginning to do the work; it was consistent and I felt good about this. If I'm having a very bad day and I'm being particularly hard on myself, I ask myself, "Jennifer, who are you at your core? Who were you when you were a child, before life started progressing from preteen to adulthood? Who were you then?" And then I remember who I was, and that's the intuitive compassion and empathetic person in me, and so I go back to that core all the time.

What I love about this work the most is the challenge of navigating the sticky and awkward moments in life with people. I like diffusing situations in a compassionate way, and that ability translated into my surrogate work. I like helping myself and helping people around me to discover all these little mini-epiphanies about our truer selves. I think a lot of people might not know themselves very well, and it takes teamwork, when someone's going through a particularly hard time, to pinpoint those epiphanies and those truisms about ourselves. If you're in a safe place, you can reveal what's really true about yourself, even if you don't think it's the best aspect of yourself.

Tova: You feel that you have the ability to empathize with people; to teach and to allow people to be patient and work at their own pace.

Jennifer: That's correct. I feel that sometimes I can see the agenda behind the mask and I'm able to gently call that out and bring it out.

Tova: What does the word *mask* mean in this context?

Jennifer: It means that the false self is in front of the true self; the false self is representing the true self that's hiding behind it. I'm able to call out the true self in a way that doesn't offend the false self. We often put on our game face and we don't even know we're doing it, because we wear it so often. So every once in a while, I'm able to see through a person's façade and coax the truer self to come out. I do this by asking the client, "Would it be true to say that maybe it could be construed this way, and not the way that you're experiencing it now?" Sometimes they pause and think about it, and it helps them progress just a little more.

Tova: What are your three most memorable experiences with clients?

Jennifer: My first clients came from Dr. Bernie Zilbergeld, whom I met when I trained with another surrogate, Vivian Resnick. I sought her out and asked her to train me. She met with me probably six times, and I needed her to help me get my foot in the stirrup, so to speak.

Tova: I want to add that the late Dr. Bernard Zilbergeld was one of the foremost sex therapists in the country and the author of *The New Male Sexuality*.

Jennifer: That's correct. I met with him and we had quite an interesting meeting. He was a gregarious man and kind of hard to deal with at first. That's not a put-down; it was just his style.

Sex Is the Least of It

We had to find a balance in how we communicated without misunderstanding each other. Assertiveness between us mixed like oil and water, so it took a while to sort out. But he sent three people to me who I worked with, out of six who I can recall were standouts. My first client was a late male virgin at the age of thirty-eight, and I was thirty-three at the time. He was extremely shy, extremely held in. When I first met him, he reminded me of a geeky Matt Damon. He wore glasses, a plaid shirt, and jeans. When he came in, his hands were sweating profusely and he asked to use the bathroom. In the back pocket of his jeans, I could see that he had a bottle of what I later learned was Maalox. He was very nervous, and the sweetest person I would ever meet in all the work I did. We worked together in Sausalito, a town in Northern California, at my dad's apartment. My dad was very supportive of what I did and he allowed me to use his apartment during the day when he wasn't there. It was beautiful apartment overlooking the Bay.

So with this client, we worked on his advancement beyond his late male virginity. He was one of the three clients with whom I ever had sexual intercourse. What was very touching about this particular man was that he often had been locked in a closet by his very stern mother. And whenever he wrote about his desires in the journal I asked him to keep, he wrote in such microscopic handwriting that I needed to use a magnifying glass to read it. I asked him why he wrote so small, and he said, "Because I don't want my mother to see what I'm writing." He was terrified that she would invade his privacy. Or that she would take away privileges that he had, because he was still living with his mother.

Tova: Did he hold a job?

Jennifer: No. He had an Asperger's-type personality, so he was socially inept. This was not of his own choosing; but I think because he was so stunted, either through trauma or the nature of his intellect, he was just born that way. I worked with him, and he actually would be nauseated when he came in, so sometimes he would get sick before we'd do any work. He'd go into the bathroom and vomit, and then we'd sit on the couch. For months we sat on the couch just talking, and then eventually holding hands.

Then I educated him about the foot baths and hand-washing ceremony, asking him for permission and getting it, educating him about giving and receiving, and talking about his desires, even if they were nonsexual. We worked on his asserting himself, and, eventually, he allowed me to give him a hand washing in the sink; and it was really touching, because he'd never had his hands touched by a woman and washed, and it was very erotic for him. He started crying when we were working in the kitchen washing his hands, and all I could do was just hold him while he was crying. It was very touching and I was crying, too.

We eventually progressed to the foot bath, and that was very hard for him: just to take off his socks and his shoes, and just beginning to take his clothes off. I worked with him for about eight months before we finally were able to undress in bed. The first time with clothes on, he ejaculated in his pants just from lying on the bed together. I didn't even touch him. We kept moving through that over the weeks, and eventually he took his clothes off. We did achieve penetration, but he was never able to really hold "quiet containment" inside me for longer than about twenty seconds.

Tova: How would you define *quiet containment*?

Jennifer: It is having a penis contained inside the vagina without any thrusting or orgasm. He was very sweet, and by the time I had known him in that way, I felt very connected to him and so compassionate towards him. He'll always stand out as the sweetest, most wonderful person I ever had the honor to work with.

Tova: Is there anyone else who comes to mind?

Jennifer: Yes. The second one I call "the breast man." He, too, was referred to me by Bernie Zilbergeld. We had only two visits. He was referred to me because he was socially inept in navigating social situations, especially pertaining to dating women. He had a history of being impatient, and his tonal range with women was not good. The first time he came in to visit me in Sausalito, he sat on my couch and we conducted the "get to know you" interview; and when I concluded the interview, he looked at me in disbelief and said, "Is that it?" And I said, "That's it." I said, "I'll go ahead and talk to Bernie, and let him know what transpired today. We'll arrange for you to come back next week, or whenever you're able."

He shook his head and said, "No, no, no, no, no. I was told that I would get to see your breasts." I told him, "This is just the first introductory interview. When we meet again, we can work on more prescribed exercises. I'll confer with Dr. Zilbergeld to discuss what he feels the next step should be and he will confer with you. Then we'll work together in our triadic relationship to make that happen." Then, still sitting on the couch, he pounded his fist on his knee and said, "No I want to see your breasts. I was told I would get to see your breasts. Quite frankly, I think this whole interview has been a big tease." Then he said, "I want my money back. I don't think I should have to pay for a tease when I came for something more." I reminded him that one of the reasons that he was there was to work on his social ineptitude with women, and that this was part of it. I explained that we were practicing in real time, and that his approach would probably not be the way to make a demand of a woman that he was dating if she didn't deliver what he expected. He got even more irritated with that and he raised his voice. I concluded the visit and said, "We'll both talk to Bernie about this and see if he wants us meet another time."

Tova: You mentioned previously that you had a second meeting.

Jennifer: We had one more meeting and it was brief. He apologized and we talked, and he said at the end of the meeting that he didn't think that we were going to make a good match, and that he would get back to Bernie and figure out what his next move would be. From what I understood from Bernie, they continued his therapy sessions, and Bernie attempted to match him with other surrogates. Bernie would continue to see him, but it wouldn't be with me as the surrogate. I don't know what happened to him, but he was really funny. I was at least pleased that he was able to apologize. It was good that he could see that much about the situation. So those were the two most memorable clients. I have lots of others, but they were the two most memorable.

Tova: Would you talk about your boundaries?

Jennifer: I realized early on, after I had intercourse with maybe three clients, this was not how I wanted to express myself as a sexual surrogate. I briefly talked to the president of IPSA about it and she told me the bad news was I would never work as a surrogate if I was not willing to engage in intercourse, and that she definitely could not certify me if I chose not to go down that path, and we left it at that. I told her that I would pursue the work while still honoring my own boundaries, and that's what I did. It didn't turn out to be difficult at all. I chose to interact with a couple of therapists, primarily Bernie Zilbergeld. Then I took a leap of faith and decided that I wasn't going to network with other therapists unless the client insisted on having me network with his therapist. So I went on my own, kind of as a maverick, and I did just fine. I continued to take personal growth classes, and while I wouldn't say that I count myself as a sex therapist or a licensed psychologist, I made sure that everyone who called me knew that I wasn't either, and I highly encouraged them to see a therapist while they were seeing me and involve them as they wished. But most of them did not wish to see a therapist because it was yet one more turnstile they had to go through. So I worked with them and honored my own boundaries. I was very straightforward right out of the gate. I helped them understand the particulars of how I work and they accepted those terms. Some people really enjoyed that, while other people felt limited; and if they couldn't work with me because they needed more, then I always referred them to other surrogates.

Tova: Does that mean you don't work with virgins?

Jennifer: Not necessarily, because if a virgin needed to work around issues of masturbation, bodily acceptance, or dating, just social skills, that certainly is something I could help them with.

Tova: Is there anything you want to add?

Jennifer: Yes. There was this one sweet thing I wanted to say about how my mother and father were when I was younger. As I said, there was no shame, no guilt, no drama that time when my mother talked to me about masturbation. When I was three years old, my father happened upon me masturbating on the family room couch, and he calmly told me, "Not there, sweet pea, but in your room is fine." And I'll never forget that because he never overreacted; he was very casual and he kept walking down the hallway, and that was it.

Tova: It sounds like that was a very special experience.

Jennifer: And the other time, when I was fourteen and really concerned because I hadn't started menstruating, I kept asking my mom, "When am I going to menstruate?" I was in ninth grade when I finally had my first menstruation. I called my mother from school, and she came to pick me up. She got me into the car and said, "I'm so happy for you. Where would you like to go to celebrate? I want to take you someplace." So I said, "I want to go to Baskin Robins." She took me there and got me a banana split sundae, and we ate it together. And that evening, she made sure that all my siblings had dinner before she, my father, and I did. She waited until then to say, "Don, I just want to tell you that our little girl has become a woman today." I wasn't embarrassed at all. I just sat there and ate my dinner, and my dad looked at me, smiled, and said, "That's really great, Jennifer." So I just ate my dinner, and my mom told my dad about our ice cream sundae, and that was pretty much it.

Tova: It sounds like your mom and your dad created a ritual rite of passage for you with the things that they did.

Jennifer: Oh yes.

Tova: That's wonderful and most unusual.

Jennifer: It was very sweet. Growing up, I was never embarrassed by my mother or my father in any of that, or about them coming to my school. I wasn't like a lot of kids who wanted their parents out of the picture; I was always proud of my mom and dad.

Contact information:

Email: sexualhealthsolutions@gmail.com

Websites: www.sexadvicenow.com and www.SexualHealthSolutions.net

Phone: 707-889-3889

Justyn Caise, Master's in Mental Health Counseling

Photo from istock

"Every blade of grass had its angel that bends over and whispers 'grow! grow!'" —The Talmud

Tova: How did you first hear about surrogacy?

Justyn: I heard about it in graduate school, when I was taking a class in human sexuality taught by Dr. Marilyn Volker. In the class, the subject of surrogacy came up and I found myself intrigued. At that time, I was in my mid-thirties and my awareness of my sexuality came from life experience. As Dr. Volker was describing the sensate focus exercises, I realized that I'd actually done just about all those exercises with my first girlfriend.

Tova: You were already involved in exploring touch in a deeper way.

Justyn: My girlfriend and I began touching each other using the sensate focus approach, light and very slow. We did the hand caress, face caress, and sensual shower. I was in graduate school for psychotherapy, and I felt the whole point of my life was to help people. I thought this could be another approach to help people at their most vulnerable. I then became motivated to take the surrogate training and learned a lot about the finer details of human sexuality. Just as important, I learned to look beyond the physical appearance of a woman. I'd say that was the most critical part of my training, being able to go deeper and connect with a woman on a more profound level. It was one of the central experiences that I gained during my surrogate training.

Tova: I imagine that also opened doors for you, to be able to heal clients whom you might not have been attracted to initially; but over time, I bet they became more attractive to you.

Justyn: I became attracted to their humanity, and there's something appealing about everyone.

Tova: Why do you think that you felt so comfortable with your body and your sexuality? Where did that come from?

Justyn: I think it just evolved over time. I couldn't point to any one experience. It was just an unfolding of years and having a few relationships of my own. It became a manifestation of my personal growth. It became abundantly clear that what other people thought about me was completely unimportant to my happiness and how I felt about myself. Because everybody can have an opinion, and sometimes I might listen to it, but otherwise I'm pretty likely to discount it.

Tova: What are the qualities that you possess—empathy, listening ability, creating rapport, or any number of other qualities that made you such a good surrogate?

Justyn: Well, I could say that all the qualities you mentioned are qualities necessary for a counselor too; and I think by the time I became a surrogate in my thirties, I had a lot of life experience behind me. Also I had grown a lot as a person, and I was able to express those traits that I found fundamental for connecting with people. I've always been a teacher, and it seems like I'm always teaching somebody something, whether it's tennis, chess, or you name it. I seem to have a natural ability for that. And I'm an easy-going guy. I don't have an agenda or an angle; I just want to do right by people, and if I can be a part of somebody's personal, spiritual, or sexual growth, that's an incredible experience, and I feel honored to be along for the ride.

Tova: Would you share with me some of your more memorable client experiences?

Justyn: I've had some experiences with clients that were pretty amazing. I was working with a fifty-five-year-old virgin who was a child psychologist and a large woman. She had never held hands with a man, never hugged or kissed anybody. She hadn't had any physical contact with anyone. On our third session, I acted on my intuition and I asked her if she would like a hug. And she said yes. I was taller, so I wrapped my arms around her from the top and she wrapped her arms around my waist and rested her head on my shoulder. As she gave me a really strong hug, I became aware of my shoulder getting wet. I just held the hug for a few minutes, and she finally pulled away and I saw the tears in her eyes and rolling down her face. She said, "I've missed so much." For me, it was very rewarding to be there for her when she had that experience. She had friends in the community who were very supportive, and she talked to them on a daily basis. She prepared herself for a sexual experience to the point where she used dilators to prepare herself for intercourse. She was very smart and I think she appreciated the fact that I was mature and experienced. She breezed through the whole process.

Another experience I had was with a woman in her early thirties who had experienced incest by her brother and uncle. She had done a lot of work with her therapist, a lot of hard work. She was sexually experienced, but she only had sex when she was high or drunk. She just couldn't have sex any other way. I worked with Dr. David Johnson on that case.

Tova: He was a therapist?

Justyn: Yes, I worked with him. In the therapist's office, this client was pleasant, but just very wary. I could tell she wanted to take this slowly. She was working through her issues, and I said, "Don't worry, we'll take it really slow." We did the sensate focus exercises very gradually, at her pace. She got to a point where she trusted me and that helped her advance rapidly, which I took as an example of my ability to make people feel safe. She was able to let go and open up, and I was pleasantly surprised. I thought it would be a really tough experience, but it wasn't at all.

Tova: She was overcoming so much pain, such a traumatic childhood.

Justyn: Yeah and she shared a lot with me too. She had created a journal that she wanted to make into a book. It was the most amazing journal I've ever seen; she had cut out pictures from magazines, and it was incredibly expressive and creative. She shared that with me and spoke about her abuse, and how she moved past it to a large extent.

Tova: Any other experiences come to mind that particularly stand out?

Justyn: In my first case, I worked with a woman who was very well educated; I believe she had a master's degree. She was forty-five and a mid-life virgin. I think she had heard of surrogate therapy through her therapist, or maybe it was in a magazine, and she brought it to her therapist and said, "What do you think about this?" It was decided that she was an appropriate candidate for SPT; she had spoken to her therapist about her shame about not being experienced at the age of forty-five, of not knowing how to kiss somebody and not knowing what it feels like. She really needed this experience. It turned out that the surrogate therapy really worked well for her and she was very enthusiastic.

But when we reached the point of genital touching, she just had a huge meltdown. She was able to keep it from me that day, but she saw her sex therapist and they discussed it. I was a little surprised, because I had spoken to her therapist and said, "Well, we did this and everything seems okay." Then the therapist called me back and said things weren't okay. That ended up being a very important aspect of my client's sexual growth. Because from that experience, she learned that even though we were discussing it the whole time, if she was feeling uncomfortable, it was okay to say "let's back off" or "let's try something else." She learned to give herself permission to be more straightforward in expressing her comfort level and her feelings.

We were able to reconnect in a couple days and she asked if it was okay for us to keep our clothes on. I said, "What do you think about us just going outside and taking a walk?" Once we were outside, I asked, "Would you like to hold my hand?" That was the first time she'd ever walked around holding anybody's hand in public. So we just did simple activities like that, and then she asked if we could resume kissing, which allowed us to connect on a deeper level. And we actually had a very positive outcome.

Tova: Through your surrogate experience, what did you learn about yourself?

Justyn: I have to go back to the ability to go deeper with a person, to connect with their heart, their soul. And maybe on another level, I perhaps increased my ability to nurture and empathize.

Tova: How about going deeper within yourself?

Justyn: I would say that I was already doing that independently of surrogacy, because I started to get connected with spirit in my thirties. My surrogate work was just one of the many things that I was doing at the time that just sort of deepened my experience of life and broadened my horizons.

Tova: And when you say spirit, what are you speaking of? Do you mean meditation or a particular church or tantra?

Justyn: It falls under the broad category of spirituality, but I definitely had immersed myself in spiritual experience, whether it was through Native American studies, sweat lodges, or where I am now, which is Buddhist or Eastern philosophy. So for me, the search for truth is a journey that will continue until the day that I die. And I think spirit is within us and around us all the time, so I was eliminating fear-based ego-generated thought forms that interfere with connection to spirit. Whether that's in meditation or yoga, that's where I found myself and still find myself now.

Tova: You are single, correct? Has your being a surrogate had an impact on your personal life?

Justyn: Only in one situation. It was just coincidence that when I was doing surrogate therapy intensives, I wasn't dating anybody. But subsequently, I met a woman and was dating her, and I got a call from a therapist who said she might have a case for me. I spoke to my then-girlfriend and said, "This is what I used to do, but it wasn't something I was planning to do for the rest of my life." So I discussed it with her and she wasn't comfortable with it, and I decided to retire. But my girlfriend came to accept that what I did had value and that I was helping people.

Tova: Many women have intimacy issues or sexual problems, such as problems of arousal or orgasm. I would think that there would be a significant need for male surrogates.

Sex Is the Least of It

Justyn: It seems that men know about surrogate work, and women don't come forward, or else they don't know it's an option. And there's a tremendous need; I've heard that as many as 40% of all women have never experienced an orgasm. That's staggering. So many women are just not in touch with their sexuality, which could present opportunities for trained male surrogates.

Tova: I always say we've made one big leap for mankind on the moon, but we've yet to experience one huge erotic explosion for womankind in the bedroom.

Contact information:

Email: besafemv@gmail.com

Mare Simone

Photo courtesy of Mare Simone

"The human body is not an instrument to be used, but a realm of one's being to be experienced, explored, enriched and, thereby, educated."—Thomas Hanna

Radio Talk Show Host Mare Simone is a Certified Tantra Educator and Certified Surrogate Partner, a profession she began exploring in the mid-1980s following a yearlong teacher-training and initiation in Tantra Kriya Yoga. Mare trained and worked directly with Dr. Michael Perry, MFCC, and is a featured surrogate in his educational video, "Sexual Secrets—A Surrogate's Guide to Great Sex." She has appeared on HBO's "Real Sex," as well as The Playboy Channel, E!, British ITV, Check It Out—with Host Steve Brulé, and in the popular Tantra.com video "Ancient Secrets, For Modern Lovers." She appeared on "Strange-Sex" on the Discovery, TLC—The Learning Channel as "The Bedroom Coach." Mare leads seminars and maintains an ongoing private practice with clients across the globe. She continues to co-facilitate seminars and work privately with students as an Advanced Certified Tantric Educator.

Sex Is the Least of It

Tova: How did you first hear about surrogacy?

Mare: I became interested in surrogacy via a classified ad in *LA Weekly*. A Los Angeles sex therapist was offering a surrogate training course because he needed trained surrogates to work with some of his patients. I answered the ad and became a trainee.

Tova: What do you think contributed to your feeling so comfortable with your body and your sexuality? Where do you think that came from?

Mare: It wasn't an easy place for me to arrive at. Although I've always been very sensual, I had a lot of religious barriers to overcome. But deep in my heart I felt I really honored the power of sexuality as being a very sacred and spiritual experience. For me it was natural, and I gravitated in that direction, although it took some time to really claim my power.

Tova: What was that journey like for you?

Mare: I was a very promiscuous young woman in my teens and twenties. For me, sexuality was about self-discovery, so I didn't feel many restrictions or boundaries. I was pretty open until I had a few challenging, somewhat damaging, incidents on my journey. They turned me towards looking at sexuality as something that needed to be healed and taught in a way that others would honor it. I was raped at the age of seventeen, and again at twenty-one; these were two totally different experiences. Each one was a crucial lesson for me that moved me in the direction of being a sexual advocate and healer. Those lessons were eventually insightful, but also very difficult in the years that directly followed. They put a damper on my passion and my expression, and on my freedom in terms of expressing my sexuality openly. And so I had to relearn, with a new structure, how to relate to my own sexuality and how to relate to others. I started to withdraw socially and became more guarded and self-protective. I wanted to seek a deeper meaning in sex, and to find men who also wanted to experience that.

Tova: What was your initial reaction to the idea of surrogacy?

Mare: I was eager to do this work. I felt that I would gain a lot of value and a deeper understanding of my own sexuality by working as a surrogate. I took it on as 'on-the-job training,' where I could learn a great deal more and learn a trade where I could help others who also had experienced sexual emotional damage in their lives. I was already studying Tantra, an Eastern spiritual philosophy. I was in a certification program for Tantra Kria Yoga and was very attracted to the spiritual side of sexuality, as well as the psychological and emotional aspects of it. Together they dovetailed nicely for me.

Tova: Approximately what year were you trained?

Mare: I believe it was 1986. I got divorced in '86 and had been married to a man with whom I didn't have a very happy sex life. After our divorce, one of his parting gifts to me was paying to send me to surrogate school so I could do the training and have a career.

Tova: Was that a startling gift?

Mare: I knew he wanted to provide for me in a way in which I could take care of myself. At first, he paid for my schooling to become an esthetician. I went to beauty school and learned a lot about skin and body care. But I found out quickly that it didn't really challenge me the way I wanted to be challenged, so I went back to him and told him I wanted to take a different kind of training. He agreed, with no questions asked. I felt the surrogate training was a gift and an opportunity for me to advance my knowledge. I secretly hoped I could help him sexually, but that never occurred.

Tova: What are the two or three most memorable client experiences?

Mare: One that stands out for me because of the progress that we made was when I worked with an elderly man who had prostate cancer. He was in his mid-seventies and I was curious to see what we could accomplish together. He had gone through radiation treatment, so his prostate had been severely damaged. And he wasn't capable of getting an erection or feeling much sensation in his genitals. We did a tremendous amount of work together that helped him to regain his sensations. And after a while, he actually started getting erections again. He was very happy about it, especially at that age. I think that a lot of his success was a result of the fact that we were able to establish a real heart connection, a depth of intimacy where he felt he could communicate and express his feelings, his despair, and all the other emotions that were trapped inside of him. In our work together, he blossomed quite beautifully.

Tova: I think that people don't often understand that the rapport in the relationship between a surrogate and the client is really one of the most significant aspects of the whole process.

Mare: Absolutely. It's a very deep personal bonding experience that provides the foundation for real emotional vulnerability and openness. And in this case, this was difficult for my client to do. It was something he had never done with the people in his life. I still remember seeing him so happy with his successful erection, jumping up and down like a little boy, and of course his erection was bouncing freely in the open air. He was just elated that he was able to feel that much again. We're still very close to this day. I feel like he's one of my great success stories because neither of us knew what we were going to be able to accomplish, and it was such a tremendous breakthrough.

Tova: What other memorable clients do you recall?

Mare: I've worked a lot with couples; I'm thinking about one particular couple where I helped the woman to communicate more openly with her partner to be able to freely express her desires, her dislikes, and her needs. She learned to share things what were really pleasing, and sometimes discovered, for the first time, what was truly pleasurable for her. She learned what was arousing for her and explored wonderful new sensations. I taught her partner that women become aroused differently than men do, and I'd demonstrate for him massage strokes so he knew how to please her. I just saw that couple a few weeks ago and they still speak very glowingly about what a breakthrough they had with me and the time that we worked together.

Tova: I think that it's very common that women have a difficult time developing their sexual voice and really asking for what they want. What are your words of wisdom for women who are struggling with acknowledging their own sexuality and are unsure about how to communicate that to a partner?

Mare: I feel that women really need to know their own bodies so that they can help their partners learn about their bodies, too. You know, men want to win. They want to be a good provider on every level, including sex. But when a man is with a woman who doesn't know her body, he doesn't know what to do. Often they'll do what worked for a former partner; but because women are all so different, men are startled and confused when the same things don't work for their current partner. Men are very vulnerable when it comes to sex, so they may feel like failures. I was also very challenged with being able to teach men what I liked because, until I took some time to discover myself, I was really hoping the man would know, and that he would show me things that I didn't know. It was only when I worked with another woman who taught me about my body that I became aware that I had been trying too hard. That was a great "Ah-ha!" for me. Then I started to realize there was a more subtle realm of sensations that were very satisfying and on a much deeper level. So I would educate women to learn what pleases them, and especially to slow down enough to really listen to their bodies. It's important to not apply so much outward stimulation, but instead to seek a connection with your partner. There's a sensual feeling that's already there; it just needs to have the blinders removed to unveil the real sensuality, the subtle but powerful feelings that a woman can have that are different from men's.

Tova: We know that men are very goal-oriented, and many men consider intercourse and orgasm to be truly the climax of the sexual act. And women experience the sexual act as a sensual journey, which is a very different paradigm.

Mare: Exactly. An intimate journey that involves the feeling of being loved and cherished, adored and honored, these are the sorts of things that make a woman blossom. Women tend to be more emotional. So acknowledging her whole being—her heart, her mind, her intelligence—those are the things that make her feel like she's being loved on a whole body, mind, and soul level. It could be anything from having a wonderful feast, a deep conversation, and lots of luxurious massage and caressing. The way that a woman blossoms sexually is when she's touched from the extremities of her body, then towards her mid-section, rather than lunging right for her erogenous zones.

Tova: How might a man help himself transition from what the Eastern philosophers call "ordinary sex," which is to say "penis and vagina" sex, to a more sensually, spiritually approach?

Mare: A man needs to learn how to get in touch with his own erotic sensations in a full-bodied way that isn't goal-oriented to discover how to expand his erogenous zones. I think a sensual massage is a wonderful way for a man to awaken his erotic, sensual nature and to explore new experiences like a prostate massage. It can help him awaken his secret chambers in an area that I refer to as the male G-spot, which is located just beneath the prostate. This is a highly erotic area for many men that allows them to feel super turned on without feeling that urge to climax. Through prostate massage, a man's erotic sensations can radiate to other erogenous zones, and his arousal is not just limited to his penis. This erotic energy can easily move up and down his spine, which helps him transcend the immediate need to ejaculate. Instead, it feels more like waves in the sea, ebbing, flowing, and spreading throughout his whole body.

Tova: What impact has surrogacy had on you as a sexual woman?

Mare: I'm really comfortable in my body and very capable of communicating what I like. I was not always like that, so I feel that my surrogate training has helped me enormously in that regard, to be able to share with my partner what I like in a way that helps him to hear me. And it's taught me to feel the level of comfort that can help others who are struggling, or who've had sexual traumas, to help them overcome their past. And help them discover that they can make new choices and create a new future that doesn't have to be haunted by the memories of the past.

I feel like I've made a 180-degree shift in my whole experience in relation to my body. I think a big part of why I'm doing this work is that I feel there are so many people who have suffered some kind of sexual violation and have shame imprinted on them. That shame goes so deep; so when they're able to open their bodies to a partner, it is life-changing.

I've been there, and felt the depths of my own despair; I've done a lot of emotional processing to break through old hurts and to open myself to my own sexual pleasure. Because of my own experience, I feel that growth is not always just about going to a therapist and talking about a problem that will create a breakthrough. Talking is not always enough. That's why I feel surrogacy is so crucial for our sexual development in therapeutic models.

I went to therapists for years, and talked and talked about my sexual fears; but I didn't have any hands-on practice except when I was with my partner. I found that when I was with him, I was still going into a place of numbness or freezing up, and recalling memories that hindered my sensations. I just didn't know how to deal with it and it was a huge source of frustration for both of us. It was a long road for me to finally feel safe and not worry that if I revealed a part of my personal history, it would create a rift in the relationship that we couldn't resolve.

Tova: How are you different now as a surrogate than you might have been earlier? What more do you bring into your work today?

Sex Is the Least of It

Mare: I have a lot more experience and certainly a great deal more comfort in this work than I did when I first got started. Now I can relate. I tend to attract people who have had some sort of sexual trauma because I'm very open about my own experiences. That's really important because there are so few people who really are open about these things. When someone is experiencing trauma in their life, they're much more comfortable with somebody who says "I've been there, too; I can understand what you're feeling. This is what I did to shed that feeling of being trapped. These are the steps I took, and I'm here to hold your hand and help you go through your process." I can provide more support, more hand holding, and closer, one-on-one intimate coaching. So I feel that I can embrace other people and help them create a new reality outside of their limited fear box.

I'm working with one client now who was sexually violated from the time he was very young, and it has traumatized him tremendously. His whole association with intimacy has meant pain. But what I'm experiencing with him now is a vibrant man who is eager to love, and eager to heal and break through, so that he can really have a deeply loving relationship. He is also very spiritual and loves to go into nature, where he experiences an ecstatic awareness of spirit and body.

Tova: So often, clients gain not only social confidence, sexual confidence, and comfort. They also become more open to that spiritual side of themselves. And they come out with a really holistic experience, not just one that's focused on sex, but much broader, wider, and deeper than that. I think it's something the general public doesn't really understand.

Mare: I think you're right about that, and that surrogacy is a unique formula for each person. You take what you've learned in the surrogate training that was created by pioneering sex researchers Masters and Johnson, and you infuse it with your own experiences, your own wisdom and awareness. There's so much pressure that men experience, and that's why there is so much performance anxiety. Just that term, "performance anxiety," establishes the idea that sex is a performance and that they are responsible for being a good lover in order to maintain their masculine image. What's beautiful about real intimacy with a partner you trust is that it's okay to stumble and to be innocent. When you're really authentic, it's a gift to be able to say to a partner "I'd really like to know what pleases you. I don't know how to touch you where you would like to be touched. Would you be willing to show me?" The added bonus gives a woman a feeling of confidence that this man cares about you enough to ask and be open enough to learn. You've created a deeper connection every time you speak from the heart.

I'm really grateful for this opportunity to share with you and the readers of this book why the role of the surrogate is so incredibly important. I hope people will realize that there is a need to learn, and to take time to ask their partners a lot of questions and listen carefully to what their partners say. Because I know the first time I was asked, "How do you like to be touched?" it was such a joy for me to be able to actually verbalize it to somebody who cared and wanted to touch me in a way that would please me. So I wish that more people would understand that surrogacy isn't just for sexually wounded people, but that it's for all people who would like to expand and explore their vibrant sexuality.

Contact information:

Email: TantraMare@gmail.com

Website: www.MareSimone.com

Sandi Sain, B.S. in Psychology & Human Sexuality

Photo by Eric Williams

"The way you make love is the way God will be with you." —Rumi, The Book of Love

Before training to become a surrogate partner, Sandi Sain was a vice president of a Fortune Top Ten company in New York City. It all began when she read a magazine article about sex surrogacy, then watched a TV sit-com with a character who had trained to be a sex surrogate. She told her then-husband that she wanted to try it, and when he encouraged her, she sought training. In 1982, after attending a six-week workshop in Manhattan by a Masters and Johnson-trained instructor, Sandy began working part-time as a surrogate while still in the corporate world. She has a B.S. from Empire State University in Psychology & Human Sexuality.

Tova: What prompted you to become involved in surrogacy?

Sandi: At first, my husband thought it was sexually motivated because I had a strong libido. But I knew many people had issues regarding sexuality and intimacy. And I thought I might be able to help them.

Tova: Why do you think that you felt so comfortable with your body and with your sexuality?

Sandi: I didn't have a problem with my body, which wasn't perfect. I've always been curvy, and I accepted it. After I left the South and moved to Hawaii, I went to work at the Playboy Club. At that time I was still a virgin and didn't know much about sex. When I did become sexually active, I liked it a lot and started studying it by reading *The Joy of Sex,* which was the only book out on the topic at the time. From then on, I continued to be an avid student of sex and sexuality. This probably was another reason surrogacy was such a natural fit for me. It's become a lifelong quest and I believe, for me, more of a calling than a decision. It has enabled me to make a positive impact on people's lives, not just with their sexuality. This is what continues to keep me involved and sustains my love of the work.

Tova: What messages did you receive about sexuality as you were growing up in the South?

Sandi: Well, they were a little bit convoluted. I was raised in the uptight Bible-belt South. When I started menstruation, my mother was very open about it and educated me on sex, pregnancy, and birth control. But other messages about sex were kind of nasty, such as homosexuals were disgusting, your body was dirty, and so on. Eventually, when I was seventeen, I ran away from home.

Tova: So you had a lot of early training to work through.

Sandi: I don't recall ever having to "work through" any emotional stuff about sex. I believed that, and the reason I remained a virgin until I was almost nineteen, was that I was sure that when I became sexually active, I would really like it and thought I might become very promiscuous. So I wanted to make sure I was out of my mother's home so she couldn't judge me. And that was what happened, I became rather promiscuous.

Tova: When you moved around to study, was it so you could learn from various surrogate teachers or was it to study with tantric teachers?

Sandi: I moved around to work with different sexuality teachers. I trained with the Body Electric school and Tantra masters, so I've branched out in many directions rather than taking a single path.

Tova: Where else did you study?

Sandi: I studied with Dr. Marty Klein, a nationally recognized sex therapist at the Institute for Advanced Study of Human Sexuality in San Francisco, and also with David Deida. These teachers taught different types of sexuality. I also studied Tantra with Charles and Carolyn Muir.

Tova: What are the qualities that make you such a good surrogate?

Sandi: When I was working in sales, they told me during a sales training course that "You have something we could never teach, and that is your ability to bond with people." But I think my most significant attribute as a surrogate is that I am completely accepting. I don't ever judge, regardless of a client's eccentricities, fetishes, or emotional issues. I'm open-minded and accepting of what they bring to the process. I've also put myself in the trenches of life experience and learned all these different things. There isn't much I haven't personally seen, heard, or done. And with a lot of it, it hasn't only been for my personal interest and discovery. Much of my personal learning has been about asking myself, "How I can I use this in my work? How can I teach this? How can I share this and help people?"

Tova: What are your most memorable client experiences?

Sandi: One of my favorites was working with a late-life virgin. He was forty-two when he came to see me. And his dream was to have a marriage like his parents; to get married and have an incredible relationship. I worked with him for many months to prepare him. At first he couldn't even be touched. He was afraid of women or anything to do with sex. He wasn't raised to think this way. It came from his own, personal interpretation of the world. I learned that nothing really bad had happened to him to make him feel this way. It was his fearful interpretation of life and relationships that had developed over time.

As we worked together, we went on "field-trip" dates together, as surrogates do with clients. We needed to go step by step; he had to become comfortable with being touched. I realized that he needed to learn how to dance to navigate the dating scene so I suggested dance lessons. We covered basics, such as how to talk to women on the phone. He'd call me and we'd have conversations, and then afterwards, I would call him back so we could critique the conversation. We did this with all his communications with women, including emails.

The reason we went through every step of dating is because he had missed this experience during adolescence, that time of budding sexuality and social development. After our work together, he started dating and had wonderful experiences, and is now blissfully married. He invited me and my husband to his wedding and it was very exciting.

Tova: Was there another memorable client experience?

Sandi: My second favorite experience involved my longest-term client. He lived in Florida and had seen different psychiatrists and psychotherapists who referred him to me, and when his job relocated to Georgia, therapists there also referred him to me. He had many issues to work through and we worked together for three and a half years. We'd take two steps forward and three back. It was grueling and painful for both of us. But as you know, in doing surrogacy work, genuine feelings develop between the client and the surrogate. It took some time for him to develop a sense of trust in me. In time, we were able to create a strong rapport; and ultimately, he was able to apply the skills he had learned to the dating world and create a healthy relationship with a girlfriend, who moved in with him and they're planning to marry.

Tova: Can you address the bond that develops between a surrogate and the client? There are many misconceptions about surrogacy, as some feel that it is predominantly a sexual process. But we know that a significant role of the surrogate is to develop a safe environment where the client can relax and feel unconditionally accepted.

Sandi: Yes, there's a trust bond; that's the biggest part of it. The first thing that comes up with clients is, "How many sessions will I need?" I tell them that I don't know, because it depends on how he progresses. Together we will make progress if we each do our part. I give homework, which I call "home-fun." I give clients things to do on their own, which could be as simple as making eye contact with a woman. The relationship between us becomes one of good close friends. When the process works well, romantic feelings develop between the client and the surrogate. As the surrogate, I am the guide and the teacher, but this a collaborative process. But the relationship is the biggest part. There is nothing but love there, and that means everything.

Many clients had said to me, "I have never felt as loved as I did when I worked with you, not even from my parents. You always gave one hundred percent and made me feel like I was the only person in the world who mattered."

Tova: Any other client experiences that you want to relate?

Sandi: Yes. I had a lovely gentleman who was married for thirty-two years. They had not had sex in ten years, so he began to have affairs. And, as a result of his guilt, he lost his ability to have erections; and then, once he did, he couldn't maintain them. I worked with him for about a year and eventually it was determined that he had a defective valve in his penis, so he got an implant. It was a terrifying experience for him, but it was something he needed to do to feel like a man. We worked together once he got his penile implant, and afterwards, he was able to become sexually active again. I had already taught him how to make love to a woman without using a penis, and explained that in Tantra, the penis is the least important part of sexuality, and that intercourse is the smallest part of sex, especially for women. People incorrectly believe that sex is a genital friction-focused activity because that's the only kind of sex we know. After this client got well and recovered, he and his wife decided that since she wasn't willing to have sex, they should divorce and move on. And he became a randy-dandy, dating lots of different women. He's now happily remarried and having a wonderful time. He calls periodically to tell me how happy he is and that I changed his life.

Tova: Do you have any particular kind of specialization in your work?

Sandi: One of the things I specialize in is working with men who are re-entering the dating world. I focus primarily on men between the ages of thirty-five and sixty-five. At that age, men often experience life transitions in which they don't know what to do, or else they believe that they've lost their ability to function as a man. In these situations, they tell their therapists, "I don't know what I'm going to do. I'm going to date, but I haven't had sex in a few years and I'm nervous about it." So the therapists refer these men to me and I help restore their confidence and their self-esteem, and teach them to love themselves. Because, relationships don't end in a day; it takes many years for them to break down. And usually when that happens, there is a lot of pain, as well as beliefs that are created that don't benefit these men. So we work together to create new belief systems and implement them, especially love and self-forgiveness. It helps to give them credit for what they have done instead of what they haven't done. And often we haven't even touched, aside from a hug when they arrive.

Tova: Through your surrogate experience, what did you learn about yourself?

Sandi: I learned everything that happens to me, personally, provides information for my work. My first husband was Catholic, and he had major sexual hang-ups. I was able to take that experience and use it in my work. He developed a porn addiction, and I was able to take that and help people with a similar problem. Having had cancer, I've been through lots of changes in my body and my abilities, and that's made me even more compassionate and empathetic towards my clients.

Tova: Is there anything you'd like to add that I haven't asked you about?

Sandi: People don't realize that surrogacy involves a long process: that it's a relationship, and that often, intimate contact is a minor part of the work. Sex is just the catalyst for them to get help. I believe that when people seek out a surrogate, it's not that we are their last resort. They're often in so much pain, we're their *only* resort.

Contact information:

Email: sandi@goddesshq.com

Website: www.goddesshq.com

Phone: (678) 886-7887

Shai Rotem, B.A. in Psychology

Photo © Shai Rotem

"The hunger for love is much more difficult to remove than the hunger for bread."

— *Mother Teresa*

Shai Rotem has an extensive background in psychology and surrogate partner therapy, as a surrogate trainer and mentor. He studied psychology at the Ben-Gurion University, also graduated as an Energy Healer in the Reidman College Tel-Aviv. He has worked with groups and individuals in the Ilanit Adult Rehabilitation Center in Israel, and has worked with kids with autism in Los Angeles. He has been a certified surrogate partner since 1997 and a surrogate trainer since 2000. He gives lectures and presentations about Surrogate Partner Therapy and healthy sexuality on a regular basis in graduate schools and clinics in California. He is the founder of the Center for Professional Clinical Surrogate Therapy in Los Angeles, California.

Tova: Shai, what were some of the messages about sexuality from your childhood?

Shai: Sexuality was always there, and sexual energy was very high between my parents. In my extended family, there was a lot of embarrassment and repressed emotions. Sex and sexuality were important but hidden under the surface. As a child I knew that the adults were trying to hide something from the kids, which made me more curious.

Tova: Tell me more about the sexual repression.

Shai: My mom was more emotional than my dad, who was very emotionally repressed. He belongs to the old generation of men who thought that expression of emotions and feelings meant weakness. I was aware something was going on under the surface that the kids were not supposed know. Around the time I hit puberty, I could not go to my dad to ask questions about sex because he was so embarrassed. My dad said when I turned eighteen, he would tell me everything. He did give me one educational book when I was around the age of eleven. I thought the book was geared for younger kids, because my understanding of sex was deeper than what was in the book. My mom never talked with us about sex. When I found a condom, she was so embarrassed when I asked her, "What is this?" I knew the answer, but she was not able to talk with me about it.

Tova: How do you think you got from that to a greater openness about sexuality?

Shai: Feeling that the adults were trying to hide something generated my curiosity, so when I was in the sixth grade, at around the age of eleven, I became aware of my erections. I had a lot of sexual energy and I didn't know what to do with it. My sexuality was repressed. I was really very innocent; I never even masturbated. Then, when I was sixteen, I had my first real girlfriend and my first sexual experience. We both were excited about it, so we explored various sexual activities. And then, a year later, I started masturbating.

Tova: So that was your first introduction to sex.

Shai: Yes, I found that sexuality was an amazing experience. I really liked the human connection, the cuddling and spooning; it was not just about sexual intercourse for me. I liked the whole thing, the shared intimacy, and the connection and the sexual exploration of two people. It felt very safe for me. I enjoyed cuddling and falling asleep together with my girlfriend. So then I started my sexual exploration and had many relationships.

Tova: What do you think contributed to your feeling so open about your body and your sexuality?

Shai: A major contribution was that my first girlfriend was madly in love with me, with my body and with my body odor, which was a great start. When I pursued surrogate partner therapy training in 1997, I wasn't fully accepting of my body, but I had a lot of diverse experiences with women. I had many experiences of emotional and physical intimacy, and several with women who had experienced emotional trauma in their past. I realized I was attracting women who had been molested or traumatized. I would begin a relationship with a woman and then later find out she was a late-life virgin or had been sexually abused. Most of my girlfriends had major issues about intimacy, communication, and sexuality, and I discovered that I was able to help them heal and grow. I liked that I was able to help them. Some said they hated men, but they didn't really. The truth was that they were afraid of men. I wanted to be the man that would help them change their minds and understand that not all men are bad or abusers.

Tova: How did you find out about surrogate partner therapy?

Shai: By the age of eleven, I was very curious about sexuality. I had a male friend who also was curious about sexuality; together we found an educational magazine about human sexuality. Once a month, we would go to the newspaper stand and buy this magazine about healthy sexuality, and we learned all about it. In one of the issues, there was an article about Masters and Johnson and female surrogate partners. I got really excited about it and thought that it would be great for me to work with a woman to teach me all about sex. Remember, I was only eleven years old at the time.

Tova: It sounds like you were very precocious.

Shai: Yes. Then, about fifteen years later, when I was studying at the university in Israel, I used to read the Sunday newspaper, which had a section about sexuality. Readers sent in their questions, and they would be answered by professionals like sex therapists, gynecologists, and psychologists. One Sunday, when I was reading this page, the doctor that gave the answer was from a surrogate partner therapy center in Tel-Aviv. There was a phone number, so I called and spoke with the office manager. I was invited to a meeting with the director of the clinic and evaluated as a prospective candidate for the surrogate training program. I went through a long process of psychological evaluation, personality assessment, and several other tests. I was accepted and took the training in 1997. A few months after I graduated, I got my first referral and began working under the supervision of the clinic's founder and clinical director, Dr. Ronit Aloni. She supervised me for nine years and I worked with younger and older clients, most of whom were virgins.

Tova: Were there any specific conditions you worked with at the clinic?

Shai: A significant number of women I worked with had vaginismus, which is an involuntary contraction of the vaginal opening muscles in response to penetration or touch. In rare cases, for some women, it happens from just thinking about sex with a man. So I specialized in working with these women. We had a specific protocol for helping women with vaginismus that was very successful. A case study conducted at the clinic followed thirty-two women with vaginismus. Sixteen had a partner, but the other sixteen without partners were referred to male surrogates at the Center. The first group that worked with their boyfriends or husbands had a 75% success rate versus a 100% success rate in the group working with surrogate partners. I also worked with a few women who were sexually abused, as well as women who were lacking social and dating skills.

Tova: When did you come to the U.S.?

Shai: I have family in Los Angeles and I visited them every year since 2000. In 2006, I went on a spiritual journey in South Asia that ended in Mexico and California. Then, later that year, I moved to Los Angeles and started my private practice as a surrogate partner.

Tova: What are the qualities that make you such a good surrogate partner?

Shai: I think that I have a good understanding of human nature, women, and sexuality, which includes human connection, intimacy, and communication. I have a big heart and a lot of compassion for people. I greatly enjoy seeing people grow, especially knowing that I was a part of their healing process. Back in 2001, after working as a certified surrogate partner for four years, I got the answer to the question, "Why I'm attracting women into my life with major sexual or emotional trauma?" The answer was that both of my parents and other people in my family were survivors of sexual abuse or sexual trauma.

Tova: What are the most memorable client experiences?

Shai: I think all of my clients were special and great human beings. But one that stands out was a thirty-year-old woman. We got to the stage where we were ready for nudity, and when we became nude, we did an exercise called body image. She had passed the sensate focus part of the process, but there was still no erotic touching. So for body image, we used a full-length mirror, and we talked about how we felt about our bodies and our genitals. I went first. I talked about the anatomy of my genitals and about how I liked to be touched. Then it was her turn to talk about her body. When she got to the point where she talked about her genitals, she pointed with her fingers and said, "This is my clitoris." I told her, "No, that is not your clitoris. It's your urethra." When I said this, she started crying and cried and cried. I hugged her and asked, "Why are you crying?" She said, "Because I feel so stupid. I have lived in my body for thirty years, and am just now beginning to understand my anatomy. Now I understand where my clitoris is."

Tova: Do you have another experience that you would like to share?

Shai: Yes, and I really want to show the humanizing element of being a surrogate. Many people believe the myth that surrogate partner therapy is just about sex; they don't realize what profound work we do. I recall a twenty-five-year-old client who was beautiful and intelligent. She was referred to me to address serious problems with relationships. She'd had sex with her mom's boyfriend and with her brother's girlfriend. She wanted to learn how to just be friends with men, without needing to have sex with them. The objective of our therapy was to create a friendship: a warm, platonic relationship between us. She learned how to feel comfortable with me and how to communicate. She learned how to feel comfortable with nonsexual, nonphysical intimacy. We went to the movies together. We went for dinner and lunch together. We went for walks on the beach, in the park, and all the things that friends do together. We were attracted to each other and we both had high sexual energy, but in this process we learned how to channel this energy into our friendship and not to follow our impulses and have sex.

Tova: Were you aware of your boundaries a client?

Shai: Yes, since she was a client, we only met for two-hour sessions once a week under the supervision of Dr. Ronit Aloni. In the therapeutic context we were able to talk about our sexual energies and about our sexual attraction without needing to act on it. We talked about our feelings and held hands like friends. She learned to just enjoy the feelings of arousal without needing to take action.

Tova: Is there any other client that comes to mind?

Shai: Yes. She was a twenty-nine-year-old virgin and the presenting problem was vaginismus. The client and I started by talking, creating rapport, and communicating. We moved on to the sensate focus very gradually, step by step. Then, I think it was in session eight, we planned to get naked. We took our cloths off, but she insisted on keeping her bra on. I asked her if she felt comfortable and ready to take off her bra. She said, "No, I want to keep it on." I said, "Fine. No problem."

The same situation arose in the following session, and each time she said she wasn't ready. This went on for three sessions, and during this time, she's of course processing her feelings with the sex therapist. When I met with Dr. Aloni, she told me that she felt the client was ready to take off her bra. So I said to the client, "I feel there is something going on with you regarding taking off your bra." And she said, "Yes. You're right. I'm so embarrassed…I feel exposed and I'm afraid."

I asked her why she had such strong feelings and she explained, saying "My left breast is huge and my right one is small, and I'm so ashamed of that." I told her that I would be very honest with her and give her sincere feedback. She agreed. She took off her bra, I looked at her and said, "You know, the physical body is not symmetrical, in every person's body there is some asymmetry: people have different-sized feet, different-sized waists, different-sized hands, and different-sized breasts." She was a virgin who had vaginismus, but ironically, as we got into the more erotic touching, there was no problem. She didn't have any vaginismus at all. And then the therapist and I concluded that the root of her problem was not vaginismus. It was her body image, and not wanting to be nude with anyone. Would you like to hear another story?

Tova: Yes, please share another.

Shai: This client was a forty-four-year-old virgin. She had very good social skills and wanted to learn how to end her fear of men. We had been working together for a while, and everything was going very well. At some point in the therapy process, she started recalling childhood memories. It turned out she had been sexually abused by her father. At the age of six, her brother became sexual with her. And that's why she was so afraid of men and had remained a virgin. When we started the body touching, these memories came back to her. After she told me what had happened to her and she unburdened herself, we were able to have intercourse. She started crying and crying. It was very sad, but also a huge relief for her. At the end of the session she said, "I feel like I gained back ten years of my life." It was a huge, transformational experience.

Sex Is the Least of It

Tova: Through your surrogate experiences, what did you learn about yourself?

Shai: I love healing people, helping women and supporting their healing journey. And I want to make people feel safe. I'm able to communicate with them about relationships and physical intimacy. Through healing my clients, I have healed myself, my fears. My parents never went to therapy to address their sexual trauma, so I inherited it. This work is my calling and my passion.

In sixteen years as a heterosexual surrogate partner, I was able to heal myself. So now, after being embarrassed to be naked in a public space, just a couple of years ago I went to a nude beach in the Caribbean and enjoyed it. I walked naked and felt comfortable in my body. That's just one instance of feeling comfortable in my skin and feeling good with my sexuality, as well as feeling confident about my healing power and my ability to help people. As I help more and more people, I realize that I'm on the right track and that I'm here to help people.

Contact information:

Email: SurrogateTherapy1@gmail.com

Website: www.SurrogateTherapy.net

Rebecca Torosian

"So she thoroughly taught him that one cannot take pleasure without giving pleasure, and that every gesture, every caress, every touch, every glance, every last bit of the body has its secret, which brings happiness to the person who knows how to wake it."—Hermann Hesse, Siddhartha

Rebecca has been a professional dancer and choreographer for more than twenty years. In 1984, she became a practicing Soka Gakkai Nichiren Buddhist, a decision which transformed her life and changed her destiny. She taught in dance schools in New York and Brazil and performed as a solo artist; she worked as a stripper in clubs, and was a performer in two world peace culture shows in Hawaii and Japan. She pursued college, majoring in Liberal Arts. Rebecca is a certified massage therapist, energy practitioner, and has worked for the past ten years as an actor/trainer for the New York Police Department, training all ranks of officers how to come to a peaceful resolution in situations involving the mentally ill through role-play scenarios. She wrote and performed *Cock Healer*, a one-woman show, which she performed for six years on the East Coast.

Tova: What were the early messages that you heard about sexuality in your home?

Rebecca: The messages were either nonexistent or relatively positive. My father was very comfortable with his sexuality and I was at ease around him. My mother was repressed. There's evidence that points to some early abuse that she experienced. Some of that's cultural. She came from an insular Pennsylvania Dutch background. There's also some evidence that I may have been the victim of preverbal, or inappropriate contact, with my grandfather, and even my grandmother on my mother's side.

Tova: When you say evidence, what do you mean?

Rebecca: I have preverbal memories. I remember being terrified when I was visiting my grandparents, which was often, in Pennsylvania. My grandfather would walk in on me in the bathroom. I was terrified because I couldn't lock the door. In contrast, I was never terrified at home. We didn't even have a lock. When I was entering puberty, at twelve or thirteen, I already had a boyfriend and I was already being sexual. I had pubic hair. They didn't have a shower, they only had a bath. She walked in while I was taking a bath and asked me if I had "cleaned myself down there." And I told her I was very uncomfortable. And it wasn't until later that I knew this was really inappropriate.

Tova: Taking those experiences into account, were there any social or sexual issues that you needed to work through as you matured toward adulthood?

Rebecca: Yes. I was sexually active very early. Although my father was loving, and was very supportive, he was often absent. I believe I really needed a tremendous amount of attention from boys and men to feel valued. I desperately wanted to be desirable. My sister, three-and-a-half years older, was very active early as well, and she had many boyfriends. And she used to talk to me about her boyfriends and gave me a little bit of sex education when I first got my period. She was the one who told me what it was, not my mother. So, I remember always wanting a lot of attention in any way possible, not just sexually.

Tova: How did you discover that your sexuality was a means of attracting male attention? Was it through a process of experimentation?

Rebecca: First, I had an amazing sexual experience with a schoolmate that was very spiritual when I was twelve. We were together for one year. My experience with him was not in the same vein as wanting to desperately get attention from other men as I got older. With him, it was before all that even happened. And it was so natural. And I was getting my period, so I knew that we couldn't have sex, because I knew there was something called rubbers, but I didn't know what they were or how to get them. So we couldn't have intercourse. But we had everything else. You know, oral sex, sixty-nine, everything. But it was so natural and just felt so loving and just so completing, so fulfilling. And then when we broke up and moved on in our lives, and I became a young adult, at about fourteen, I remember grieving over the loss of that, and feeling that I would never experience anything like that again. At that time, all my friends were going to parties and dances and flirting, and it felt so juvenile and so pointless to me. And I felt like I'd already been there and done that. I was also dancing in clubs, going to discos when I was like fourteen and fifteen, and dancing with much older people, and feeling that was one way in which I felt very special and very sexual, very alive, that I could use it and express it through my dancing. My first actual sexual experience was with a much older man when I was sixteen.

Tova: And then, then at what point did you move into more mature relationships?

Rebecca: I would say my more fully adult experiences happened when I was twenty or twenty-one. I lived with a man for about a year and a half, right after leaving my parents' home. Our experience together felt more like having been married.

Tova: Had you worked through the attention-seeking need?

Rebecca: I was still promiscuous. I still had affairs while I was with this man towards the end of the relationship while I was doing some print modeling. I was working at a photography school where I was photographed for teaching purposes. I loved that attention. I had slept with some of those men. I was also still dancing professionally, and then I also started stripping at twenty-two. When I did that, then it was like the lid came off. I had a lot of sexual partners.

Tova: Was that another manifestation of seeking attention?

Rebecca: I believe so. I think it was a combination of seeking attention and just really loving and enjoying sex. I also loved dancing. I loved stripping. I felt very powerful and very desirable. I'm very talented as a dancer. So I felt like I was giving a service, and in one way, and at the same time, getting well paid for it.

Tova: How did you first hear about surrogacy?

Rebecca: I had left my last corporate job and answered an ad to go to Brazil to teach and perform. This was in the early 1990s. When I came back, I wasn't sure what I wanted to do. I felt sick and discovered that I had gotten a tapeworm while I was there. At first, I thought that I actually might've gotten AIDS. I didn't. We didn't know enough back then to know that I couldn't have transmitted the disease. There was no way. I had no needles. No drugs. I was terrified that I might be dying. At that time, I was a practicing Buddhist. My prayer became, "If I'm not sick, then I must find a way to create value out of my sexuality. I must find a way to use it that will help myself and others heal.

Tova: Tell me about how you became involved with Buddhism and what has that practice meant to you?

Rebecca: I was always seeking. I'm the daughter of a Presbyterian minister who was a civil rights activist through his ministry. He was part of the outer circle of Martin Luther King. I grew up in Washington, D.C., where our home was the community center for everything from the Poor People's Campaign to the March on Washington to Cesar Chavez. And I feel that there's a direct connection between my father's ministry and my future work. It was helping others, just in a different arena. He was a model for that, and he was also a model for Buddhism, even though he was Christian, because he practiced it as a humanist. He practiced his religion in terms of trying to help underprivileged people.

I internalized that, and when I came to New York to dance when I was twenty-three, somebody introduced me to a particular form of Buddhism. I learned that it was about basically transforming one's life from within with no external deity; I felt like it was what I had been seeking. It was in complete alignment with the spiritual philosophy of the way I was raised. I believe I transformed my destiny. At the time, I was very self-destructive, taking a lot of risks. I was just asking to get hurt, and in fact, it happened: I was raped on my way to do a party. But I survived it. And I told him that what he had done was horrible and his Karmic retribution would be worse. Cause and effect, you know? I did not turn him in to the police, although I had the chance. I actually introduced him to Buddhist practice. My wisdom told me that was the right thing to do.

All of that was a big turning point for my life and my sexuality. I was guided by my faith, and I felt like, "Okay Rebecca, you took a horrible situation and created something amazing out of it." This was a wakeup call because I kept tempting fate. And so my prayer became, how can I really begin to appreciate the value and dignity of my life so that I can honestly remain on this earth? It was a slow transformation, but I gradually became healthier. I just started chanting, just started practicing. That was a huge shift in my life.

Tova: Then one day, along came the *Village Voice*.

Rebecca: Yes, then I saw an ad in the *Village Voice* for surrogacy training in 1993. I was looking for a way to create value out of my sexuality. This seemed like the answer to my prayer. I walked into the Sex Therapy Clinic of Eva Margolies on 34th street. It was a very nice professional office setting. She told me what the work was about, accepted me into the program, and began to train me. There were a number of other surrogates working, and so I was trained within that community.

Tova: Because many of the surrogates in this book have come from different schools of training, what was your training like and what did it include? You represent the New York "School" of surrogacy.

Rebecca: The New York School. Who knew? Right. That's what it became. The clinic was called the Clinic for Sexual Recovery. Love that name and always did. I was trained for about two to three months. I would come in a few times a week, and we attended staff meetings in which Eva would have me take notes and read. I read about Masters and Johnson, as well as her book, *Undressing the American Male*. I spoke with the other surrogates, and they helped me understand what the basic sessions were, including educating me about the major sexual dysfunctions and the symptoms associated with them. And then we practiced the exercises that became the foundation for the process, the breathing, the sensate focus approach to touching. I did role plays with the other surrogates. They would play the client, so I could practice how to respond effectively in different situations.

Tova: Did her training follow the fourteen-to-sixteen-session protocol of Masters and Johnson? The hand caress, the foot caress, the face caress, etc.? Was it that kind of rollout for you?

Rebecca: No. It wasn't exactly. In fact, what I realized later was that Eva had adapted Masters and Johnson and created her own surrogate program based on it. So it had all those exercises, but slightly different versions. It wasn't just the hand caress. It was called "the massage" instead. Sometimes the words were different. It didn't follow M & J exactly, the wording and the chronology, but it was close. She developed exercises that I believe she had learned while working previously with another sex therapy clinic that utilized surrogate partners. From that original clinic, she and another sex therapist went on to develop their own clinics that included surrogate partner training and treatment options for clients.

Tova: Then you started an internship with a new client?

Rebecca: Right. Basically, I would be given one or two people to start that were just getting started themselves. Because the early sessions were just meet-and-greets and straightforward teaching sensate focus, so I could learn how to teach these basic foundational exercises. I took to it like a fish to water. Once I started doing that, then it came very natural for me. Then she gave me more patients that were ready for more advanced exercises.

Tova: You worked within the triadic model?

Rebecca: Yes I did. Eva was my supervisor. She would conduct the initial intakes and determine if prospective clients were appropriate for the program. Then she would refer the individual to whichever surrogate she felt was the best match. I would meet him. If after the first meeting, it seemed like we could work together, the patient would be assigned to me and we would get started. I would write up reports after every session so that she would have my progress notes before her next session with him.

Tova: Why do you think you felt so comfortable with your body and with sexuality?

Rebecca: I think the main reason is because, by that point, I had already been exposed to some therapeutic healing work for myself. You know, for my own ability to rejoin my own body.

Tova: In the form of traditional therapy?

Rebecca: I did traditional and nontraditional. I did the Reichian model of bioenergetics, which is from Dr. Lowen, who had studied under William Reich. It was about combining both mind and body in the session. That made a big difference.

Tova: What are the qualities that you possess that you think made you such a good surrogate?

Rebecca: Compassion. I'm a good teacher and coach. I'm enthusiastic. I believe in the model of teaching skills, practicing them, and then sending someone on their way; being a part of the process, not the guru; rather joining in to support the other person's process, so that they can fully be able to fly on their own. I'm passionate about the surrogate process because I believe it is a model that really does help people heal and live a more fulfilled life. I remember being startled when I realized that through this simple process, people got better. It blew me away.

Tova: What are the two or three or four most memorable clients that you can recall?

Rebecca: One that touched me deeply was an Irish-American man in his late twenties. He had never been in any kind of therapy before, and probably never would've, but he started having erection problems. He had a girlfriend. We came to find out that he had stomach cancer a few years ago and that it was now in remission. He'd have to go in every so often and have his stomach and lower abdomen probed. He acted like it was nothing. When Eva was taking his history, he downplayed the cancer. He and I worked together for a short time. We did spoon breathing, just lying side by side in the nude. I was just touching his back lightly. In about the fourth or fifth session, he just started to sob. He was so ashamed that he lost control, he ran to the other side of the room and curled up. I told Eva what had happened. He saw her for a session. We realized that the touch released something deep inside of him, and that he was finally able to grieve, and experience the fear and his mortality. After that, he didn't return.

Tova: So that was a real catharsis for him?

Rebecca: Yes. That was the most traumatic. Through touch, we created a safe enough space for him to express his feelings.

Tova: Anyone else?

Rebecca: Yes. There was this really interesting, wealthy, older man who was eighty-one. He had already been in therapy with a number of the surrogates. He liked the idea of therapy, and I think he really didn't want to graduate. He had erection problems and sometimes rapid ejaculation. But the real problem for him was that he wished he was twenty-one. He bought a pump. We would begin our sessions by looking at art magazines because he fancied himself an artist. At the same time, he would be pumping himself up to get an erection so that we could do some mutual touching and he could feel youthful. I liked him. It was just a little distasteful, because the pump made his penis kind of clammy. But it gave him confidence. It made him feel like he could be intimate with a woman, which brought him pleasure. I admired him too, because he was already eighty-one, and he was still wanting to experience erotic satisfaction. The urge for touch doesn't die.

I worked with many patients who had many different types of diagnoses. I worked with a late virgin who was in his early forties and a lovely guy, a photographer, and gentle soul. He had infantile syndrome, because he could only get erections by rubbing his penis on a bed. He had never been able to have an erection from a hand stimulation or a vagina. He wanted to stay hard enough to actually have an orgasm inside a woman. He wanted to learn how to get used to the hand for masturbation, or a vagina, so that he could date and have a fulfilling social life.

His touch skills were good. I helped him explore different masturbation styles. He also needed to get used to the environment of a vagina. It was a slow process of adapting to new sexual behavioral styles. But then one day it happened. He was able to have an orgasm inside of me. We were so excited, it was like we wanted to break open a bottle of champagne.

Tova: The goal is to prepare the client to go into the world and live their lives with hope and human connection.

Rebecca: I had worked with Eva for four years. Then I stopped my surrogate work and pursued other passions of mine: writing, acting, and I even created a one-woman show that I performed in New York and up the East Coast, called the *Cock Healer*. Surrogacy was something that was just a good fit for me. That's why I use the word "calling." Now that I am working as a surrogate again, I know without a doubt that it's definitely a calling. Now I have the advantage of age, experience, and wisdom.

Tova: So you've come full circle in using your sexuality.

Rebecca: Yes. I've come back to the work.

Tova: You're working with the Institute of Mind Body Therapy.

Rebecca: Yes, I am. I'm excited to have a personal practice again, and at the same time, be part of a larger community that is focused on raising awareness and training and broadening the scope of this work.

This work can be accessed by many more people and help a larger population. And that was something that was missing years ago when I was training. Then, that was a dream. Today, it's possible. Since *The Sessions*, public awareness of surrogacy has been heightened. And the Internet provides all kinds of opportunities for surrogates to present their work.

Tova: Through your surrogate experience, what did you learn about yourself?

Rebecca: I learned that I could effectively help people. I learned that there's a humility in this, because I can offer a tenderness and a soft, safe place for patients. I learned that I can work with more patients, and that does not dilute my effectiveness. I can be intimate in a way that respects my boundaries and that I can serve others. It makes me more whole because of it.

Tova: You mentioned you're married.

Rebecca: I am.

Tova: How does your coming back into surrogacy sit with your husband?

Rebecca: It sits well. He has watched and learned over the last year, particularly since *The*

Sessions and the media attention that I received. He and I had many conversations about what I used to do. He saw that I was getting inquiries for help in New York, and there was no one here, and we went through periods where I was trying to refer them to IPSA, and that went nowhere. No response. So over a period of months, he and I spoke, and I finally decided that I really needed to help these people.

He really supported me in working through my feelings, the logistics, and the tech support. I said to him, "What do you think? I can't do this unless you're comfortable with it." And he said, "Well, these people are really suffering. I can see that, and you can help them. So, I'm honestly not threatened by that." I was like, "I guess that's a yes." He's good with all that because he trusts me. He knows that I wouldn't do anything unless I felt it was right for me. He's really got a kind heart.

Contact Information:

Email: intimacyexpert@yahoo.com

Website: www.savingintimacy.com

Dr. Cheryl Cohen Greene, Doctor of Human Sexuality (D.H.S.)

Photo courtesy of Dr. Cheryl Cohen Greene

The Sessions

By Jonathan Maseng

Cheryl Cohen Greene has spent the last forty years having sex with people for a living, but she's not a prostitute. Greene is one of a small number of specialists in the United States known as Sex Surrogates whose job it is to help clients with sexual anxieties become more comfortable with their bodies and their sexuality, even if that means sleeping with them. And while that sounds like a fascinating enough story in and of itself, it's Greene's interaction with one patient in particular, Mark O'Brien, a brilliant author crippled by polio, that has catapulted her to fame through her portrayal by Helen Hunt in her Oscar nominated role in The Sessions.

"It's all about shame and guilt," said Greene, speaking by phone from her home, her Boston accent thick as ever, even after decades out West. "Most of us do not feel a very deep level of comfort with who we are."

That's where Greene comes in. "What I try to help them do is stay in the moment, in their body, feeling the sensations, being able to relax and communicate," she said, of her work with her nearly one thousand past clients. "What they need to do is stop trying to be what they think other people expect, and learn about themselves enough to be able to present who they are in as natural a way as possible."

Even in the liberal bay area, where Greene has done most of her work, it hasn't always been easy. People have hurled insults like "you're nothing but a prostitute using another name," and even questioned whether what Greene does causes more harm to her clients than good. Through it all, Greene has shrugged off the criticism, knowing that her work is righteous, and has helped countless men live more fulfilling lives.

A friend of Greene's once came up with an analogy that she loves to share. He said that going to a prostitute is like visiting a restaurant. "You look at the menu, you see what they're serving and you choose, they prepare it, they hope you love it, and you want to come back and refer a friend." Going to a sex surrogate is like going to cooking school. "You get the recipes, you get the ingredients, and you learn how to mix it and make the dish, and then you go out into the world and you share that with other people. You don't keep going back to cooking class."

That's the ultimate goal for Greene with her clients, independence. As it's noted in The Sessions, a surrogate is only supposed to have six sessions** with a client, after that, the client is expected to head out into the world. "That's the goal. Can a person transfer what they've done with me to another relationship?"

Even amongst Greene's hundreds of clients, Mark O'Brien was a special case. "Ten percent of the people I've worked with were disabled people physically... noticeably disabled. The rest of us are disabled in our sexuality just by living in this culture," said Greene. When O'Brien came to her, he was nearly forty and had never had sex with a woman. He and Greene began a process that is lovingly presented in The Sessions, to help him learn to appreciate his own body and sexuality.

"In the movie, Mark and I fall in love, or there's a tenderness that develops," said Greene. "It did develop, but it didn't develop quite the same way." And though Greene noted several inaccuracies in the film, they didn't seem to bother her. In fact, in some cases, she found the use of "poetic license" ended up impressing her. "Mark and I became friends and when I ended therapy, I didn't walk away from him the way it happens in the movie. I always cry when I see that scene, it's just so touching, but it isn't the way it ended."

One scene that Greene noted was accurate was a scene in which Helen Hunt holds up a mirror for John Hawkes, who practically channels O'Brien, so that he can see his body for the first time since he was a child. It's juxtaposed with a scene of Greene going into the Mikveh to convert to Judaism. It's one of the more powerful scenes in the film, and according to Green, "It's actually real." Though she notes that in real life, "I was pregnant when I got into the Mikveh; eight months pregnant. I had a three year old daughter and she went into the Mikveh with me. And I wish Rhea Pearlman had been there. The woman who was there was scary."

Greene spent time with Helen Hunt to prepare her for the role. "I met with her at a raw foods restaurant in Santa Monica, and I had never had raw food. I'd had salads, but I didn't know... it was fabulous," said Greene, laughing. "She was just so real with me, no pretense. She's a marvelous person."

Greene even went to Hunt's mansion to show her how to do the sensitive touch that Greene used on O'Brien. Her client for the demonstration? Hunt's partner, writer/producer Matthew Carnahan. "If Helen wins, I would be ecstatic," Greene said. "If she doesn't win, I'm still so honored."

Greene also met with the film's writer and director, Ben Lewin, when the project was in its infancy. Lewin, who grew up in Australia, and was stricken with polio himself as a child, first learned about O'Brien and Greene though the magic of google, of all things. "I still believe that electricity is produced by monkeys running inside barrels, but the internet certainly changed my life in this respect," said Lewin, speaking by phone.

Prior to doing The Sessions, Lewin, who'd once had a busy career, hadn't been able to find work for nearly a decade. He kept busy by selling high end watches, among other things, though, as he points out, chuckling, "I wasn't out of it. I wasn't getting any work."

Now riding high on the success of The Sessions, Lewin, who is remarkably nice, and humble, commented that "there is a kind of pleasure in being reinvented. My agent kept telling me, oh before you were Ben Lewin; now you're BEN LEWIN."

According to Greene, Lewin was unsure of what to expect when he met with her. "He said, I don't know what I expected you to be. I thought for a while maybe you were somebody who had a thing for having sex with disabled men."

Lewin says that Greene's help was invaluable to making the film. "After meeting her, I really began to see the film as a relationship movie, and more of a two-hander than a biopic," said Lewin. Meeting Greene also helped in another way. Lewin had brought along a friend from Australia with him to meet Greene, and after their meeting, the man opened his checkbook and wrote a check for 20% of the film's budget. "He was the audience, and there was an audience for this unusual story. So meeting Cheryl was a threshold event."

For Greene, the attention is wonderful, but she knows that her interaction with Mark was just one part of a very interesting life. She's recently published a book called "An Intimate Life: Sex, Love, and My Journey as a Surrogate Partner" that deals with her relationship with O'Brien but also delves into her interactions with many of the other clients she's helped over the years.

If there's one message Greene thinks people can take away from her work with O'Brien, it's that "there is somebody out there for everybody. It's just whether they pass like ships in the night or they come together and they meet. The meeting is what I pray for them to have, and Mark got it, and that was beautiful."

Cheryl Cohen Greene contact information:

Sex Is the Least of It

Email: cherylcohengreene@gmail.com

Website: www.cherylcohengreene.com

** The limitation of six sessions is not representative of traditional surrogate partner therapy.

Linda Poelzl, B.A.

My Life as a Sexual Surrogate: It's More Than One Big Sex Party

15-year sexual surrogate therapist Linda Poelzl is mild-mannered, but speaks rather bluntly when describing her intimate work: "We're not having sex all the time, but there is sex involved" she says. "People assume sex surrogate therapy is one big sex party. And clients often assume they can get a few sex lessons and then they are fine, but it's usually more complicated than that."

Poelzl works alongside psychotherapists (but refrains from dealing with Freudian analysts, explaining, "I like to work in present time") who refer their clients to her, though she also advertises through her personal website. (http://www.waterdragonwoman.com/)

Poelzl has worked in the field of human sexuality for nearly a quarter century and has been independently (and steadily) supporting herself as a sex surrogate since becoming certified fifteen years ago. She is one of the few remaining in this fringe line of, yes, legal sex work. There is no guarantee for "full sexual service" but as Poelzl admits, "It's certainly not just hand-holding."

Her $300 per-hour rate is not covered by any health insurance plan (nor will it likely ever be) and she estimates that she's seen between 300 and 500 clients over the years, many who are in their 50s. A sexual surrogacy session is usually two hours, with an average of fifteen sessions, but there have been notable exceptions: Poelzl's most committed client is going on his 94th visit.

She feels "safe and proud" of the work, though admits to feeling affected at times. "It's so tricky when you are dealing with sex—boundaries can get blurred. It can be hard to date."

Sex Is the Least of It

The International Professional Surrogate Association (IPSA) is the only existing organization that certifies sexual surrogate therapists. Prostitution and fear of legal repercussions have taken a toll on the profession. Consequently, Poezl's line of work is both highly risky and thinly populated. "We are a dying breed," she says.

How did you become a sex surrogate?

I was a volunteer with the San Francisco sex information switchboard. Sex therapy and sexual dysfunction was part of the training. A colleague talked about sex surrogate work and I was immediately intrigued.

I was a massage therapist and instructor in 1978, and I've always been able to help people relax and accept their bodies. I was going to sex parties, too—I was engaging with other people, not so much intercourse. I was soon able to engage with people who I wasn't necessarily attracted to. In combination, knowing that I could do this sexually made me feel like I was qualified, even before I went through training with IPSA in '95. The day after becoming certified, I got started. It's the kind of thing you have to have a lot of life experience to do. It was a ten-day intensive training. We are screened, gave our history and documented just why we felt we were qualified. Some people didn't pass the test.

Can you describe the process?

A lot of people think, "sex, sex, sex!" But it involves less sex than with an entertainment sex worker. Certainly it's not just hand-holding. I work with psychotherapists who refer their clients to me—but I don't work with Freudian analysts. Sex surrogate work is about a relationship with less focus on psychological processing. It's helping a person relax and talk about their feelings. I teach them about touching, body language, how to show confidence…once you get some, that is.

We then get into nudity. People tend to get impatient, they want to just get to the good stuff. But just because I am an expert doesn't mean I know everything about my client. When I have a new partner, I'm learning their body, so hand-guiding or making sounds is key. Sometimes it can be a little clinical and not always sexy. You are learning something, so communication is needed. I'll teach them things like initiating touch and sensual skills first, and then "How do you know when a woman wants to be kissed?" Some of it is role play—like being on a date.

How much of the time is physical?

With some clients, there's less actual sex. Some people can be touch-phobic and very anhedonic—they literally won't feel pleasure. There can be a lot of touching, but it's gradual. I use a lot of sensate focus: concentrating on sensations, and taking turns giving and receiving. During sex, people are touching each other at the same time…we work up to that.

How do you rate success?

Some particular sexual dysfunctions can be fixed. But it depends on the issue. Some issues are easier to clear up than others.

Does your work kill your own sex drive?

I am older and my sex drive is lower. Most clients are over 45; some are 60 or 70. Baby boomers still want to have sex. I've learned a lot about elder sex.

Feelings on Viagra?

When Viagra first came out, I thought it was great but I was worried it would put us surrogates out of business. I have clients who were prescribed drugs for erectile dysfunction and have used the drugs in conjunction with their work with me. Usually it's not just a physical problem—and using these drugs tend to annoy post-menopausal wives who are happy that they are having less sex and suddenly their husbands want a lot of sex. For them, it's a burden.

Have you ever refused to work with a client?

There have been a few over the years. They needed more psychotherapy, and I felt they weren't ready for sexual surrogate work.

Have you worked with any couples?

I had a couple in their 30's who were in an arranged marriage. While they were very fond of each other they were having trouble; they had no previous sexual experience. They walked in, took their clothes off and said "we want help!" and I pretty much taught them body mechanics. They were desperate and willing. It was a matter of teaching them about…adjusting.

I imagine that there might be some clients you've had whose partners aren't as open to sex surrogate therapy?

Yes. I have worked with clients who have partners that are uncomfortable, sure…

Then would you encourage them to disclose their surrogate therapy to their partner?

I don't really care if a client tells their partner or not. But what does concern me when they choose not to, is will they feel guilty and not be able to connect with me on the level that's needed in order to work through their issues?

How would you protect yourself from a jealous lover?

Well I have a confidentiality agreement. I spell it all out in a paragraph, differentiating my work from prostitution. It's not a contract for sex:

Sex Is the Least of It

"CONFIDENTIALITY AGREEMENT: I understand that the surrogacy sessions are for the purpose of expanding my ability to feel physical pleasure and emotional fulfillment through greater intimacy and increased sensation and to overcome sexual dysfunction. I acknowledge this session series is not for the purpose of sexual gratification or entertainment and may or may not include sexual intercourse, manual, or oral stimulation. I understand and will abide by the above agreements."

Do you allow clients to keep in touch with you down the road, once the therapy is over? Who decides when the therapy has run its course?

As with any relationship, it's unusual to end it well. Generally, when there is a lot of sex in our sessions, we are done. I work with the client in order to acknowledge that it was a professional experience, but I usually have a period of no contact with a client for a couple of months. They can come back if they need maintenance, but when I get cards and emails from people who end up married, it's always nice. There are some people who need maintenance, and it helps them to have some outlet.

Where do you see sex surrogate therapy headed in the next, say, five years?

We are a dying breed. I think some of that has to do with the fear of liability that psychotherapists have; there are people who think this work is excellent, but fewer therapists want to risk their licenses. Maybe I'll look into training people. We need young blood!

Courtesy of TheFasterTimes.com, http://www.thefastertimes.com/oddjobs/2010/04/07/sexual-surrogacy-more-than-just-hand-holding/

Contact information:

Website: www.waterdragonwoman.com

International Surrogates

Amit, M.A. , Israel

Photo from istock

"I will not play tug o' war. I'd rather play hug o' war. Where everyone hugs instead of tugs, Where everyone giggles and rolls on the rug, Where everyone kisses, and everyone grins, and everyone cuddles, and everyone wins." —Shel Silverstein, cartoonist and composer

Amit holds a B.A. and a Master's degree in psychology. He's a sex educator certified to teach workshops on sexual issues to children in schools, particularly lectures about safe sex and sexual behavior. Teens frequently visit his website where they post questions that he answers for them. He is a licensed masseur and is currently working toward certification as a sex therapist, as well as a family and couples therapist. In his spare time, he is a salsa instructor.

Tova: When you were growing up, what were the early messages you heard from your family about sexuality?

Amit: Growing up with my parents, sex was a very open issue. They always told me that if I had any questions whatsoever, I shouldn't be afraid to ask them. They bought me books about sex in my early years, and I used to sit and read books in the bookstore's sex department. My parents are still very loving and romantic, always touching, kissing, and hugging. Sex was never a forbidden subject and I grew up in a very open-minded family.

Tova: Not many people have that kind of positive early influence. But were there any social or sexual issues that you found you needed to work out as you moved toward adulthood?

Amit: Yes, there was one that affected me very much, actually, and it's a long story. I have only one brother who is three years younger. He's got green eyes and he's very beautiful; he was the most popular boy in his class and in his school. And every day when we came home from school, there were girls waiting for him outside of our house, hoping he would take off his shirt. He's actually modeling now and he's also very smart. He has an M.A. in Business Management and is CEO of the company where he works. But he always was and still is very beautiful. So among his friends and our family, he was known as "the pretty one." Since I have a very high IQ, only three points less than the genius. I was the smart one.

Our parents were very supportive and they loved giving us all sort of compliments. But the problem was that they always gave us the same compliments: they always complimented me on my brain and my brother on his looks. So, as I was growing up, I was wondering why nobody ever said anything nice about my looks; all I ever heard was good things about my brain. Eventually I assumed that I wasn't good-looking based on the good things my parents said about my brain, my abilities, and my personality, but not my looks.

Growing up it became a vicious cycle, one in which someone thinks he's not good-looking, so he projects that image. Such a person broadcasts this message about himself to everyone in his surroundings, and when girls see someone projecting that image, they receive it and transmit it back. This reinforces what he thinks about himself, which is that he's not good-looking. This process is repeated over time and he begins telling himself, "See, that girl doesn't think that I'm attractive. I guess I'm right for thinking that I'm not attractive." When I reached the age of seventeen, I was convinced that I was ugly. I didn't just think it; I was sure of it. It was a clear fact, at least in my mind. And by the way, it's not true. I'm actually good-looking.

Tova: We all perceive ourselves in certain ways, and very often our perceptions are very different from what the outside world sees.

Amit: At the age of seventeen, I wouldn't let anyone touch me, because I thought that if they did, it would be only out of pity. And I didn't touch anyone because I thought that they would be disgusted by my touch because I was ugly. So obviously I didn't do anything with girls. But at that point in time, all the chat rooms on the Internet started up, and I thought to myself, "This is a great opportunity for me to impress someone with my personality, the way that I talk and think, and how I treat women." This would happen without the need for them to see my face; there was no video chat at that time.

Sex Is the Least of It

So I actually met a girl online who was very impressed by what I'd said in the chat, and at some point she wanted to meet me. When I told her that I didn't want to meet, she insisted; so I met her. I was convinced that once she saw me, she'd scream and run away. But she didn't; she stayed and we talked, and then we started dating, which went on for about two months. She was my first kiss, and in two months I got to undress her, took off her shirt and bra. But after two months, she said she needed to tell me something. She said that the only reason that she'd been seeing me was because she wanted to meet my brother. You can imagine how this affected me and my first intimate experience with girls.

It took me some time to recover from that blow. But when I did, I went to a self-awareness workshop called "It's My Choice." It's a workshop that helps you understand why you believe certain things about yourself, and why you think the way you do. They teach that "if you choose it, you can change it." That's when I came to understand the effect of all the issues surrounding my parents' compliments. It was there that I started to realize that what I thought about myself might not be true, and that I might actually be good-looking and not as ugly as I felt.

Two metaphors represent the progress that I made in that self-awareness workshop: one is a dam, which signifies the dam of beliefs I had built around myself for a long time. But then that workshop broke a hole in the dam and everything started to flow outside of me. The other metaphor is a pendulum. I was stuck most of my life on the extreme side of the pendulum, and when the workshop released me, I started flying toward the other side.

I went from being someone who couldn't touch other people to becoming a certified masseuse. From being someone who didn't want anyone to see him, who couldn't be seen by other people, I became a dancer and a dance instructor. And from being someone who didn't allow anyone to touch him, I started to enjoy and ask for all sorts of contact and touching. Those were the issues that I had to overcome when I grew up. Those childhood messages really had affected me, but in the end, I think it turned out to be to my advantage.

Rather than investing so much effort in my appearance and spending time courting women, I was instead focusing on developing my personality, my manners, and my romanticism; working on my ability to write and to listen, to appreciate and to support, and all those things that teenagers who think highly of themselves usually don't spend time developing, at least not at a young age.

Tova: Those are many of the qualities that women find very attractive.

Amit: Yes, but at the time, it had the opposite result. I was really supportive and smart, and I helped my lady friends with everything that they needed, but when you're young and in school, those qualities send you straight into the "friend zone."

Tova: Yes, but I'm sure as you've gotten older, those qualities have become an asset.

Amit: Yes, when I got older, those qualities started to pay off. But that's what I'm saying, that I managed to develop those good qualities when I was young and thought I was unappealing. Now that I realize I'm good-looking, a lot of women are really attracted to me and I know how not to abuse it.

Tova: How did you first hear about surrogacy?

Amit: People always used to open up to me and tell me things because I actually listened, unlike a lot of other boys. Because I tend to listen, to help, and to support, people find it easier to open up with me. Since I don't regard sex as a forbidden subject and I love talking about it, and since I make people feel comfortable talking about it, they open up about sex with me. Actually, it was my friends who started me on the path of becoming a surrogate. I'll tell you a story about how it happened: I had a lady friend who had a birthday, and her female roommate had a birthday at the same time.

They invited me to their place to celebrate, and at some point, my friend left to go to sleep and left me with her roommate. Later on, the roommate and I had sex. And in the morning, my friend came to me and asked me, "How was it?" I was kind of surprised that she actually knew that something had happened. Then she told me that this had been her plan all along, because her friend was twenty-six years old and still a virgin. She knew that if she was with me, then I'd be able to overcome her roommate's fears and all of her objections. They both knew that was the plan, and that I was her present. But I didn't know that.

So as it turned out, I was a surrogate before I even knew what a surrogate was. My friends always told me that. And at some point, a lady friend of mine told me that I should actually work as a professional surrogate rather than just help people that way in my personal life.

Tova: So it was actually a friend who told you about surrogacy?

Amit: Yes, a friend told me about it, and she was taking the surrogacy training. She said that she thought it would suit me, so I read a bit about it and then went with her to the course.

Tova: When and where did you take your training, and how long have you been working as a surrogate partner?

Amit: I trained at Ronit Aloni's Clinic. As for how long I've been a surrogate, my diploma says November 2009. So I've been doing it for just over three years.

Tova: What do you think made you feel so comfortable with your body and your sexuality?

Amit: Well, first of all, I have great genes from my father. So growing up I had a six-pack, but I was unable to appreciate it. When I did the training, I started to look at my body objectively, and then I could appreciate it.

Sex Is the Least of It

Tova: What are the qualities that make you such a good surrogate?

Amit: I make people feel comfortable. I'm also able to calm people and talk to them in a manner that will make them feel at ease. I listen to them and I know how to support them. I know how to accept them, no matter what they tell me. I'm not judgmental when they tell me something that they did, something that they think that they did wrong, or when they tell me something that they think I can't handle. But I can handle it. That's the best way that I can explain it.

Tova: That you're accepting.

Amit: Yes. Accepting is a good word. So I'm accepting of everything that they tell me. I'm not judgmental and I'm a very warm person. I know how to love and how to transmit love. I appreciate touch. I know how not to scare them. I know how to read body language and how to read people, how to address their needs. I enable people to be what they want to be, or feel what they want to feel. I help them to understand things about themselves and allow them to explore themselves without judgment.

Tova: I'm interested in hearing about your most memorable client experiences.

Amit: The experience that stands out is the one in which I fell in love with the client. And I had only one of those. Usually I know how not to fall in love, but this one captured my heart, and it was very sad when we had to end the surrogate sessions.

Tova: How was this handled therapeutically when you were aware that this was becoming more than a surrogate-client relationship and that there were really genuine romantic feelings involved? Did you go to the therapist and talk about it? How was that whole situation handled?

Amit: Well, first of all, we know from the start—both patient and surrogate—that this was a relationship with an expiration date. I believe that as a surrogate, you shouldn't put too many boundaries or limits on how you feel because the women that I work with feel those feelings. So if it's going to be genuine and strong, they will feel it and they will respond in the same way. Anyway, getting back to your question, I processed those feelings with Dr. Aloni when we met weekly.

Tova: You're referring to Dr. Ronit Aloni, who is the founder of the Sexuality Center in Tel-Aviv.

Amit: Yes. I had a meeting with her because she was my supervising therapist. She always makes sure that I'm okay and that I'm maintaining my boundaries and ethical conduct. She allowed me to feel, but within those boundaries.

Tova: Did you feel that the client reciprocated those feelings?

Amit: Yes. No doubt about it. She was even more in love with me than I was with her. But from my experience, I think that 97% of all my patients fall in love with me. They fall in love during the treatment. Maybe only one didn't. All the rest, they fall in love.

Tova: With this particular client, were you able to go the full length of the therapy or did you need to remove yourself from the case? Did the romantic feelings become part of the process?

Amit: During the meetings, we'd always lie together and talk about the fictional future, one in which we would elope somewhere and live abroad. But we both knew that we were just fooling around and that this was not something that was actually going to happen.

Tova: So these feelings were all processed in the therapy and you were able to take the therapy to its conclusion with her?

Amit: Yes. We did complete the therapy.

Tova: Was it difficult?

Amit: It was very difficult, especially because the main issue for the surrogate is personal relationships. We don't tend to have those and they're not easy to find. It's rare to find people who can live with the fact that their partner is a surrogate. It means you need to find someone that you like, who likes you back, and can deal with the fact that you are a surrogate. Like I said, it's very rare.

Tova: Yes. It takes a lot of understanding.

Amit: Yes, a lot. So it was very sad. It was quite hard. That treatment finished about two months ago. I had a birthday a week ago. And she actually gave me letters to open on my birthday. I opened them last week, so that brought me back a bit. But it's become a very loving memory. Unfortunately, that's all that it will be.

Tova: Are there any other experiences that stand out for you?

Amit: Yes. There was a patient who was a tough case. On our first meeting, she shrunk into a little ball. She clung to herself and looked at me. That was how she was for the first five meetings. It was a long treatment, one that lasted for a year. But at the end, we remembered how she was when we started the treatment compared to how she was at the end of it. When the treatment ended, she felt free to be naked around me; she was hugging me and she was the complete opposite of that little ball when she started.

Tova: Had she been traumatized as a child?

Amit: Sexually abused? No, I don't think so. I don't recall her being traumatized by that. She just grew up with tough parents. She was a bit deformed, but nothing too serious. Only she had a big head, so it wasn't easy for her growing up. That's why that comparison between how she started and how she ended was really a memorable thing.

I also remember another client: with her, in every session, we would have an objective or a specific lesson that we were not allowed to go beyond, no matter what. What you need to understand about those objectives or targets is that it's not something that we *have* to do. It's a very important point, because we, as surrogates, don't have to do anything. If I don't want to do something, then I will not do it. I'm pretty sure that you are addressing the issue that people compare surrogacy to prostitution.

Tova: Yes.

Amit: One of the major differences, among other things, is that we don't have to do anything we don't want to do. So in that session, the objective was to French kiss and I remember that she wanted me to French kiss her three minutes after we met. I told her that I didn't want to, "I don't feel like it because you just walked through the door." She wanted to fast-forward to the French-kissing part. I told her that this was something that you worked towards, and that after the mood is set, you need to start kissing lightly, then evolve into French kissing. Her presenting problem was that she couldn't make an emotional bond with men because she always had sex with them the first time that she met them. With most clients, we need to draw them out to do something comfortable; but with her, we needed to put on the brakes.

Tova: Did a client ever express her appreciation by giving you a gift?

Amit: I have in front of me a gift I got from a patient, which is my first memory. She had a great talent with stories, and she wrote me a story about my life. It's about what I told you about my brother and everything that happened with him that affected my self-esteem. She wrote this story and she framed it and gave it to me. It's a very touching story and she concluded it like this. "You ask from where I know this soul? Well, I had the luck of running into him, and I wish that I could be with him because in my eyes, he's the one and only. But as much as I would love us to be forever together, I know that there are many other sad people who need his help."

Tova: Is this your mission in life?

Amit: Yes. It's my calling.

Tova: What are the qualities or abilities you need to be a good surrogate?

Amit: I think what's important is the ability to separate your surrogate life from your personal life. I need to fully understand my boundaries and not let my feelings overlap from one part of my life into another. That works for me. I don't know how it works for other surrogates, but for me, it helps me to be able to go on with this. I had a girlfriend once, and when I entered the clinic, I put all of my feelings for her in a box and locked it somewhere in the back of my mind. Then I took out the box for my client and opened it up, which allowed me to fully reconnect with her. After one and a half hours, when my session was done, I left the clinic. I closed that box and opened my girlfriend's, the one that contained all of my feelings for her.

Tova: It's a special balancing act.

Amit: Yes, and it's very much needed, I think. I don't tend to work with a lot of clients at the same time, so it's challenging. And as I said, the main problem for surrogates is the impact on their personal lives. If someday I choose to stop being a surrogate, this will be the reason. I always say surrogates are intimacy coaches, but it's at the price of our own personal lives. And that's a price I pay willingly most of the time. But I think, now that I've started training to be a sex therapist, I will still be able to help people change their lives and still have my own personal life. I don't know which one I will choose: to remain a surrogate or to focus on being a sex therapist. Because I think there's a big difference between influencing someone with your words in therapy and changing someone's life with your hands or your actions as a surrogate. It's important that people understand how surrogacy can change people's lives.

Dafna, M.A., Israel

Photo from istock

"... Becoming an integrated person means becoming comfortable with truth..." —Caroline Myss

Dafna has an M.A. in Education and has taught theater and dancing for five years. In addition, she has taught yoga and meditation and has studied art.

Tova: What were the early messages you heard growing up in your family regarding sexuality and intimacy?

Dafna: I was raised in a very progressive home, so I had a very positive feeling about sex. I'm the youngest and have two brothers and one sister, all older than me. The examples I had were not just from my mom and dad, but also from my siblings. My brothers would have talks with my mom and share intimate details about their girlfriends with her, and she would listen with a lot of love and empathy, and maintained a positive attitude. She also accepted the girlfriends into our home in very loving ways. My brothers would walk around half naked and it was no problem. It was something that they considered very natural to do. I also saw my brothers kissing their partners when I was a little girl, and I believe that living in this kind of relaxed, positive environment made me very comfortable with sex, sexual behavior, and intimate communication. There was no guilt or shame around sex, although, in looking back today as an adult, I recognize some kind of emotional suppression and unspoken issues.

Tova: Given the fact that you had a very open and accepting family, were there any social or sexual issues that you needed to work on as you grew toward adulthood?

Dafna: Yes. The issue was that I imitated my mom's sexual behavior. My sister, who was more conservative, considered my mom a little over the top when she wore provocative clothes and flirted with men. And at parties, my dad would dance with other women and be very warm with them. So I got the message that they both felt really free. Consequently, I looked at this as beautiful behavior of my parents and wanted to imitate them. I know that is why, in my younger years, I was probably more provocative and less sensitive about how my behavior affected other peoples' feelings. In time, I learned that I needed to be wiser in handling my sexual behavior and sexual energy.

Tova: That was an important piece of maturity for you.

Dafna: Yes, and actually I'm still learning that. I'm learning to notice, to be more sensitive, and to respect socially acceptable codes of sexual behavior. But still I have my small social group, and there my natural behavior is accepted.

Tova: Do you consider yourself a sexual rebel or someone who needed to become more sensitive to social norms?

Dafna: Yes. I feel that practicing being more conservative in my sexual behavior has been a gift for me because it taught me how to consider other people's feelings. I'm not a rebel. I'm an educator, and part of my teaching is to live my truth and be sensitive to the feelings of others. And yet, the society I choose to live in is still not ready to accept my lifestyle. But I am aware that following accepted social codes helps me integrate and build bridges to other people.

Tova: How did you first hear about surrogacy?

Dafna: I heard about surrogacy when I was twenty years old, from a friend who had begun working as a surrogate. He told me about the profession and the role of the surrogate, and I became very curious to know more. By that point, I already knew that I wanted to do work connected to human sexuality, although I didn't yet know exactly what that was.

Tova: How did you find Dr. Ronit Aloni's Sex Therapy Clinic in Tel Aviv?

Dafna: I called the clinic and said that I was interested in working there in the area of sex education. I set up an appointment with the clinic's manager, Dr. Aloni, and we talked. Finally I decided to participate in the surrogate training in 2011 and enrolled right away.

Tova: You're involved in the field of education and work in surrogacy at the same time?

Dafna: Yes, I am.

Tova: Why were you so comfortable with your body and your sexuality?

Dafna: As I became more mature, I experienced a lot of joy through my body and from my sexuality, and it became a playground for pleasure and exploration.

Tova: When you started working as a surrogate with your first few clients, did anything surprise you?

Sex Is the Least of It

Dafna: I knew from the beginning that I wanted to take it slow, I didn't want to have more than one client at a time, because I wanted to be sure that I was totally present in the experience. I also wanted to be sure that I was capable and could really do the work. What surprised me was the gradual buildup of the relationship created between me and my clients and how that led to intimacy, becoming friends, and creating a rapport. We started slowly developing trust, rather than immediately getting into erotic activity.

Tova: Like in a relationship.

Dafna: Yes, like what happens in a relationship and when forming a close friendship, by sharing stories, experiences, and feelings. I needed to focus on getting close to a person in a nonsexual way. I learned in my training that less than 10% of the entire process involves direct sexual contact.

Tova: That's a very important point you make, because many people have the misconception that a surrogate is having sex with everybody all the time, and it's actually quite the opposite.

Dafna: Yes.

Tova: It's the relationship, the trust, the support, and the emotional intimacy that are so essential. The physical intimacy is really a very small part of the process and may not take place at all, depending on the client.

Dafna: Exactly. And when we get to the point where we express our sexual energy, we are already close and trusting friends. As a result, the sexuality flows fluidly.

Tova: What are your most memorable client experiences?

Dafna: One stands out: he was a thirty-seven-year-old virgin and a very successful man, but hadn't had an intimate connection with a woman. He had a high level of anxiety and a lot of guilt and shame about sexuality. We created a strong bond of trust and became very good friends. Slowly, he was able to release his anxiety a bit more each time we saw each other; he began to thrive and really grew in the process. He's now in a relationship and very much in love. He is living with his partner and very happy. There are no sexual issues there anymore.

Tova: Isn't that the ultimate reward for a surrogate, to know your client has gone on to lead a happier life, and that you have been an important part of making that happen for him?

Dafna: Yes. I still feel that we have this special connection, even though we're not in contact. I have a special place in my heart for him.

Tova: Does any other client stand out for you?

Dafna: I had another client who was about twenty-nine, and he'd had a brain injury that left him disabled. He was taking medications and functioned well in his life, but he didn't have enough confidence to approach women because he lacked social experience. He also had a problem with his short-term memory, and the therapist said that he had a flat affect, meaning that he showed very little emotion.

He was extremely happy, but in a way that wasn't connected to reality. When I met him, I felt he had a big heart and a great soul. His eyes were shiny and he smiled, and I immediately felt very close to him. But I didn't know if I could be physically attracted to him because he's not a guy that I would choose in my personal life. And yet, because he has a big heart and a big smile, and is so optimistic and loving, I was able to do beautiful work with him. I came to feel very close to him emotionally. We enjoyed listening to music and singing, and we danced together. I felt that my heart was opening through these experiences, and then the physical attraction unfolded for me. After his therapy, he grew in his confidence and self-esteem. His strong qualities and traits, such as being optimistic, positive, and having so much empathy, are gifts for women. After completing the surrogate partner therapy, he went out into the world to search for a partner. He gained a lot, and I, too, learned something very important: that being friends is a very good basis for developing a physical attraction.

Tova: Is there any other client who comes to mind?

Dafna: Another significant experience was with a twenty-four-year-old man who was a virgin. He was filled with anxiety and he had a backstory: when he was in kindergarten, he played doctor with a girl, and it took place in her house. He was lying on top of her when her parents found them, and her parents' reaction made him feel so guilty and ashamed that he couldn't create an intimate connection with anyone after that; he had been so totally traumatized. But he felt safe enough to share this with me. I felt that there was a shift in his trauma and in his body memory. So we started at the beginning. It was important to me that he always felt comfortable with the work we did and not be tense or anxious.

Tova: You gave him permission to connect with his sexuality in an accepting way.

Dafna: Yes, what was most essential was to give him the opportunity to dare to do what he really wanted to do. One time he said, "I want to draw your body." And so we did that. Experiences like that helped him to become more open and less ashamed. I wanted to legitimize his good feelings about sex.

Tova: What did you learn about yourself through your experiences as a surrogate?

Dafna: I learned that I love people and love the variety of people on this planet. I feel that I know more about human behavior now and have more compassion and acceptance for the people around me, whether I meet them at the clinic or somewhere else. I know that most human beings experience some level of shame or fear about sexuality, and I believe it's my role to help more people let go of these negative feelings, fears, and behaviors. I want to help change their lives.

Tova: So, just as surrogates' clients grow through the work, surrogates grow as well.

Dafna: Yes. Learning and growing go both ways. And giving and receiving benefit both people. When I finish therapy with a client, I write him a letter and thank him for the specific things that I learned from him. I do this as a reminder of their strength and to support their confidence.

Tova: Is there anything else you would like to add?

Dafna: Yes. I want to say that being a surrogate is fascinating. It's the most incredible experience I've ever had. I'm very happy with my decision to become a surrogate. It feels like it's the first step on my path toward personal growth through intimacy and sexuality. I know that my journey has just begun.

Dr. Tara Long, Holland

Photo courtesy of Dr. Tara Long

"The essence of education is the education of the body."

—*Benjamin Disraeli*

Dr. Tara Long is a mentor, trainer, and sex educator for adults who want to enrich their intimate relationships, connect more profoundly, and develop their sexual, creative potential with greater awareness and joy.

As an international lecturer and sexuality educator, she works from a transpersonal and somatic perspective. She integrates both Western and Eastern sexuality in her educational approach.

She has been educated as a professional dancer, choreographer, neuropsychologist, and clinical sexologist. She obtained her doctoral degree as a doctor of scientific psychology in the field of cognitive creativity research. She trained as a Jungian and transpersonal therapist.

She is the dean of the Connection University of Advanced Erotology, whose vision is teaching conscious sexuality and contributing to a more peaceful loving world.

Tova: Where did you receive your training?

Tara: I was trained by the Connection University for Advanced Erotology. I studied Sexual Shamanism with Dr. Ray Stubbs, Sexual Tao with Mantak Chia, and also regression therapy. I acquired my Ph.D. in 2009, through a co-research project with City University, London, University of Amsterdam, and CUAE. My degree was a Doctor of Science in Psychology.

Tova: How did you learn to connect with your sexual energy?

Tara: I was never aware of it until I was twenty-five. I fell into the world of Tantra by pure chance. At the time, I was working as a dancer and choreographer, and studying as a dance scientist at a modern dance institute in London, when I injured my back. My dance institute was close to a little Chinese shop with acupuncture and herbs, and I decided to go there for acupuncture treatment. I was told that I might experience some pain, but that it would go away. During the night, I had this incredible feeling in my pelvic region and I was shaking in my bed. I had never had such an incredible reaction in my body. But although I was scared, I also noticed a deeply energized feeling moving up from the bottom of my spine to the crown of my head. It felt like kind of an orgasm, very intense. The next day I went back to the shop and asked the Tibetan Doctor what had happened.

She said, "Have you ever heard about Tantra? I have a meditation group that meets every week and we do this kind of energy-moving work. You are welcome to join us." I attended her group for about a year, and then she referred me to a Buddhist monastery located in Scotland. At the monastery, I was also trained in Tantra, based on sexual energetics, and learned how to move that energy throughout my spine and entire body to expand my awareness and consciousness. I did this really just for my own personal development.

I studied Tantra for seven years, and in the meantime, also graduated as a neuropsychologist. I decided to leave behind my dancing after a period of serious illness and realized I wanted to connect with people, with their hearts and through intimacy. I started giving my own Tantric sessions and the clients came to me more and more. In just three years, I had developed a full-time practice. In my tantric sessions, I included slow healing massage, helping people connect with their bodies, and making them aware of the power of their breath. Many of my male clients had sexual problems, such as premature ejaculation, some had a lack of sexual desire, and there were women with vaginismus who were totally blocked.

Tova: Why do you think that you felt so comfortable with your body and your sexuality?

Tara: I was raised as a dancer and so I worked with my body as a serious instrument for many years. I learned to know my body from the inside out. Secondly, I think it was my upbringing, especially the relationship with my father, which was very positive; he affirmed my self-esteem. I don't think that so many fathers are as emotionally intimate as my father was with me. He was always there in a very supportive way. On the other hand, my mother was a very strict, disciplined person; she was very scientifically gifted, so that brought me a kind of balance. Somehow in the personality differences that I saw in my parents, my creativity, freedom, and sexual liberation were born.

Tova: How did you first hear about surrogacy?

Tara: In 1998, I met with Cora Emens, the first person in the Netherlands to work as a sex coach and sex surrogate. Some years later, in 2004, we organized a support group of practitioners who were working as sexological body-workers, tantric practitioners, or sexual initiators. I felt that more physical contact, not just touching with my hands, could be very helpful for some clients. So I started working with more physically intimate contact to see how that benefited my clients, and to find out how I felt about it. I discovered that it was no problem for me to do this kind of work; I felt no shame, no guilt. I knew I needed more education in this area, so I attended the Connection University. I met a regression therapist and health psychologist, and together we designed the first surrogate protocols used in Holland. We trained a group of (integral) sexologists, sex educators, sex surrogates, and therapy supervisors.

Another reason why I went into surrogate work was because of my husband. After he and I had our first child, I found that my husband has autism. He has Asperger's syndrome, but it had never been diagnosed, and he was already fifty-two years old. This was a big blow; I had just become a mother of a beautiful daughter. But my husband couldn't easily relate to her, and it was so painful to see him suffering with that, not being able to be emotionally intimate or physically loving with our daughter for about nine months. I felt this lack of interaction would be bad for my daughter and tried many things to help them relate to each other.

I asked him to see a psychiatrist, who tested him and found out he had Asperger's syndrome. The psychiatrist told me that autistic people are very fixated in their responses and cannot change. But by using my Tantra and body-work skills, taking very tiny steps, like just letting him talk to her for a minute, he learned how to slowly move forward with me and with his daughter. He learned by making mistakes, falling down, and standing up again. But most of all, he learned through my physical love and patience. Contrary to what the psychiatrist said, my husband was able to change. Now he is a wonderful, loving, and caring father for his two daughters, and he is really enjoying being a parent. This was possible because I worked with him in a physical way, not just by talking.

Tova: Did that further motivate you to practice as a surrogate?

Tara: My husband said, "You really should help people who are frozen, who are clumsy, who are lonely, and inexperienced. You are the most wonderful teacher. It's going to be important work for your life and for other people's lives."

Sex Is the Least of It

Tova: What are the qualities that make you such a good surrogate?

Tara: I think the most important thing is to be able to make yourself vulnerable to another human being. In my sessions I feel my own ego vanishing as I serve as a sensual guide to help my clients discover their sexual energy. I can feel intimate with people who I normally wouldn't feel attracted to. I think it's important to share genuine love. When you are caressing a client, they are not only experiencing the sensate focus touch, but a strong energy is transmitted through this touch. Other qualities that I think are important are spiritual intelligence, body intelligence, and sexual intelligence.

Tova: Do you also need compassion?

Tara: Yes, compassion and a strong feeling of empathy. You also need to be very patient, because you are co-creating a process of change with your client and you need to go at his pace. It's a unique bond between two people who come together, which creates a sort of organic transformation. Also, I feel that I am receptive, sensitive, and very authentic with my clients. To be a surrogate is to be an artist. And a surrogate relationship is sometimes more real than a normal love relationship between partners, because the surrogate partner relationship with a client is always honest and transparent.

Tova: Tell me about the three or four most memorable client experiences you've had.

Tara: I'll tell you about three: two where I was successful and one where I failed. You learn from your failures as much as from your successes. I'll start with a case I had four years ago, working with a man who was a sex addict. Normally in the case of a sex addict, in clinical, psychotherapeutic terms, touching or intimacy is exactly the opposite of what you should do with them.

However, I had read very interesting research at that time stating that sex addicts could be treated by transpersonal therapy and by learning Buddhist meditation. This could help them from acting out their addiction. With this client, it was not easy for me to read his body language. Even when I did some sensate focus exercises, I had the feeling he was hiding something, but was not yet willing to show what it was. He did a lot of traveling for his work, and he had a fear of being alone at night. His routine was to pay an escort to spend time with him in the evenings. When I asked him why we had developed this addictive behavior, he could not answer. He said that he was happy and had had a stable childhood, but now he wanted to end this compulsive behavior.

When he arrived, he told me that he was searching for the best escort service. I decided to try a very experimental approach with him. I wanted to understand his routine with an escort, how she acted and how he acted with her. I proposed that we arrange two appointments at a hotel, and that I would present myself in the role of an escort. I would not be there to give him any therapy, not to provide any feedback, but just to observe how he acted. Well, this perfect gentleman transformed into someone quite primitive during our hotel meeting. At the beginning of the meeting, he was very sexual, but by the end, what struck me was that he was actually looking for an intimate connection.

Tova: In your first meeting, were you sexual with him?

Tara: Yes. This was the agreement, which I know is totally against every surrogate protocol. That's why I said this was very experimental, but I just followed my intuition.

Tova: What about the second meeting?

Tara: We decided to have another meeting, but then in the middle of the encounter, we would make a transition from being sexually intimate to being emotionally intimate. In the middle of the session, I would start to do different things to see how he would react. We met at the same hotel, and halfway through our encounter I said, "Let's take our clothes off and just hug." He came close to me and I hugged him. He felt so bad emotionally that he cried in my arms for a very long time. It occurred to me that he had never learned how to be intimate. So we restarted our sessions working with very simple things, like talking to each other, holding hands, embracing each other with our clothes on.

After about 11 months, he felt he could be more intimate with himself and with other people. He started to connect with his family again. But I still felt there was something unresolved. Sometimes if a client remains stuck and we cannot find the deep reasons for his behavior, either through physical work or through traditional therapy, I use regression therapy. I told him I had a feeling that we hadn't found the core reason he became addicted. I asked him if we could use regression therapy and he agreed, because he truly wanted to know the real reason for his problem.

Then the whole story came out. When his child was born, his wife had to move to America to work on her Ph.D. She left him with their baby daughter, and during this time, he lost his job and was feeling very bad. He told me that the baby would cry for hours sometimes and that he didn't know how to console her. Out of frustration, he started hitting her so severely that her backside was black and blue for days. This situation repeated itself for months, until he wife returned from the United States. And he kept this horrible secret locked inside of him for twenty-one years. He told me that after he had been so vicious and so aggressive with his child, whom he loved, he couldn't connect with people anymore, especially not with women. In that session, he cried from the inside out because he was in such emotional pain. Because my session with him was running long, I called my supervisor and asked her what I should do. She decided that I should stay, because something very significant was opening up for him. From that point, we were able to build a real relationship. He realized that because of his guilt, he had prevented himself from giving and receiving love.

Sex Is the Least of It

Tova: What most people don't understand is that a surrogate can dramatically change a person's life, and that the process is not only about sex, but more about emotional intimacy and connection. Is there another experience that stands out for you?

Tara: Yes. This experience occurred with a female client. People often think that female surrogates only treat men. But that is not the case for me. Sometimes women feel more comfortable with a woman at first, before they move on to working with a man. So one day I got a call from a man who said, "My wife has vaginismus. I can't make love to her; and she was traumatized because she had been abused by men in the past. She even had been forced by a former boyfriend to work as a prostitute for more than 11 years. She has worked with trauma psychologists and sexologists, but no one has been able to help her. I also have a problem; I'm autistic and I can be very impatient and sexually aggressive. I'm afraid I might reinforce her trauma more deeply."

In accordance with our ethical protocol in The Netherlands, I was not allowed to help these people with touch therapy, because there is a regulation that people with compromised intelligence cannot be treated using this technique. The man's wife had difficulties expressing herself, but he could express himself verbally extremely well. He had a problem controlling his anger and also his sexual desire. They were quite opposite types: she was an introvert and he was an extrovert. He was fixated on sex and she was not interested in sex at all. They had been a couple for about one year, and she was traumatized as a result of being abused by pimps in a brothel. She was kept in a small room and forced to take on ten clients a day. By sheer chance, she was rescued by the vice department of the Dutch police.

Tova: What kind of therapeutic help did she receive after she was rescued?

Tara: A team of five mental health professionals treated her. None of them was able to successfully resolve her trauma. When I saw her for the first time, she was extremely scared. She sat in the corner of the couch not able to even look at me. There were social workers in the room with me who were caregivers for the disabled. I tried to make contact with her, but all these people were talking, as was her autistic boyfriend, who was very controlling. I said, "Dora, my name is Tara and I would love to hear some words from you." With tears in her eyes she said, "Tara, can you help me?" She started talking and was very aware of her situation. She was obese and said, "I'm eating because I want to die. I don't want to feel anymore." I contacted the Trauma Center that had been treating her. The Center's social worker and I agreed that my sessions with Dora were to be recorded on camera so that what I did was fully transparent. For the first two sessions, I worked with her and her husband because they both wanted it that way. But as it turned out, he was more unstable than I realized.

Tova: What kind of work did you do with her?

Tara: I did de-armoring and energy de-blocking, because there was so much physical pressure in her belly that it blocked her from being able to have any feelings in her genitals. She really loved massage, so I did that several times and included a sensate-focus hand caress. I also gave her husband a back massage, which was very relaxing for him and made him less aggressive. Then I taught him how to give her a massage without being too rough. I taught them how to do sensate-focus exercises together, and taught him how to stimulate her; this enabled him to become more emotionally intimate.

In the third session, I really wanted to start addressing her trauma. I taught her how to do a meditation breath, which she continued while I massaged her. She felt many blocked areas in her pelvic region, so I began to do pelvic floor release. She started to shout, cry, and move her pelvis. After a while, she began to experience physical pain. Then the tears began and her horrible memories came to the surface. I covered her up and she felt cozy. This was the most healing transformation I have ever done. After two days, I called her and asked her how she was doing. She said, "I don't feel pain anymore and I feel really light."

Tova: Did you also help her with her social skills?

Tara: Yes. She started learning how to cook so that they didn't have to be dependent on all these caregivers. She started exercising and lost weight. After many weeks, when I went back to their home, she said, "Tara, I want to show your something. And I want to do it in the bathroom." She said, "Look, I got a vibrator with a turning head from my husband." She took it into the bathroom with me and she started pleasuring herself. She said, "I do this every day now, because you said I should love myself. But that's not what I wanted to show you." And then she ejaculated and we both started to laugh. I asked if she had intercourse with her husband, and if so, was there any pain? She said, "We did and there was no pain at all."

Tova: Do you ever work without a supervising therapist?

Tara: I understand that surrogate therapy is a triangle as described by Masters and Johnson, the client, the therapist, and the surrogate. But in the beginning of my work, there were no supervising therapists that could mentor me. Just five years ago, I started to work with educated supervisors.

Tova: Do you prefer working with a therapist?

Tara: Yes, because it makes the process much lighter. Otherwise, you have to switch all the time from one role to the other. This takes a lot of energy and the ability to keep your boundaries very clear. Working with a therapist has great value. The client needs supervision to process his psychological issues, and the surrogate needs the assistance of the therapist to guide her.

Tova: Have you ever fallen in love with a client?

Tara: Yes, I felt so deeply in love that I could hardly forget the client. But because of our protocol, after closure of therapy, the surrogate and the client cannot contact each other. I never forget that I'm married and that I have two wonderful children, but sometimes it is a conflict.

Tova: Do you talk to your therapist about that?

Tara: Yes. I spoke to my therapist and told him how I felt. He said, "I understand that you both have strong feelings for each other because you have so much in common. If you need me, call me again." But the bottom line is you have to deal with those feelings yourself. There's no supervisor who can take those feelings away, and it simply takes time to heal. Eventually, you will disconnect.

Tova: Is there anything else that you would like to add?

Tara: I didn't tell you about the case where I failed. This was a case with a thirty-seven year old Belgian client who was sexually inexperienced. He had never had a long-term relationship and had only had sex one or two times with a prostitute, which was unsatisfying for him. When the therapist and I started to work with him, he told us he had a great interest in the sexual Tao system, and I knew that was a way I could connect with him. So I worked with him by teaching sensate focus exercises and socialization and also using the Tao system. He had taught himself how to have total body orgasms and to move his sexual energy throughout his body. But sexual intercourse was virtually impossible for him and this really puzzled me. I wondered how someone who had accessed such high orgasmic states could not function in regular intercourse.

I thought perhaps it was shame, his upbringing, or maybe a lack of education. But there was nothing unusual about his upbringing, and a urologist said that there was nothing wrong physically. He was very handsome and I knew that women must have been attracted to him. During the course of our therapy, he found a lovely girlfriend with whom he was deeply in love, but he could not have intercourse with her. However, he was very good at fulfilling her with his hands and his mouth, so they were intimate together. He said, "Tara, I'm not satisfied. I want to have regular intercourse with my girlfriend." I decided to use a technique that involves very slow sex without ejaculation. The first time we did this exercise, we were lying together like two spoons.

Tova: You were spooning?

Tara: Yes. He was behind me and got an erection just by our gently moving together. In the next session, I suggested that we try intercourse using only very slow, gentle movements. But I believe he thought that I had set that up as a goal that, if he failed with me, he would fail forever. During the session, everything went well. We started with slow pelvic movements. Then he lay on top of me and I felt his erection; I asked him, "Do you feel ready for penetration? Does it feel right for you?" He said yes, and then I reminded him, "Put on a condom because we practice safe sex."

The moment we unwrapped the condom, I saw him turn pale, and I could see his erection subside. I understood that the condom was a problem for him, but I explained that I never work without a condom. I told him we could just lie together and that I didn't want to force anything; that maybe the next time this would feel more comfortable for him. Then he started to cry. He said, "I'm such a failure; I'm a loser." No matter what I said to him, I couldn't reach him anymore. And we had been working together for nine months. When the session was over, I felt that he would not be coming back. Despite everything the therapist or I did to reach him, with emails and calling, we never heard from him again. We didn't understand why. Both the therapist and I had such a good relationship and trust built up with him. I felt a sense of rejection and I started to doubt myself.

Tova: Would that have been closure for you, if he had indicated why he would not come back?

Tara: That would have been very meaningful. I know before we started our sessions that he went to an escort who specialized in working with virgins. He told me that the manager of the escort service called him before what was to be our last session and said she found a really nice woman for him. So maybe that was the reason. I really don't know. He just never came back.

Tova: What do you believe is the role of the surrogate partner?

Tara: The value of the surrogate is that we can offer clients an intimate, embodied experience and a relationship based on trust. When you learn something by hearing, seeing, or talking, it's too limited, especially when you're describing a sexual experience that should integrate all our senses. In healthy sexuality, we feel, we hear, we smell, we make noises, we talk and touch. So to provide that richness for some clients is really incredibly effective and constructive. The surrogate needs to be able to handle all of that and to encourage the client to make mistakes, because it's all a part of learning. The client wants to feel that he is loved and that he can be completely authentic. That experience is healing in itself. The surrogate provides a warm surrounding and the therapist provides the analytical part, helping the client reflect on what happened during the sessions.

Contact information:

Email: tara@love-in-action.nl; info@deconnection.org

Websites: www.love-in-action.nl (in English soon)

www.your-love-life.nl (with an English summary!)

Marion Van der Stad, Holland

Photo courtesy of Marion Van der Stad

"Sometimes we make love with our eyes. Sometimes we make love with our hands. Sometimes we make love with our bodies." —*Author Unknown*

Before becoming a surrogate, Marion worked as a personal spiritual matchmaker in her own Dutch practice, Aquarion, School for Love & Leadership. After seven years, she began helping single men and women develop their dating and relationship skills. She gained additional experience through her studies in Gnosticism and Tantric sexuality followed by leadership trainings. She has made intimacy the core of her work. She coaches her clients to greater freedom, true sensuality, and the art of joyful sexuality.

Tova: When you were a child, what were the early messages that you heard about sexuality and in your home?

Marion: The overall message was that I should not do it. And I understood later why, because my parents as well as my schoolteachers were terrified of my becoming pregnant. My mother especially said things like, "It's dirty and you should be a virgin until you marry." But she couldn't control her three daughters. We did not follow her advice, except for my second sister, who really was a virgin when she married at the age of 20. When it came to romances, my father called us bad names in his fear, like sluts and other derogatory terms, when we playfully and innocently started kissing boys. How to make babies was discussed, but not sexuality itself or birth control. My parents did not know how to be open about it, although they loved us. They made sex a shameful thing as a way of protecting us. So I had to find out about it myself, the difficult and unsafe way, burdened by their fear, groping in the dark.

Tova: Do you think this was due to your religious background or was it just the attitude of your parents?

Marion: It had nothing to do with religion. In fact, my parents were very free in their religion. They were free thinkers and stepped out of the Church Community. Although in the days when I was growing up, it was thought best for me to have a proper fiancé and get married. Living with a man unmarried would have been a shameful thing to do. I got married at the age of twenty-three and became mother of two children, a son and a daughter.

Tova: How did you discover your sexuality as you were growing up?

Marion: Well, as a teenager I loved to kiss and cuddle and fool around, as green as I was. I didn't know much about my body. Once I got hold of some 'dirty' little books, which I secretly devoured with great appetite, experiencing new sensations in my body. So that was my beginning. Then at age nineteen, when I was far away from home working as an au pair girl in Geneva, I had my first sexual affair with an Italian boyfriend whom I had fallen madly in love with. I was really lucky not to get pregnant. I simply trusted the way my boyfriend handled the situation without using condoms. This is how naïve I was.

Tova: So at some point you discovered that your body felt good.

Marion: Yes, and it functioned well. I had discovered it when I was about fourteen. I liked the feeling in my body when boys kissed and touched me. I got thrilled and longed for more. Maybe because my parents were so strict, I was rather rebellious and explored all those feelings secretly. My two elder sisters had the same experience, so I didn't feel completely alone. Later in life, after my marriage ended, I discovered books, courses, and works on sexuality, male and female trainers who helped me tremendously in trusting not only my own femininity and body, but also my whole being, my sexual being included. I am most grateful for their teachings.

Tova: Tell me about your current work as a surrogate?

Marion: I began working as a surrogate in 1999. Now my practice has changed. I have clients I work with in one-to-one settings, mostly for dating and inspirational talks on sex, and I have clients that I refer to intimacy coaches for hands-on body work. I particularly enjoy working with older clients thirty to seventy-five years of age. My clients are extremely sensitive and shy, even those who are married with children. Shyness robs people from being able to make love and engage in sex and life like other people. I am so touched by this that I am writing a book on this subject. In Holland, we find the term "surrogate partner" rather cold, so we prefer the word "coach," which sounds much warmer.

Sex Is the Least of It

Tova: What did you do before you became a surrogate?

Marion: Initially I was a trained private secretary. Because of my own life and sorrows, I became interested in the psyche. I even had the chance to work for nine years in a university clinic as private secretary for psychotherapeutic professors. Some years after my divorce, after an eighteen-year marriage, I started my own matchmaking agency for spiritual people in 1992. It turned out that a lot of my male clients had no experience with women or with sexuality at all. I understood their need to gain experience with sex because they were stressed and often deeply depressed about dating. After some years, I befriended a female tantric masseuse.

Both of us watched the documentary, *Private Practices*, with sex surrogate Maureen Sullivan. We got so inspired, we wanted to integrate this kind of work, so I referred some of my male clients to this colleague for hands-on sessions. I realized that I also needed to find a woman who would specialize in engaging in intercourse as well. So I put an ad on the Internet and trained those who responded as female coaches, and later on also male coaches. Together we created our own sensate focus exercises into programs we call Intimacy Coaching and Surrogate Partnership.

Tova: Describe your process.

Marion: I do client intakes and assessments that can take from four to six hours. I listen to their history, their social and family contacts, dating and sexual situation, and their hopes. And I listen to the secret content of their lives, which they are often sharing for the first time. I find out if they have had any experience at all with kissing, or other physical contact with the opposite sex. With men and women who are either virgins, poorly experienced, or elderly, I often start by inviting them to do a little touching with a feather and the fingertips. Then we usually progress to holding hands, sitting next to each other on a sofa, and chatting informally together. All of my clients, because of poor life experiences, feel like failures when I meet them, so I always go slowly and teach them to relax and breathe.

Tova: And how do you proceed?

Marion: After the intake, a client starts to work with a surrogate. There seems to be a commonality in the program ingredients that we use: learning to hug and to embrace, feeling the skin and brain responding, being comfortable in each other's arms, touching with clothes on, and then, when appropriate, undressing, sharing body awareness. Then we progress to sexual bonding and sharing it in intercourse. Our clients learn how to give and receive sensual caresses coming from a peaceful body, mind, and heart.

Tova: Do you have the involvement of a therapist?

Marion: Therapists who refer to us for a program, most of the times step aside for a while. After the intake, I become more of a supervisor than a surrogate. I use the word supervisor rather than therapist. I work in the traditional triadic system of client-surrogate-supervisor. This three-way relationship safeguards everyone. As the supervisor, I ask the client, "How are you progressing? What would you like to know, to do now; what are your fantasies and what goals would you like to set for yourself?" I always encourage them to speak as honestly as they can to me, to the surrogate, and in their lives. The surrogates report back to me their observations of the client, the sessions, and how the two of them are creating a bond. We have specific rules and health codes for clients versus surrogate partners and vice versa.

Tova: Can you describe what those rules are?

Marion: There are practical guidelines for how clients and surrogates should relate to each other regarding hygiene, ethical boundaries, communicating with me, and appointments. The main rule is honesty. Integrity and respect of privacy are highly valued. I see my intimacy coaches and myself as role models for clients. We all radiate with warmth and openness.

Male coaches work with men as the giving and sensitive guides and with women as a surrogate boyfriend. The female coaches are receptive, playful guides or surrogate girlfriends. In 2007, I co-founded the Dutch Foundation of Intimacy Coaches and Surrogate Partners (NOVIS) of which I have been the chair ever since. Recently, I have begun training surrogate partners from other European countries as well.

Tova: Why do you think you felt so comfortable with your body and your sexuality?

Marion: I was trained in body awareness through Tantra. There are many excellent teachers in Holland and throughout Europe. One of my primary Tantra trainers was a female psychologist, and after that, a male psychotherapist who taught me how to ground myself in sexuality. Other Tantric teachers taught me to understand the shadow sides of myself. For me the goal is always to look within and trust my whole body. I learned that I am perfect as I am, even with a rather painful body.

Tova: So after your Tantra training, you started feeling very comfortable with your body?

Marion: Yes, I speak freely about the sacredness of sex and about my journey of discovery. I've also profited from many Landmark trainings; I attended one in New York where I learned what leadership means. After that, I added the School for Love and Leadership to my practice name.

Tova: When you talk about leadership in the context of love, what do you mean?

Marion: Generally speaking, I mean that you follow your inner core, you become the leader of yourself, of your own life, your own body, mind, and soul. You follow the wisdom in your heart combined with the wisdom of your sexuality. Leadership means being in charge of yourself, and understanding, loving feminine as well as masculine energies throughout your body, including mind, heart, and genitals.

Sex Is the Least of It

Tova: What surrogate experiences would you like to share?

Marion: One of my most memorable experiences when I started surrogacy was with a thirty-eight-year-old woman in the process of becoming a man, a transgender individual. She was taking hormones and was about to have her breasts surgically removed when she came to see me. She said to me, "Since I am still a woman, I would like to work with a woman about female feelings." She started as a scared and troubled person. After some sessions, she was able to feel safe with me, unlike with her mother, who had been a tremendous threat. I opened my arms and she came into my embrace. She lay against me for hours. At one moment, she said to me, "Now I'm getting sexual feelings," and I said "Oh, this is great…enjoy it," and she did.

She was allowed to feel her feelings, whether female or male, without needing to take any sexual action, nor did I; it was the warmth of body-to-body contact. I was sorry to hear that she wanted to turn herself into a male, because I think she could have gained much as a woman. But her decision was made already. She was on medication for some time and had passed all the required tests, so I did not attempt to change her wishes. Her experience with me was the start of resolving some of the damage inflicted by her mother. She left feeling mature and self-centered.

Tova: Did she continue with her sex change?

Marion: Yes, later on, she proceeded to have her breasts removed and she was completely fine turning herself into a man. I saw him several months later, and he was very happy, joyfully running around in just a shirt and pants. Being in a more male body made him feel free.

Tova: Do you have another experience that you would like to talk about?

Marion: Yes, this was with a seventy-two-year-old male who was still a virgin, referred to me by a therapist. He had been with a girlfriend for twenty years until he was sixty-five; he had worked as a government official, she was a physician. They had been lovers up to the point of penetration, but never beyond. She wanted him to caress her to orgasm, but then wouldn't let him enter her, and she would not touch him in return. After all those years, he still reacted as a victim, not knowing who to turn to with this kind of intimate misery. Finally, he started to talk about it with the therapist.

Tova: He realized he had been deprived?

Marion: Yes, he very much longed for sexual openness and fun. At the end of that relationship, he had lost the ability to have erections, probably because of feeling rejected for such a long time; he literally had dried up. When he visited me, I said, "Let's start very gradually touching each other's hands so you can feel safe with me." We began with the caresses, and slowly he began to regain his self-confidence. And I found out that he was quite a good lover indeed, more in giving, of course, since that's what he was used to.

Tova: Was he able to restore his erections?

Marion: Not yet. Just at the moment of penetration, he would pull away, lose the erection, probably because of so many years of his arousal not culminating in intercourse. I was able to help him regain his respect and his sense of manhood. When he left treatment, he felt fabulous. I heard from him later that he had met a girlfriend in her seventies, and that after some months, their love was consummated.

Tova: So you had a tremendous impact on his life.

Marion: Yes, a very big change. And I learned that you are never too old to learn to love. I think one of the great services that surrogate partners offer is to help people open their hearts and trust themselves, including their private parts, particularly when they have been wounded over and over again. We help them change their negative beliefs and slowly show them that they are worthy of love. We encourage them to not take anything personal and to make social friends with more people, not just love relationships. I very often see that when they feel their confidence renewed, they are able to find a partner of their own. The sexual aspect of surrogacy is not necessarily a part of our work. I see to it that they are cared for until their treatment ends with a proper aftercare and farewell.

Tova: I assume that aftercare is about making sure that they remain social and helping them with their dating skills?

Marion: Yes, to make sure that they really have learned to take their lives to a higher level and continue to practice social skills. We look at the whole person. Late-life virginity is the hardest issue to deal with for many clients, as they could keep hiding alone even after they've experienced intercourse just out of habit. Even when a person feels that he or she has gotten in touch with sexual feelings, there may still remain clumsiness in dating. We rehearse what it's like to be on a date, to talk informally, appear inviting, dealing with the first kiss, holding hands in public, experiencing whatever discomfort may arise and staying with it until it becomes more familiar. We also go outside and hold hands, visit them at home, do makeovers. We have dinners with them and go on practice dates. If necessary, we encourage them to live on their own, if this was not the case before, and to buy a double bed instead of a single one, although a partner is not yet in sight! We get them ready to date.

Tova: What are the qualities that you think made you such a good surrogate?

Marion: Two of my best qualities are that I am warm and trustworthy. I know how to make people feel safe as they get out of their comfort zones. I help them move away from the lies they've told themselves which have damaged their self-confidence into the essence of love. Because of my knowledge of sacred sex, I guide them into a higher level of lovemaking through spirituality which strengthens them even more

Sex Is the Least of It

Tova: Through your surrogate experiences, what did you learn about yourself?

Marion: I learned to become more patient, focused and in harmony with myself. I also learned to work with a client at his or her pace. I am grateful for those talents and feel joy on the successes of clients who broaden their view of the world to include more joy and happiness. This touches me deeply. I feel I am contributing to a better world and to peace itself. I also feel help from other realms. Through my studies, experiences, and of course my clients, I grew from a doubter into a believer.

Tova: Is there anything that you would like to add to what you've already said?

Marion: A documentary made by British filmmakers for Channel 4 was made in 2007 about my work. It is called "Virgin School." Since the film was made, I have continued refining my methods to even higher standards. And, in addition to working with Dutch people, I have created special courses for people who travel to us from all over Europe for private treatments. I run the only organization that offers such intensives in the Netherlands.

Recently I added the use of morphological techniques, which encourages people to let go of their emotional blocks in a safe way. It saves time and money, and can even be done by Internet sessions. I'm planning webinars in both Dutch and English to teach these healing lessons.

Contact information:

Websites: www.Aquarion.nl (Dutch) or www.surrogatepartner.nl (English)

Former Surrogates

Mukee Okan

Photo courtesy of Mukee Okan

"Knowing others is wisdom, knowing yourself is Enlightenment."— *Lao Tzu*

Initiated as Swami Muktananda Saraswati, February 1984, by Swami Satyananda Saraswati, Biha School of Yoga. Bihar School of Yoga: world's first Yoga University. The most well-known international educational training facility in scientific, systematic yoga practices in the world (http://www.yogavision.net/).

Tova: What messages about sexuality did you get from your family as you were growing up?

Mukee: I am a first-generation Australian, but my parents grew up in Estonia. I love them very much, but they passed on their Lutheran upbringing about sexuality. This meant that little was said about it until they found out I was having sex. That's when I discovered that they did not believe in sex before marriage. My parents grew up with stricter, more traditional values and ideas about sex, whereas in Australia, we are very connected to nature, and there is greater physical freedom and more relaxed attitudes about sex.

Tova: Did you hear negative things about sexuality at home?

Mukee: My parents weren't able to communicate anything to me about sex. There was no conversation at all about sexuality. But I was self-pleasuring and having orgasms from the time I was a little girl.

Tova: Where were you born and where did you study?

Mukee: I was born in Sydney, Australia, where I lived until I was about twenty-two. I studied architecture at Sydney University. When I completed my degree, I moved to the bush in Australia and lived in a subtropical rainforest area where I built a house.

Tova: Tell me about your spiritual journey?

Mukee: I went through a major spiritual transition there in the subtropics, which began when I started going to yoga classes in the local ashram. I studied with the Bihar School of Yoga as a beginner and was initiated as a karma sannyasin in that system by Swami Satyananda Saraswati. I was given the name "Swami Muktananda Saraswati." *Swami* means master of oneself and *Muktananda* means the bliss of spiritual freedom. I'm mentioning this because it began the total transformation of my hippie lifestyle from sex, drugs, and rock 'n' roll into a totally different dimension. It was a spiritual awakening for me, and soon I was looking for a new place to live that had a Satyananda yoga ashram. I went to New Zealand, because I wanted to be in a place that had an Ananda yoga ashram. I ended up living in the ashram for almost four years, and that was the first time I was able to connect with my inner awareness. What's that got to do with sexuality and becoming a surrogate? Well, in my yoga practices, I learned that the practice enhances one's sexual energy tremendously, even though our daily program was not designed specifically for sexual relationships.

Tova: So at some point, you went from an inner awareness of sexuality to an external expression of it?

Mukee: Yes. Sexuality was not addressed directly in that lifestyle. However, I use everything I learned in my life. I use all of my training in everything I teach and coach, and do in surrogate work. Also I still do the yogic practices on a regular basis myself.

Tova: At what point did you move from New Zealand to the United States?

Mukee: I moved from Australia to New Zealand, lived in the ashram, and then came to the U.S. Then I embarked on the study of Quodoushka, a type of spiritual sexuality, and went on a ceremonial medicine journey. That was a second awakening for me, and so I apprenticed to the lineage of the Sweet Medicine Sundance Path, a matriarchal shamanic body of teachings. I decided to move to Los Angeles, where the main teaching center of the Deer Tribe Métis Medicine Society Shamanic Lodge of Ceremonial Medicine was located. This is an extraordinary body of knowledge, and Quodoushka, the spiritual sexuality teachings, are the catalyst and one part of the vast teachings. In the first Quodoushka program I attended, I met Stephanie Wadell, who was a surrogate partner. It was through my connection to Stephanie that I then found out about the IPSA (International Professional Surrogates Association) program, whose training I did in 1995.

Tova: Were you living in Los Angeles then?

Mukee: No, I was living in Phoenix, Arizona. The Deer Tribe center had moved to Phoenix from L.A., so many of us moved there as well.

Tova: When did you start working as a surrogate?

Mukee: I completed my internship in about six months, but my biggest challenge in Phoenix was finding a therapist who knew how to work with a surrogate partner. This wouldn't have been so difficult if there were trainings for therapists so they could learn about the process and how to work with surrogate partners. Because of this dearth of trained therapists, I would begin to work with a client and then the therapist would abandon us. The SPT process can't work unless it's a three-way relationship of therapist, client, and surrogate partner. You can't go into deep healing practices with people, for instance with adult virgins, without the support of a therapist.

Tova: Were you able to cultivate working relationships with any therapists?

Mukee: No, it remained a challenge. Because I am also a Quodoushka teacher, I began focusing on those programs rather than trying to be a surrogate without any support. We definitely still need more training for therapists on how to work with surrogate partners.

Tova: Why do you think you felt so comfortable with your body and your sexuality?

Mukee: A lot of it has to do with growing up in Australia and how much we lived in nature; on the beach, in the water, and in the wilderness. I had discovered orgasms when I was as a child, so sexuality has been a natural part of who I am. In high school, I was expelled because I was involved in a sexual relationship; then, when I went to my new high school, a lot of the girls began to confide in me and tell me very personal things. So people have always felt comfortable coming to me to share traumas or very difficult situations they experienced.

Tova: You were an intuitive sexual healer starting from a very young age, then?

Mukee: Yes, I suppose you can say that. My last year of high school, I lived with my boyfriend, because my parents wouldn't let me stay in their house unless I agreed to live by their stipulated rule of no sex before marriage. So I moved out, and a lot of the girls at school would ask me precious, innocent questions like, "What does he expect from you because you're living with him? Does he expect sex from you?" and so on, as if I didn't have a choice. They asked all these precious, innocent questions because they trusted me not to judge them or gossip to others.

Tova: What personal qualities do you have that made you an effective surrogate?

Mukee: I have an ability to heal, whether it's healing relationships or healing personal intimacy. When a surrogate is with a client, there's a mutual giving and receiving. It is a real relationship. It's probably the hardest job on the planet, after being a mother. I'm very empathetic; if someone starts crying, I feel like I'll cry too. I'm also able to be with someone and totally accept them exactly as they are. In relationships, we often have expectations and opinions about how everything should be; but as a surrogate, I'm challenged to face my expectations and opinions, and to keep myself present in the physical and grounded in the reality of what is.

Tova: Can you recall some of your most memorable experiences with clients?

Mukee: One of them was a man in his late forties who was a virgin. He had been in an incestuous situation with his mother and her boyfriend when he was about fourteen years old, and I don't think that he allowed himself to be touched by anyone since then. He would sit in my living room, where there were two couches at right angles to each other; and for all but the last session, he sat in the space between the two couches. He'd have sweat pouring down his face and all over his body, just from sitting alone in a room with a woman. I used a lot of my yogic background to guide him in relaxation, and used breath awareness to move his attention to different parts of his body and do some simple movements. He joined a therapy group for survivors of sexual abuse where people shared their experiences. He always sat where nobody else could be next to him; but one day he told me that he had sat with women on either side of him on a couch. That was a tremendous victory and a huge step in his growth.

He and I practiced a series of sensate body focus exercises. He joined another group of mostly women and they held hands in a big circle at the end. He and I practiced how to hold hands and I encouraged him to always communicate with his circle if someone was holding his hand too tightly. For him, it was a revelation that he could say no to somebody, or "I'm not comfortable with that," or "That's too tight." Little by little, he became more at ease and comfortable in our sessions and began choosing more intimate sensate body focus exercises. He had just chosen to do the next session in the bedroom, still fully clothed. But then, for some unknown reason, he changed therapists. The new therapists didn't believe in surrogate work, so unfortunately we ended our sessions very abruptly, with no proper closure.

But it was incredible to see his transformation as a result of the intimacy of our conversations and our simple sensate focus touching. I always gave him choices; he learned that he could say yes or no, and that it was entirely up to him. And what was extraordinary was that he started taking dance classes, which encouraged him to become more confident in social situations. We practiced dancing together, so he could experience how to control the space and how much body contact was okay for him. It was always his choice what we did in each session—either what we did last time or a new experience. When we danced together, I encouraged him to press against my body and to make physical contact. We were fully clothed, and many of the things he and I did together were not comfortable for him. But he stayed with it and that was so great.

That's why I find it so disheartening when a client who is making such wonderful progress transfers to another therapist who doesn't understand the value of surrogacy, and this terminates the client's growth. The problem is that some therapists are fearful of the law and the lack of a sufficiently clear distinction between surrogate partner work and prostitution. The therapist often has no knowledge, training, or experience with how surrogate partner therapy really works. It all comes down to education for everybody.

Tova: Is there another experience you want to share?

Mukee: I worked with a young man who had cerebral palsy and was a virgin. He was sexually precocious, and young people today can access all sorts of stuff about sex online. When his therapist introduced us for our initial three-way meeting, he was depressed and introverted, and taking several prescription medications. I saw him about once or twice a month for about six months. We did the simplest sensate body focus practices and rehearsed social conversations, such as asking a woman on a date. His therapist and his parents were amazed at the change in his demeanor. He became a happy young man and was confident that he would have a relationship with the right woman for him.

Tova: Did your sessions include sexual activity?

Mukee: No, we did not have sexual intercourse. We went at his pace and did some intimate practices together. One of the most successful things for him was to practice calling a young woman and inviting her out to dinner. I also gave him a few tips, such as cleaning his apartment. On the date, he cooked dinner at his place and they watched a movie. She wanted to have sex, and I was so proud when he told me his response to her was, "I'm not ready for that." As part of the sensate focus practices, he learned about communication and agreements which involve clearly communicating the territory of your mutual exploration. That was a great step for him.

Tova: You taught him to find his sexual voice.

Mukee: That's right. He was able to communicate what was right for him. He eventually graduated from his education program and moved to another state.

Tova: Are there any other experiences you want to talk about?

Mukee: Yes. There was an older gentleman who hadn't had a sexually intimate experience with a woman for a very long time. The focus of his treatment was his lack of confidence and need to revive and polish his social skills. The main thing about this experience was how well he blossomed and how his self-confidence grew. He was able to initiate dating; he joined some clubs, such as hiking clubs that helped him meet women. Through intimate communication and the nature of the exercises, I helped him learn to value himself again as a man.

Tova: Did you ever have a client who was particularly moved by one of the sensate focus experiences, perhaps someone who was not used to being touched?

Mukee: For the clients I've spoken about, the sensate touching was a unique experience that opened up their awareness about themselves and got them in touch with their body and feelings. But I'd rather talk about a situation that points out the importance of working with a therapist trained in SPT. Once, a therapist wanted to refer a client to me and said that her client was very advanced and didn't need to start at the beginning. When I met him in the therapist's office, it was clear he was not willing to start with the beginning steps of SPT. I said I wasn't able to work with him unless he was going to let me guide the program. So I did not work with him and his therapist, who supported the client's position through a lack of understanding and education about what surrogate partner work is.

Tova: What did you learn about yourself through your surrogate partner experiences?

Mukee: I learned about my ability to be present, to be in the moment with my client; that I am very open and receptive; and that I'm also creative in guiding the SPT process. I greatly appreciated the courage it takes for someone to reach out and enter into this kind of therapy, which is a tremendous act of faith. I learned that I'm able to listen in a nonjudgmental way and be totally accepting. And although this is a step-by-step process, it is not an agenda set in stone; so as a surrogate partner, you always respond to the needs of the client, within certain clearly communicated boundaries.

Tova: Is there anything else you would like to add?

Mukee: Yes, I want to applaud the courageous people who enter into surrogate therapy and make the choice to grow and change. Surrogacy also is good sex education, something which is missing all over the planet. It's important for parents to educate children, but healthy sex education comes from all of us and every person is an image-maker of sexuality for young people. Often, sex and sex education has becomes a political and moral issue. I see that as a waste of energy to fight against; that's why I have dedicated myself to sexual healing education. My mission is to facilitate profound sexual well-being experiences for men, women, singles, and couples, and to produce outstanding educational programs for all. I envision a global network of sexual healing centers dedicated to transforming lives through enhanced sexual well-being.

Contact information:

Email info@mukeeokan.com

Website: www.mukeeokan.com

Alicia Snow, M.A.

Photo courtesy of Alicia Snow

"If anything is sacred, the human body is sacred."

— *Walt Whitman*

Tova: What early messages did you hear about sexuality in your home?

Alicia: I was fortunate to grow up in an open-minded household. Both of my parents were considered rather progressive for their time. They conveyed an attitude of open-mindedness and mutual respect as we were growing up; they never made us feel inferior. They weren't prudish or easily shocked. I was the first born of three daughters. Both my parents instilled confidence in all of us, and gave us constant encouragement. They were supportive and willing to listen to us, and encouraged us to explore and to think for ourselves. I think that influenced my concept of sexuality and being a confident person. Then when I was in high school, I read a lot about other cultures and developed an interest in reading erotic literature. That served to further broaden my horizons and expand my exploration of my own sexuality, as well as my understanding of my body. When I went to college, my interest deepened as I continued reading and I was fortunate to have professors who validated my philosophy of life, sexuality, and relationships.

Tova: You were very fortunate to grow up in such a progressive home.

Alicia: Yes. That was in stark contrast to what a lot of my friends experienced. Many of them loved to come to our house because my parents were so open, accepting, and welcoming. They were good role models for a healthy relationship, so that was another fortunate thing, because many of my friends grew up in homes where there was conflict and divorce. My parents are still married after fifty-three years. My dad was an idol to me. It wasn't until I got into high school that I realized not every man was like him; he could solve any problem, fix anything, and still have a calm temperament. So it was a bit of a surprise to me to find that not all men are like that. Through my parents' example, I learned to be more tolerant of others, valuing them for their own unique qualities.

Tova: What kind of work did you do before you became involved in surrogacy?

Alicia: I didn't actually have much work experience before I became involved in surrogacy because I was fairly young.

Tova: How old were you when you started?

Alicia: I was twenty-one. I had experience working in a medical office starting in high school. I also worked for an acupuncturist/chiropractor, then worked briefly as a waitress. I did the office work and the waitressing in my late high school and early college years, and started in surrogacy toward the end of my college years.

Tova: How did you hear about surrogacy?

Alicia: It was an ad in the school newspaper at Cal-State Fullerton. It said something like, "Surrogate partner training/sexual enrichment class now forming," and listed a phone number for the Riskin-Banker Human Sexuality Center. At that time, if you said the word "surrogate," most people associated it with surrogate motherhood. But I was majoring in psychology and had done a lot of reading about sexuality, so I had an idea about what surrogate partner therapy entailed. Whatever this class was, I thought it would interest me and possibly be useful in my psychology studies. I'd been looking for opportunities to get some kind of work experience in the field, so the timing seemed right.

Tova: So it was a stepping stone toward further studies in psychology.

Alicia: Exactly. So I called to inquire about the class. They offered a surrogate training course, which I took and completed in 1983. I was trained at their office in Orange in a class of about twelve people, with a few trainers leading the class. I was trained by two very experienced surrogates, Clover Behrend and Paul Gethard. The training consisted of a series of intensive weekends over the course of a month, culminating in the final weekend held at a different location. We had full days of practice sessions that included rotating partners. We learned a number of the sensate focus exercises that are basic to the entire program. We practiced verbal feedback and communication skills, simulating the experience of therapy sessions.

Tova: Why do you think you felt so comfortable with your sexuality and your body?

Alicia: I think a lot of that has to do with the fact that I grew up in a household that didn't stigmatize sexuality; it was considered normal and natural, not something to be ashamed of. My mom made it easy for me to talk to her about anything. Also, the reading that I had done encouraged my exploration. I think all of those things contributed to my feeling confident and comfortable with myself in general, which in turn contributed to my having a healthy relationship with my body. I had always been a "people person," and I've found that people feel comfortable opening up to me, talking about fairly intimate matters and asking for my advice. I knew that I had the ability to make genuine connections with people, including intimate connections. So when I took the surrogate training, I felt that I'd found my niche.

Tova: What are the qualities that made you such a good surrogate?

Alicia: I think empathy is a big one. I have a good intuitive ability to understand the feelings of others, and even experience them on some level. And that leads to being compassionate. I think compassion is a very important element in being a good surrogate, along with being nonjudgmental. I'm able to interact with a variety of people from all walks of life and not judge them for whatever kind of life they've lived. I treat them all with respect, and I think that leads to their feeling more comfortable with me. I believe that my clients felt valued as a person. I also have a well-rounded education and worldly experience, and I think this helped me relate to different kinds of people with a variety of lifestyles and interests. Whether someone was a college graduate or a high school dropout, a captain of industry or a worker bee, I could relate to them on their level and they'd feel we were peers. I was able to find something in each client that I could genuinely connect with. My interest in them was sincere, not an act. A big part of being a good surrogate is respecting people and helping them feel valued and accepted.

Many of the men I worked with had negative past experiences due to their sexual dysfunctions or social awkwardness. They'd often been ridiculed by insensitive partners. One thing that makes surrogate work so successful is that clients realize they're safe and accepted; surrogates and clients establish a strong bond of trust. That trust allowed my clients to learn, explore, and grow in a nurturing environment. They didn't have to be ashamed. I wasn't there to criticize them, but rather to help them. Another important element is communicating clearly, offering guidance to clients in a gentle way, without hurting their dignity or making them feel inferior. Much of surrogate work is helping to improve a client's self-esteem. My role was as a coach, a mentor and a partner.

The deep connections I made with my clients really stand out for me, even after many years. I've maintained limited contact with a number of them and clients occasionally contact me long after the end of therapy. I get emails and sometimes handwritten letters to let me know how they're doing and to express their thanks. They emphasize that they really appreciated the time we spent together, and they tell me that they were able to form healthy, happy relationships because of what they learned from me. It's incredibly rewarding for me to get that kind of feedback.

Tova: The lessons they learned from you lasted years and decades beyond your therapy with them.

Alicia: Yes, it's very gratifying. I feel so honored to have worked with individuals during crucial times in their lives, when they were gaining self-confidence and learning to be comfortable with their own sexuality and social skills. Occasionally I get notices that clients have gotten married or had children, and it's nice to know that they look upon their experience with me as something that had such value in their lives.

Tova: I think what you're saying is so important, given the fact there's so much misinformation and misconception about surrogacy, the most formidable of which is that surrogates are escorts with a fancier name.

Alicia: Exactly. There are those who think of surrogates simply as glorified prostitutes. I do my best to dispel that misconception because there is so much more to the work than just sex. I worked every bit as much on the social aspect of a person's psyche as the sexual aspect. Like all good surrogates, I addressed the entire person. Whatever limitations they had, whatever trouble they were experiencing—whether sexual, social, physical, or psychological—we addressed all of it. That's why it was so important to work in such close conjunction with a licensed sex therapist who supported and managed the entire therapeutic process.

Tova: What stands out for me in doing these interviews is the common thread of compassion that everyone talks about.

Alicia: Absolutely. Compassion is the essential foundation for successful surrogate partner therapy.

Tova: The intimacy has to rest on a foundation. It has to find its footing, and the footing is in the social skills that enable a person to go out and create their own relationships.

Alicia: Exactly, and that's something I experienced in a number of cases. Clients would come in presenting with a sexual dysfunction, such as premature ejaculation or erection problems. We'd do the sensate focus exercises and get them to the point where they could function successfully and feel confident in their sexual ability. But our work was not done. Then we had to ask, "What are you going to do with your new skills? We also need to work on the social aspect, because now that you're more comfortable with your sexuality, the issue remains: how are you going to get someone in bed? Now we're going to work on improving your social skills, how you would ask someone out, practicing conversations, and where would you go to meet women."

I've gone on practice dates with my clients where we'd actually leave the office and drive down the street to a restaurant, then just have lunch or dinner, which allowed me to observe and coach them in a social setting. Sometimes we'd go into separate rooms in the office and talk to each other on the phone, making small talk. It's something many people take for granted. But to someone who lacks self-confidence, even a simple conversation can be terrifying. We even practiced dancing; I'd put on some music and we would dance. All of these activities are important parts of typical dating scenarios, and practicing them helps alleviate the anxiety that comes from their novelty. I had clients break into a sweat because they were terrified of just holding my hand. They were so inexperienced and awkward in social situations that they were panic-stricken. What good is it going to be if you can function in bed but you can't even get past the dinner conversation? There was no way for clients to gain the experience they needed just by talking to a psychiatrist or therapist. You can read books and you can watch videos, but unless you have actual experience with a supportive, encouraging instructor, and actually go through the steps yourself, it's just not enough.

Tova: What were your most memorable client experiences?

Alicia: Many of them tend to be ones that were challenging. For me, the clients who started from a point of very little experience, especially late-life virgins, were particularly memorable. I'm talking about adult virgins over the ages of thirty, forty, and even fifty, who were very inexperienced. I developed a specialty working with these clients, and our practice was sought out specifically for our expertise in that area. We actually had clients come to our office from across the country. Other clients who stand out for me are the ones who were physically challenged. I worked with a number of disabled clients, including paraplegics and quadriplegics whose physical restrictions presented unique challenges. One of the most memorable clients I worked with was one I met just at the beginning of my surrogate work. He was thirty-six years old, very smart, and had a good job as a chemist. He was successful in his career but miserable in his life, and he'd been sexually abused as a child by his parents. He had a number of physical ailments, including a condition called spina bifida, which is a congenital disorder in which some vertebrae never fully form and remain open in the spinal cord and can cause paralysis, incontinence, and deformities, such as club foot, which this client had. And like many with this condition, he lacked bladder control, so he always carried a spare pair of pants with him. He'd never learned to drive and took the bus everywhere. Because of the sexual abuse he'd endured by his parents from a young age, he had serious psychological issues that needed to be addressed. So he was one of those whole-person cases that needed help on many levels. The therapist and I encouraged him to have a surgical procedure to correct his bladder control problem, which was successful. But even after the problem was corrected, he still took the extra pants with him everywhere he went. It had become so ingrained that it took a while for him to finally feel confident enough to leave his spare pants at home.

Tova: It shows you how deeply ingrained habits can be.

Alicia: Yes, absolutely. We also encouraged him to take driving lessons, which he did. I went on some practice drives with him, which was a little unnerving at times, but it needed to be done. We both had a good sense of humor about it. He needed to learn how to dance, too. Nothing fancy, but just being able to feel comfortable enough to move around a little and not feel totally embarrassed. We also had practice dates, so he could go through all the usual behaviors. He had been an alcoholic, but he stopped drinking on his own. He exemplified the successful client who is transformed as a result of surrogate partner therapy. He was a remarkably sensual person with a natural sensuality that had been suppressed. Once his self-esteem and confidence improved, his sexuality and sensuality flourished. He became more successful at work, getting promotions and forming relationships. It was quite a rewarding case and I don't think any other kind of therapy would've produced this level of success.

I had another client that I'll never forget. He was in his mid-twenties and a remarkable person. He was quadriplegic due to muscular dystrophy and used a motorized wheelchair; he could move his fingers enough to be able to work the controls. He had a tracheotomy and so his breathing apparatus was attached to the wheelchair. He wore a catheter that fit over his penis and a bag to collect his urine. Obviously, he had some very clear disadvantages when it came to dating. But he had a healthy sex drive and was interested in forming relationships. He was actually brought to us by his mother, who wanted him to have a safe learning experience, and I give her credit for that.

Working with him was challenging because I needed help getting him out of the chair in order to do our sensate focus exercises. He had such a positive attitude and he was very smart. He'd invented a medical device for tracheotomy patients that was being patented. He also had a good sense of humor and was well-read. We developed a very comfortable relationship, laughing at the awkwardness sometimes as I was trying to straddle him or move his limbs around to accommodate me. We had fun and didn't let his physical disability cast a pall on our enjoyment of each other's company or the sensuality we shared.

Our work culminated one day when I went to his house so that I could see him in his own environment, and in his own bed. His mom was there when I got there. She showed me how to use the hoist to lift him from his chair onto his bed, and then she left us to be alone with each other. We had several hours of private time. We did a lot of oral sex, with each of us being active at different times. We had intercourse and he was able to experience pleasure and orgasm. Realistically, we didn't think he'd have many opportunities to have the kind of interaction with anyone else that he had with me. I knew that I was providing him with an experience that he might not have again—at least not in that way. It was a very gratifying and emotional experience working with him. He was an inspiring person who made a lasting impression on me.

Tova: You've highlighted something so crucial, acknowledging the sensual and sexual needs of the disabled, who are, for the most part, thought of as sort of nonsexual, or sex neutral. The need for touch is so profound and so deep, and it can significantly enrich the quality of a person's life.

Sex Is the Least of It

You truly did give him a gift because he probably would not be able to replicate a safe, accepting, intimate experience in any other way. That opens up the subject of acknowledging the needs of the disabled and people with special needs.

Alicia: Yes, absolutely. In addition to working with adult virgins, I gained recognition for specializing in working with the physically challenged. A sad note was that I learned that the client I just described passed away a few years after our work together. So I know that those times we had were the only close, intimate sexual encounters that he had. And I'm glad he got to have them. His mother was grateful that her son was able to enjoy a natural part of life that he needed for his well-being.

Tova: How wonderful that she was able to acknowledge his needs and was so open, rather than being judgmental or feeling that it was something he didn't really need.

Alicia: I know that some disabled people will go to a prostitute looking for sexual experience, which is understandable, because they think, "I'm probably not going to meet a hot chick in a bar. I'm probably not going to have the kind of experience that I'm seeking, or it won't come easily to me in my day-to-day life. Miss Charming just isn't going to knock on my door and say, 'Hey, you want to go to a movie?'" They recognize that they have special challenges, so it makes sense that they'd go to someone who provides sex for a living.

A disabled man may go to a prostitute who will give him some kind of sexual stimulation, but she's not trained to deal with all the other components of his needs, and she can't provide an overall education of the type he needs, especially the social aspects. Most prostitutes, even kind-hearted ones, just want to service the client and get paid. Unfortunately, I've heard stories from disabled clients who've experienced psychological trauma from going to prostitutes. The client with spina bifida had been to a prostitute and she wasn't compassionate. She was impatient and critical, and he felt berated and humiliated; so it ended up being a very damaging experience for him. Going to a professional surrogate partner and working under the guidance of an experienced sex therapist, clients are better able to have a compassionate experience in a safe environment with someone who's educated and trained to deal with the kinds of problems they experience. Surrogates work with the whole person's psychology in a therapeutic setting.

Tova: Thank you for addressing the issue of prostitution. I think you've beautifully articulated the difference between someone going to a prostitute for sexual contact compared to working with a surrogate for an intimate relationship.

Alicia: That's right, because there is quite a difference. Going to a prostitute is really just about getting sex; there is a time clock involved. Prostitutes make their money seeing as many clients as they can, and as quickly as they can.

Tova: That "come on, let's get on with it" attitude only adds to the discomfort and shame that a person may feel with a prostitute, whereas a surrogate is trained in a therapeutic, gradual process. And before the surrogate even gets admitted into the training, they're interviewed, screened, and evaluated. Their best tools are their qualities of empathy, acceptance, and the ability to establish emotional rapport. And within those boundaries, intimacy can grow and flourish between client and surrogate partner.

Alicia: Another important quality of a good surrogate is her own emotional health. Surrogates should not be working with clients to address their own problems. Prostitutes may have serious mental health issues and are not in a position to be counseling clients.

I give clients credit for just finding us at the therapy center and walking through our door. I know it takes courage, because they often don't know what to expect. Sometimes they come to the therapy center not even knowing about surrogate partner therapy. They come to see a sex therapist, and then the idea of working with a surrogate partner may be introduced if the therapist thinks it's appropriate. I think they're pleasantly surprised when they discover that they're going to be working with a trained surrogate in a very warm and welcoming environment. Clients are often a little hesitant at first, because they think, "What's going to be expected of me?" Then they're happy to learn that nothing is expected of them except their willingness to participate honestly, and that we're going to be practicing a series of gradual exercises that will progress at a comfortable pace for them. They can make mistakes without criticism, and they can ask any questions they might have. Nothing's going to be considered stupid or off-limits. It's all in the realm of learning and exploring in a non-threatening environment.

Tova: Through your surrogate experiences, what did you learn about yourself?

Alicia: Over time, I became more comfortable with my own body and with my own sexuality. I became more confident and trusting in my intuition. It became clear that for me, working as a surrogate was a good decision and the right thing to do with my life. Being in a nurturing capacity and helping others was really my true calling. I realized that I was destined to live an unconventional life. When I started my work as a surrogate, I had just completed my Bachelor's degree in Psychology and subsequently got my Master's degree in Clinical Psychology. I went on to pursue a Ph.D. in Psychology and finished the Ph.D. program. The only thing that remained before getting my Ph.D. was to finish my dissertation. But that was about the time that I realized that I had already been applying my best skills in working with people as a surrogate partner. I decided not to complete my Ph.D. and struggled with whether I should finish it. I finally concluded that while it might be nice to have those letters after my name, it wouldn't serve any real purpose. I already had a Master's degree, which is not too shabby. But I did an internship as a therapist and worked well with people in that capacity, but there were too many instances in which I realized that I could better serve them and connect with them by being their surrogate partner and let someone else provide the psychotherapy. So what I took away from that was that it's okay to start out with certain goals and adjust them as circumstances change, or as awareness and interest intensifies in other areas.

Working as a surrogate helped me to feel very comfortable with myself and with a variety of people. I find that there's something I can connect with in pretty much everyone I meet, and this goes for my personal and professional life, beyond working with clients. I know I'm living a meaningful life. And I feel gratified to know that I've played an important part in many people's lives, participating in their personal growth and sharing a memorable part of their journey.

Tova: When did you stop working as a surrogate?

Alicia: I retired from surrogate work in 2007.

Dr. Barbara Keesling

Photo courtesy of Barbara Keesling

"Sometimes, reaching out and taking someone's hand is the beginning of a journey.

"— Vera Nazarin

Dr. Barbara Keesling, who holds a Ph.D. in Health Psychology from the University of California, Riverside, is the author of two books: *Sexual Healing: The Complete Guide to Overcoming Common Sexual Problems* and *Sexual Pleasure: Reaching New Heights of Sexual Arousal and Intimacy (Positively Sexual)*. She first heard about surrogate partners in 1979 and decided to investigate. At a human sexuality class in 1980, she heard guest speakers who trained surrogates and had a sex therapy center in Orange County, California. She joined their surrogate training program, followed by an internship in the fall of 1980. She started working as a surrogate in early 1981, more than thirty years ago. Barbara retired from surrogacy in 1992.

Tova: How did you first hear about surrogacy?

Barbara: I read a *Los Angeles Times* article about a couple who both worked as surrogate partners and were trained in a Masters and Johnson mode. I was fascinated, and by the time I got to the end of the article, I knew I could do this. In the two years before that, I'd met several men who had sexual problems with their erections or premature ejaculation. It was frustrating, and I knew that there was help for them out there because I had heard of Masters and Johnson, but when I found that you could get a job actually helping these people, I was so interested that I took a human sexuality class and asked the instructor if she was going to talk about surrogates. She said, "Yes, we're having two guest speakers who train them." So I took the class in the spring of 1980 and met surrogate trainers who had a sex therapy center in Orange County, California. I signed up for their surrogate training program, trained between June and August of 1980, followed by my internship in the fall of 1980. I started working as a surrogate in January of 1981, over thirty years ago.

Tova: Before this, you had worked as a mail carrier, correct?

Barbara: That's right. And I didn't have tons of sexual experience at that point, but enough. I'd always been interested in reading about sex, because I grew up in a really religious, restrictive environment where we didn't get any sex education. So anything that I learned, I had to get on my own, and I learned a lot from reading books. When I started working as a surrogate, I had probably had about twenty-five sex partners at that point.

Tova: So you felt that this was kind of a calling for you?

Barbara: By the time I got to the end of that newspaper article, I said, "This is the job for me." It was like an "Ah-ha" moment and a turning point for me. I went out of my way to find out more about it.

Tova: Where did you train?

Barbara: I trained at the Riskin-Banker Center in Orange County, California. If I hadn't done the work there, I probably would have found out about Barbara Roberts' Center in Encino, California, and trained there.

Tova: How did the program work?

Barbara: I think we had eight people in the class, and both a male and a female trainer, and so there were four men and four women. Probably six of the people didn't want to work as surrogates and were doing it as a "SEE Class," or Sexual Enrichment Experience. We had a workbook with a lot of the Masters and Johnson approach to sex, like the sexual response cycle and female and male anatomy. It met once a week for three hours, like a regular college class, and in every session, we'd do an experiential exercise where a man and woman would pair up, having different partners each time.

We went through all the Masters and Johnson sensate focus exercises: the face caress, the back caress, the front caress. I think the training at that time lasted about ten weeks. Then we did an intensive weekend as a graduation, where we had a couple of other, more experienced surrogate partners come in and work with us, and show us some other techniques. We did a lot of role playing about having a sexual dysfunction, and each of us would take turns. For example, I would portray a woman who had difficulty with orgasm, and the men would portray those who had erection problems.

Tova: Who supervised you when you started working with your first few clients?

Barbara: At that time, I worked with three therapists: Michael Riskin, James Gibbons, and Ron Gib. Later on, Anita Banker got her license and I worked with her, too. The first few client sessions that I did were what we called a "generalization," which is where a client had already gone through the whole sensate focus program and had his problem resolved. Then the client wanted to work with one or two other surrogates for just a few sessions, where the client structured the session to practice ejaculation control, or relax and get an erection, but with a different surrogate. That's the point, that you're a true substitute. It's easier to do generalizations than to start working with a client from square one. I did a few generalizations in the beginning, and then my supervisors felt I was ready to start working with a client for the whole process.

Tova: Was that typical of their process, to have a client working with a surrogate, and then at the completion of that therapy, have the client go through a few sessions with another surrogate?

Barbara: Yes, that was very typical.

Tova: And that was done so the client could have the experience of being with another woman?

Barbara: Yes, one reason was that the client could have experience with another woman and reinforce his success. But also it was done when the client had become too attached to the original surrogate partner, so that they could gain confidence from being able to perform with another woman. This was done because sometimes a client would think, "I can perform with her, but what's it going to be like when I go out into the real world and I'm with someone different?"

Tova: Why do you think you felt so comfortable with your body and sexuality? You said you came from a repressive background, so where do you think that came from?

Barbara: I actually started having sex fairly late, at eighteen, which I consider my first sexual intercourse experience. But it was not for lack of trying on my part. I was ready a couple years before that, but I couldn't convince anybody to do it! When I had my first boyfriend, we were together monogamously for about a year, and then I just got curious to start having sex with other people. When I met him I was eighteen, and he and his friends were nudists, which I had never been, but I was open to it. We didn't go to formal nudist camps or nudist events, or anything like that. But whenever all his friends would get together, they would have naked parties. Hot-tubbing was really popular in the seventies, and all his friends were getting hot tubs, so everybody was just really comfortable being naked. And so I did, too, from being with them. So six years before I started working as a surrogate partner, I had already been a nudist.

Tova: And you feel that started the process of opening you up?

Sex Is the Least of It

Barbara: Yes, definitely.

Tova: So what unique qualities do you have, such as your temperament, your empathy, or your ability to establish rapport with your clients that you think made you such a good surrogate?

Barbara: I would say my personality is a little bit different from a lot of the women that I met who worked as surrogate partners. I know this is going to sound funny because I did sensate focus for so many years, but I'm not really a touchy-feely person. I generally connect with people more on an intellectual level. So I tended to get along much better with older people, even in my twenties and thirties, when I often got along with people in their fifties and sixties, because I would always start with talking about events in their lives. And I'm not saying that the touching part wasn't important; it certainly was. But I would not consider myself to have huge amounts of empathy compared with other people. I was always just a bit more matter-of-fact.

Tova: What kind of issues did your clients have?

Barbara: I worked with a lot of people who had sexual anxiety. And for some reason, I worked really well with those people and was able to teach a lot of really anxious people how to do relaxation exercises. I don't consider myself a really relaxed person—I'm kind of hyper—but I was very good at that.

Tova: So there was a lot of talking in your sessions, perhaps maybe more than with other surrogates?

Barbara: I would say so, although we certainly spent all the time we needed on touching, sensate focus, and body contact, and the sexual involvement when that became appropriate for the client.

Tova: What are the two or three most memorable client experiences that you recall?

Barbara: My most memorable client was Aaron. He had severe cerebral palsy and we were originally contacted by his mom. This was probably in the late eighties, and he was about thirty years old. His mom came in and talked to this one female therapist I was working with and said, "My son is trying to live independently as best he can. He grew up in a facility because they thought he was retarded and he wasn't; he's actually really smart."

Although we hadn't worked with someone who had this problem before, we were willing to try and see how it would work. Aaron was very severely disabled. He was in a motorized wheel chair, so he could get around by himself, but of his four limbs, he only had voluntary control of one arm part of the time. His face was in spasm all the time and he couldn't really close his mouth all the way, so he drooled and his whole body was all twisted. I started working with him and he couldn't afford sessions every week, but he did the original stuff fairly quickly within a couple months.

In every session, when I touched him, he was fine. But when he had to touch me, I had to take hold of his hand and rub it all over me because he really didn't have enough control over it to do it himself. So we went through the whole back caress, front caress, and genital caress. His penis was totally normal because it doesn't have muscles in it, so it wasn't affected by his disease. And so we got to the point where I could do oral sex with him, but he couldn't do it with me because his face muscles were just way too out of control.

When we got to the intercourse part, I had to do all the work. If I got on top of him, that was fine. But if we wanted to put him on top, then I had to lift him on top of me. He wasn't a big guy so I could do that. But it was great. And when I saw the movie *The Sessions* the other week, I realized that Aaron was worse off than the guy in the movie. Aaron couldn't really talk. He sounded like he was grunting, but it didn't sound like words.

After several years, he got intercourse experience and lost his virginity. At that point I'd see him just two or three times a year because he didn't have much money. We would just try to do a different position or something new, and I got to where I could pretty much understand what he was saying.

I really admired Aaron because he graduated from community college, then from Long Beach State in California. He did it by typing with one finger at a time on his computer keyboard; he had a little gadget with holes in it that he put one finger into to type, and he managed to graduate from college. He did guest speaking to classes and I think he's still alive, because we live in the same town and several years ago our local papers published an article on him because he had written poetry and stories. He was smart! He got through college, and he's been a writer.

Tova: So he was your most memorable client.

Barbara: Yes. I've had other clients with physical problems, paralysis, ALS, MS, a lot of different things. But he is the most severely disabled person that I worked with.

Tova: Were there one or two other experiences that stand out in your mind?

Barbara: One of my favorite clients was Howard, which isn't his real name. He was one of my first clients in January of 1981, and I did not see him through the Riskin-Banker Center, but with a therapist at UCLA. Howard had a really bad case of premature ejaculation.... He just didn't make any progress at first.

I saw him for a few sessions, and every time I would touch him, any place on his body, he would ejaculate. And I could tell he really wasn't motivated and that he wasn't doing the homework using the PC, or pubococcygeus muscle exercises I asked him to do (which are the same as the Kegel exercises for women), or the self-touch exercises or anything else. After maybe two months, Howard quit therapy. But it was clear he had a lot of other issues. He was married and had managed to impregnate his wife twice, and had sons who were about ten years old. He was forty when I saw him, and I was twenty-five.

A couple years later, he called and I was working with a different therapist. He came to see us and this time did the entire program with me and the other therapist and was absolutely great. At some point, his motivation had changed and he had fantastic results. Reflex ejaculation like his is really tough to deal with. But he did so well that he could have sex in any position for fifteen to twenty minutes if he wanted.

That was thirty years ago and I stayed in touch with him. We'd do a session maybe twice a year. And, he'd sometimes just call me. He had this tradition where he'd always call me during the Jewish holidays. I don't know why; I guess because he was Jewish. But he actually got so good at sex that he started having sex with his secretary, and his wife found out and divorced him. I said, "Howard, I'm really sorry, okay? I trained you to be such a great lover." Anyway, they should've gotten a divorce long ago.

Tova: I think you said something very important, and that was when he came to you again, he had motivation. He had commitment. And so often, in any therapeutic modality or method, people think that the therapist is going to cure you. Surrogacy is no different. They might go in thinking, "Here I am, cure me." And the truth is, the client has to come in with a level of deep commitment. Because there are going to be rough patches and uncomfortable sessions, and they need to have the commitment that will hold them in the process.

Barbara: I know that is exactly what happened with him. Sometime in the two years when I didn't see him, he got very depressed. When he came back and was successful, he told me, "Barbara, if I hadn't made it through this time, I was ready to kill myself." He said he could not live that way anymore, he was so miserable.

Tova: Through your surrogate experiences, what do you think you learned about yourself?

Barbara: That's a really good question, because, even though I technically retired in 1992, occasionally I would take a case. Back in the eighties, I was seeing ten to twenty clients a week, which was a lot. Then, in the nineties, I was keeping it quiet that I was still working as a surrogate. A couple of therapists knew I was still working and they would refer clients to me, but I'd see only one client at a time. When I was a surrogate, it was great, because I not only saw my clients, but was also married for a lot of that time. I had a good sex life with my husband and we had an open marriage, so I had other partners all through that time.

My sex life was fantastic, and I know part of that was from doing the surrogate work because of the sensate focus. It was just so easy, and I miss that aspect of it. What I learned from doing surrogate work, in answer to your question, is that I needed that focus. It's not the same if I go into sex with a lower level of consciousness, the way I did before I was a surrogate. I don't necessarily need to have a long-term relationship with somebody. But when I'm having sex, I'm totally focused on the other person. I don't play music in the room; I don't have the TV on. I'm not thinking about anything else. I'm just there with that person. That's the main thing I learned. It's important to have us both focused on each other; I am so picky about partners at this point that I don't think anybody could live up to my expectations.

Tova: Do you feel that your experience as a surrogate has had an impact on your personal life?

Barbara: Absolutely, and mostly for the good. It made my sex life fantastic for decades. But there are some experiences that ruined me for being with other men. And it's not the way you would think. If I met a guy I really liked right now and we decided to have sex, if he had erection problems, I wouldn't be freaking about it; I'd be totally fine with that and we could deal with it easily. That's the legacy of surrogate work. But if I was going to be with somebody long term, I would want somebody who had the level of experience that I have. And that's really hard to find.

Tova: I'm wondering if, when you were a surrogate, you had any significant relationships. Did you tell your partner about them, and were there any ramifications in your personal life because you were a surrogate?

Barbara: I was married from 1981 to 1991 and those were the years that I worked the most.

And I met my ex-husband through the Riskin-Banker Center because he'd gone through their class right before the class I took. Because he had taken the training, he completely understood what I was doing and what it was all about. And we had an open marriage, so that part was fine. But I didn't always tell a new man I met outside the marriage that I was a surrogate. When I did, there'd be one of two responses: "Oh no, she knows all this stuff." The other was: "Well, if I can satisfy her, this is going to be great." So yeah, it never caused a problem in a relationship. I never had to hide it.

Cecily Green

Photo from Cecily Green

"And the day came when the risk to remain tight in a bud was more painful than the risk it took to blossom."

—*Anaïs Nin, author*

Tova: Cecily, you go back to the founding days of surrogacy. How did you first hear about the program?

Cecily: I had been taking a graduate course in psychology at UCLA and we had several people come to give presentations about their work with patients in the field of psychology. There was one particular therapist who was doing therapy that involved working with his patients in a swimming pool. It was called rebirthing.

He asked the class if there was someone who had a heated pool so he could demonstrate what he was talking about. I had a home with a fifty-foot heated pool. I asked my classmates if they would like to have the therapist come to the house and everybody was very excited, so we set the date.

Tova: Were the people nude or in bathing suits?

Cecily: The people came expecting to be nude. The therapist assembled everyone in our den and he began talking about the history of sex therapy. He felt that much of people's discomfort with nudity and sexuality was rooted in very early experiences. He asked if people would be willing to share their attitudes about sexuality. It was absolutely fascinating. People talked about their first consciousness of sexuality. The last person to speak had his leg amputated during World War II, and he was very comfortable with his body. He talked about not having any problem with being nude around people that he knew. But he said the thing that bothered him most was…, he paused, then he reached up and threw his hair piece across the room! It was an incredible emotional experience for everybody who witnessed that.

Tova: What was your original profession?

Cecily: I was an executive in business for twenty-five years. Then I was diagnosed with breast cancer. Someone from the American Cancer Society had heard me speak in a class designed for health care professionals who worked with dying patients. During that time I was also dealing with the death of my mother. I'd read in the UCLA catalogue about a class covering the psychological care of the dying patient and his family. During the two-day class, the psychologist never once talked about the psychological care of the dying patient and his family. After a coffee break, I spoke with him and asked if he was going to share his experiences working with his patients, all of whom had life-threatening illnesses, because those insights would help us respond more effectively in dealing with the dying. He said that he would actually not be talking about that, but would cover more about theory and history. He encouraged me to share my experiences with the class.

So I talked about things that I had observed and how I felt about my own impending death, and about my mother. Some women from the American Cancer Society approached me and told me about a new program they were developing; and they felt that I would be the perfect person for the job. I had been involved for a year in Reach-to-Recovery, a program for breast cancer survivors, and I was very comfortable talking about how I felt; pretty soon I got a reputation and was invited to speak at various hospitals for women who had lost their breasts. I ended up working as a volunteer with the Cancer Society for twenty-five years and designed a number of their programs. I trained other volunteers and continued to give presentations to hospitals and doctors.

At my UCLA class, I had met a man and we got to be friends. He asked me, "How are you going to take the lessons you've learned from this class and apply them to your new profession?" I told him that I wanted to find somebody who had experience in addressing cancer patients and intimacy. He said he knew a therapist who teaches sexuality to adults who have problems with their own or a partner's attitudes and behaviors regarding intimacy after surgery. He said this therapist was going to do a presentation in Santa Barbara, and the therapist was Barbara Roberts, who had been a sex surrogate trained by Masters and Johnson. I attended her presentation in Santa Barbara and was introduced to her. She invited me to attend a presentation at the Miramar Hotel in Los Angeles, where surrogates and their supervising therapists were conducting presentations for physicians in the field of sexuality.

Tova: What year was that?

Cecily: That was 1974, I think. I went with my husband and it turned out that I knew a lot of people who were there. It was a marvelous presentation, and several days later, I received a call from Barbara, who wanted to talk to me about my interest in relationships and intimacy. And she was the one who invited me to attend the SEE Class.

Tova: And what was the SEE Class about?

Sex Is the Least of It

Cecily: It was about learning to be comfortable with your own sexuality and with your partner. We were taught to pay attention to our body's responses, and we did various exercises like the hand, face, and foot caresses, and it progressed to nudity.

Tova: What are the two or three most memorable client experiences that you can recall?

Cecily: I worked with a client who had a lack of intimacy in his marriage because sex was physically painful for his wife.

Tova: What was the specific problem that he needed to work on?

Cecily: He needed to learn about sexual response for a woman. He had to learn what to do, and how to talk openly about things with his wife as to how he could become an effective sex partner for her. He was so excited about the experience that he encouraged his wife to have her own sessions, and she did. She spent several weeks with a male surrogate, with Dr. Roberts as the supervising therapist. It turned out that she had major problems, but it was not just because of her husband's clumsiness and difficulty in communicating. She had been raped by a therapist, which left her totally negative about anything to do with her body. But she was able to work through that experience in therapy and release the hurt. This was such an awakening for her that she told her son about it. He wasn't comfortable dating and was very shy, so he went through an intensive experience, which is a very concentrated approach in which the client and surrogate meet for maybe four hours a day for two weeks.

Tova: You had an impact on the whole family.

Cecily: Yes, the whole family, And we stayed in touch for years. Every time I went to Chicago each year to see my family, I always saw them, too. Unfortunately, the wife developed breast cancer. The thing that made it so meaningful for me was that, because she knew about my experience with breast cancer, we knew each other intimately and we became very close. We could talk about anything

Tova: So working with you really was a life-altering experience?

Cecily: That's right. But the most outstanding thing that happened was when one day I was leaving Barbara Robert's clinic and I turned on the radio. I was searching the dial for something that I'd be interested listening to and I ended up with Dr. Laura, a local Los Angeles talk therapist who answered questions from listeners. That day she was conducting a college show, and I thought that might be worth hearing. I'd never heard of Dr. Laura, so it was just by happenstance that I found her.

The first caller that she interviewed was a former client of mine. And although no names were ever mentioned, I could tell it was him from his description of his experience in surrogate partner therapy. He was an older man, a widower who had lost his wife. He'd met her when he was close to thirty and they were married for many years, until she became ill and died. He was incredibly lonely and didn't know how to meet people, and he didn't do anything socially. His doctor referred him to a psychiatrist, who then referred him to Barbara Roberts, and I was chosen to be his surrogate. So the thing that is so incredible about it is that I happened to turn on a station that I'd never heard before, and heard this man talking about how his sex therapy experience had changed his life.

Tova: Through your surrogate experiences, what did you learn about yourself?

Cecily: I think the most revealing thing was that I had the capacity and patience to recognize how important it was for a person to be comfortable in his own skin. And, how important that comfort was to leading a nourishing life.

Clover Behrend, B.S. in Education

Photo courtesy of Clover Behrend

"Few of us have lost our minds, but most of us have long ago lost our bodies."—*Ken Wilbur*

Before becoming a surrogate, among other work, Clover was a public school teacher.

Tova: How did you first hear about surrogacy?

Clover: I grew up in Michigan, and when I was married for the second time, I moved to Illinois. Then I came to California in 1970. By the time I came to the West Coast, I had a terrible self-image, especially after my second divorce. I was feeling like such a failure, so I became involved in the human potential movement and did some other work to try to rebuild my self-esteem. I attended a place called the Elysium Institute in Topanga Canyon in the early seventies and eighties; I spent many happy weekends there and attended many helpful seminars. It was a clothing-optional growth center, and the people were wonderful and very accepting. Little by little, I started to rebuild my self-image. I bought a small condo in Fountain Valley, California, and it had a Jacuzzi in the back patio. I started hosting an event called the Clover Patch, which was a clothing-optional gathering here at my home, where people came and enjoyed the Jacuzzi, singing, massage, and conversation. That lasted for about ten years, and I Invited Dr. Anita Banker and Dr. Michael Riskin to come to one of the gatherings. They were sex therapists at the Human Sexuality

Center of Southern California, and they really liked what they saw. My house was a sanctuary gathering, not a swing party. They liked the comfort and warmth, and the sense of community that we had established. They asked me if I would be interested in training to be a surrogate. I had never heard about surrogacy and they explained it to me. And I thought, well, why not try it? So I took the training in 1982 and did the clinical internship with them. After the internship, I began working part-time as a surrogate partner.

Tova: As I understand it, at the end of your training you engaged in some short-term therapy with clients who had already gone through the process.

Clover: Yes, that was part of the internship.

Tova: What was the rationale for that?

Clover: The reason for that was to diminish any really heavy emotional involvement between the client and the primary surrogate, because the purpose of surrogacy is to empower your client. He needs to be able to go out on his own and find a partner of his choice and not to be tied to the surrogate. It was important for him to learn how to generalize his experience. So, at their ending part of their therapy, they stopped working with the primary surrogate who had taken them all through the exercises. Then the client worked with one or two other surrogates for just a couple of sessions to make sure that they could function with anyone they chose.

Tova: Where did you meet Paul, your husband?

Clover: I met him when he came to Clover Patch. When I did my training, Paul was willing to be my training partner. So I did a lot of the exercises with him, like face, hand, and foot caressing. We started dating and we've been together for more than thirty years. Paul took the surrogate training a year later. Then we both went on to do surrogate work, but obviously not together. We each had our own clients.

Tova: How did you and Paul handle that? What was it like, knowing that he might be having intercourse with a client?

Clover: Well, Tova, we never had a problem with it because we knew our boundaries, and that when we were working as surrogates, the needs of our clients came first. We also knew that our relationships with our clients were short-lived; and we only saw them under the supervision of a licensed sex therapist and never outside of those sessions, even though we bonded with clients during the sessions. It was really kind of neat, and we're so happy that it worked out that way.

Tova: Why do you think you felt so comfortable with your body and your sexuality?

Clover: I grew up in the 1940s and '50s in Michigan, and at that time, sexuality was rarely discussed. Social nudity was unheard of; and then I came out here to California and got involved in the Human Potential Movement. I had always been kind of a rebel for most of my life, and when I moved out here, I heard about the clothing-optional Elysium Institute, where I finally had the opportunity to get comfortable with my body. I had not been very comfortable with my body before that, but when I got to Elysium and I walked on to the beautiful grounds and saw all these people, so happy and comfortable, it was a revelation. They were just regular, ordinary people who were very comfortable in their own skin. After a couple of visits to Elysium, I became very comfortable with my body and my self-image. So surrogate work was kind of the next step for me to help other people become comfortable with their bodies and with their own sensuality and sexuality.

I want to add one thing that's important to me: I don't like to use the term *sexual surrogate*, because surrogates do so much more than just work with people's sexuality. I prefer the term *surrogate partner*, and then I have to explain that doesn't mean I'm carrying somebody's baby.

Tova: What are the qualities that made you such a good surrogate?

Clover: I think I'm a really good listener. I have a good sense of humor and I was able to establish a strong rapport with my clients. I'm a firm believer in Masters and Johnson's sensate focus with non-demand principles. I think one reason I empathized so much with my clients was that for many years before my training, I was an orgasm-faker, someone who pretended all the time that I was having these wild, wonderful orgasms but never had one, except through masturbation. So I'd been there myself, having been sexually dysfunctional for quite a long time. And that's the same sort of pressure for performance that men put on themselves.

One thing that Paul and I have done since we stopped doing surrogate work was to compile a course of study, including the M & J (Masters and Johnson) exercises, and we've conducted workshops, both at the DeBeneville Pines and for church groups, using sensate focus for people who are functional. Why wait until people are dysfunctional to learn these concepts?

Tova: Clover, what were some of the most memorable client experiences that you can recall?

Clover: Let me talk about a client named Michael, who had been in all kinds of talk therapy because he thought his wife had put a hex on him when they got divorced. That was because after their divorce, everything collapsed for him: his whole life, his career, his happiness, and his ability to enjoy sex with a partner. He really believed that she had cursed him and caused all of these problems. Dr. Riskin and Dr. Banker didn't have any idea what to do with him. But I was a practicing Wiccan, so they asked me to write a ritual to purge the client of the hex.

Tova: Would you explain what a Wiccan is?

Clover: Wicca is an eclectic spiritual path that means many things to different people. For me, a Wiccan is a person who follows some of the old ways and believes in the power of Earth energy and creating for yourself what you want in life. Some people use the word *Pagan*. A Wiccan can be very ritualistic and therein lies a lot of the power; it's the power of suggestion couched in rituals. So I wrote a very long, involved ritual and performed it with him. From what I could tell, his life started to improve. Michael and Anita called it a *hexorcism*. It was just kind of an amazing thing.

Clover: The other client I'm thinking about found it impossible to urinate in a public place or any place other than his own apartment. That naturally put a real crimp in his dating life, because when he went out to dinner with a date, he'd have to go right home if he had to urinate. He and I had several sessions together, which involved what's called progressive desensitization to help him overcome his fear of using public restrooms. I started by having him drink a whole lot of water as we chatted about how the week went. Then he would go upstairs, close the bathroom door and urinate. That was a big step for him.

Then, in the next session, we'd do the same thing: a lot of liquid, a lot of nice talk. Again, he would go upstairs to the bathroom. But this time he left the bathroom door open and I would still stay downstairs in the living room while he urinated. In the session after that, he would urinate while I sat at the bottom of the stairs, which was not that far from the bathroom. Slowly, but surely, I was able to get closer and closer to him, and he was still able to urinate. Then Michael called Paul in and they played the game of dunk the bottle cap. Paul and the client would stand at the toilet with a beer bottle cap floating in the toilet. Then they would try to urinate and sink the bottle cap. Can you imagine?! There was a lot of laughter, and Paul made it very light and very funny. By that time, the client was having no problems urinating in public restrooms.

Tova: That could have taken him untold numbers of years to work that out in talk therapy.

Clover: That's right. The last client I want to talk about was one of the original Viagra test subjects. He worked with quite a few surrogates, but still had problems with performance anxiety. So he started using Papaverine. Do you remember that stuff?

Tova: Those are the injections made directly into the penis?

Clover: Yes. The problem was, he had trouble injecting the Papaverine into his penis. And his girlfriend wanted no part of anything like that. So I worked with him for quite a few sessions to help him inject the Papaverine into his penis. The curious thing was, even after the injections, if he continued worrying about his performance, he wasn't able to have erections anyway. And that is very typical. He had an extreme case of performance anxiety. Then, when Viagra came along, he started doing very well with it, along with my constant reminders about not getting into a performance mode that would create anxiety for him. But, as you know, individuals who have heart problems should not use Viagra, and he had arrhythmia. It meant he had to drop out of the clinical program, and he still had erectile difficulties, even with the medications, if he got tense. So we worked intensely with the sensate focus, non-demand exercises. He was able to complete the entire process and eventually got married.

Tova: What do you attribute to the fact that he was able to see successful results with you?

Clover: Well, I don't really know. But I'm a very patient person, and he was just delightful. We had a very strong rapport, and from rapport can come trust, which is so important.

Tova: Through your surrogate experience, what did you learn about yourself?

Clover: I learned that if people just get out of their own way, their bodies have a wisdom, and they know how to respond. If we just relax and have fun with our sensuality and sexuality, and if we stay away from the performance mode, everything works the way it should. Concentrate on the moment, and enjoy the sensuality. Do not have any goals in mind; just let it flow. It was a blessing to be able to participate as a surrogate partner.

Dr. Susan Kaye

Photo courtesy of Dr. Susan Kaye

*"Be not ashamed women, You are the gates of the body,
and you are the gates of the soul."*

—Walt Whitman

Susan Kaye, D.H.S., Ph.D., is a sexuality counselor, educator, coach, and professor. She has a degree in Human Services from Villanova University and a Master's and Doctorate in Clinical Sexology and Sex Education from the Institute for Advanced Study of Human Sexuality. She is an Esalen-trained massage therapist and Tantra teacher/practitioner.

Tova: How did you first hear about surrogacy?

Susan: I was working as a massage therapist in Philadelphia and one of my massage teachers heard about a surrogate program being taught by Dr. William Stayton. He was giving a lecture on surrogacy at the University of Pennsylvania. My massage teacher suggested that I attend the lecture because she felt it was the work I should be doing. She gave me Dr. Stayton's phone number. I called and told him that I wanted to come to his lecture.

At the lecture, there was a surrogate with a client she had worked with. His name was Robert. He was a forty-two-year-old virgin. She described the work they did together and he expressed how she had changed his life. I felt, what greater gift you could give someone than the gift of relationships?

Tova: What prompted you to become involved in surrogacy?

Susan: I could see the loss that Robert had suffered through most of his adult life by not being able to be in relationships, and it struck me, this was work that would really make a difference in people's lives. I told Bill that I wanted to do this, and he said I needed to attend a therapeutic session with him so he could be certain of my intentions and that I would be therapeutically sound to do the work. He asked me to attend a Sexual Attitude Reassessment (SAR), which exposes participants to a wide variety of sexual practices and lifestyles, and provides an opportunity for them to evaluate their own attitudes about sexuality. I spent a weekend in New York with a senior surrogate to find out more about the work and the type of clients generally accepted for surrogate partner therapy (SPT). I decided to go for the training, which consisted of two weekends. I was trained with a male surrogate candidate by Bill and Ray Noonan, an already trained surrogate partner, as well as a female trainer.

Tova: Why do you think you felt so comfortable with your body and your sexuality? Where did that come from for you?

Susan: I have no idea! I sure didn't get it from my genetics or my nurturing. Neither of my parents finished high school back in Mennonite Lancaster County, which is part of Pennsylvania. It was all very old-school. Mom was a housewife and dad had a paving business. They were never very demonstrative with affection, or with touching or affirming that bodies were ok. They didn't talk to me about anything regarding bodies or sexuality or relationships. The only thing my mom taught me when one of my early boyfriends had broken up with me, and I was upset and I tried to talk to her about it, was, "Don't ever come around crying over a boy." So that was my training as far as how you handle relationships.

When I was fifteen, I got my first real job working in the dietary department of Pottstown Hospital. I took the food trays around to feed the patients of the hospital their dinner and I saw a lot; I made a commitment that I was not going to end up there. I started to study about how to stay well and honor my body. I became a vegetarian and practiced yoga in the 1960s when I was just nineteen years old. I always felt that the body was meant for good things, and I wanted a personal relationship in which I felt that my partner and I were on the same team.

Tova: What are your qualities that made you such a good surrogate?

Susan: I have deep empathy for people or animals in pain. I just have that naturally going on, maybe because the training healed my own pain. I believe I create safe environments with my massage work, and still do that with my Tantra healing. People feel safe with me. People always feel accepted, and even sex therapists tell me things they've never told anyone before. People reveal their feelings to me, whether we're at cocktail parties or in my office. I accept who people are, and at whatever level mentally, physically, and emotionally, because much of what people struggle with is accepting themselves, especially from the neck down. We get so much fear, guilt, and shame around living in our bodies, exploring our bodies, and celebrating our bodies. I give permission to folks around body issues and their fears and concerns from the neck down.

Tova: You felt so strongly experientially and academically that you pursued your Ph.D.

Susan: Yes. And that's the work I do, now that I'm no longer a practicing surrogate. I still do some hands-on work with people as a practitioner of White Tantra.

Tova: That's the more spiritual type, correct?

Susan: Yes, it's more spiritual. It's about getting your erotic energy into your heart energy and how that works to have more fulfilling, satisfying, connective relationships. Not just first chakra or erotic energy, but how we come from our hearts and combine that energy with our erotic potential. In the merging of heart and erotic energies, we get to enjoy the other 90% of our wonderful body parts, not just the 10% of the genital region.

Tova: What would you say are the two or three most memorable client experiences?

Susan: I remember Tom (not his real name), a teenager who'd had a head injury in a car accident. One little bump on his head and he was brain injured. He had to be retrained to do simple things like tie his shoes. His diagnosis was that he would always be limited to functioning on the level of an eighteen-year-old and he had never had a sexual experience. At that time, in the mid- to late 1980s when I worked with him, we were actually recognized and subsidized by a rehabilitation center in Philadelphia: The Moss Rehab and Bryn Mawr Rehabilitation Center, which paid for his surrogate therapy. It was marvelous. We don't have that today.

So Tom wanted to have a sexual experience, but what the rehab staff also felt would be of great value was to teach him socialization skills, which I really feel is the crux of surrogate therapy. As a surrogate, you are a substitute partner. That plays out in many roles and in many valuable ways of connecting to another human being. We did a lot of socialization, because his behavior could be inappropriate. He'd blurt out things to girls or try to grope them. We started out working just in the rehab center; then we'd go out for lunches or go out to a mall, or we'd go bowling or to the theater—places where he'd need to be appropriate. We worked together for at least a year or more.

Sex Is the Least of It

The whole time we were together, I gave him homework assignments, such as encouraging him to meet people. He eventually did meet a woman who he ended up living with. We've lost touch and I don't know where he is today or how the relationship turned out, but he was able to have experiences he probably would not have been able to have if Bryn Mawr had not been interested in using my services.

Tova: That must have been very moving for you.

Susan: Yes. I worked with a lot of people with head injuries, multiple surgeries, or who were in wheelchairs. People would say to me, "Wow. It must be hard to work with those kinds of disabilities," or "How could you work with someone whose faces are disfigured with several surgeries?" But you love your clients from a deep-heart connection. People ask me if there was anyone I couldn't work with. The only people I refused to work with were those who were not as invested in their progress as I was, or who were not committed to their own growth. If they weren't on the court with me, then I couldn't work with them.

Tova: Is there anyone else you recall?

Susan: There was a sixty-seven-year-old man whose wife left him, saying that their sex was awful. And after they'd had five children, she really put it to him in a way that brought him to his knees, saying she left him because sexually he was not a good match for her. He had struggled a lot with sexuality as a young man: he was in a boy's school; his mother was not really available. He came from money, but he had no love-connection or mothering from either of his parents.

His wife was his first sex partner. He was shocked to learn that he really had failed as a sex partner, so he wanted to learn about intimacy and then maybe look for a new partner. We worked together for probably a year and I took him to strip clubs and introduced him to this whole sensual world. He was a Quaker and his family was pretty closed about exploring sexuality. As it turned out, he met a woman: they were getting married and I was invited to the wedding with all of his children; I was like the guest of honor. They all knew who I was and they were so appreciative that I'd made this new life possible for him; he and his new wife were so grateful. It was very moving.

Tova: He was very open about who you were and wanted to tell people about it; this was something that shouldn't be hidden.

Susan: Yes. He was very open and very appreciative of our work together.

Tova: Does anybody else come to mind?

Susan: Yes. Masters and Johnson referred a client to me who lived in St. Louis. We worked together sometime around 1986. And guess what! I actually just had dinner with him in Atlanta recently. We've kept in touch over the years, and that was the second time I've been to Atlanta to see him. Some of his family live in Philadelphia, and when he'd come up for Thanksgiving, we would get together. He was struggling with his sexual orientation. And back in the late 1980s, there wasn't much help. There was no Internet to connect with like-minded people, nor was there a movement for gay and lesbian rights like there is today. When we met, he had graduated from law school and his family was expecting him to get married and have kids. So he wanted to try to be with a woman. He had gone through aversion therapy, he had gone through shock therapy, he had beaten himself up physically and emotionally, and this was his last ditch effort with M & J (Masters and Johnson) to change his sexual orientation. M & J arranged for us to work in an apartment for two weeks. We had to report every morning and late every afternoon about the assignments they had given us. John and I laugh now, but he was so scared and feeling like he wanted to leave a couple of times. But we did manage to get through it. When we had completed all of the assignments, he knew that he wanted to be with men. He was able to come out to his family and he invited me to Thanksgiving dinner at his sister's home with his parents there. He had told them the story about our work and they were so appreciative. It was all very sweet, and I love it that we are still close. Actually, I still hear from several of my former clients.

Tova: What was it like working with Masters and Johnson?

Susan: It was pretty amazing. I'm grateful that I got the opportunity. One of my claims to fame is that I had a gynecological exam from Dr. Masters, because all the surrogates who worked for him had to have blood work done and be physically sound to work with their clients. The same was true for their clients to work with us surrogates. They were very professional. I met Virginia Johnson; it was quite an honor. I was pinching myself while I worked with Dr. Johnson in the clinic's apartment.

Tova: What did you learn about yourself from your surrogate experience?

Susan: I value that people working with me instantly feel safe and trusting and accepted. And that's really what I feel I bring to the table. Those attributes have really shaped my work. I guess what I learned about myself is that it's healthy for us to have comfortable relationships with our bodies. I feel that is the contribution I have made: to lessen the fear, guilt, and shame about our bodies and sexuality, in living life in celebration from the neck down, rather than being celibate.

Tova: Is there anything you would like to add?

Susan: There's so much to say about the work, and about the women and men who are surrogates and who are truly angels. I'm on my way to Widener University, teaching with my mentor Bill Stayton, who is almost eighty years old and still on the stump and advocating for surrogate work as a minister of positive sexuality. I feel very privileged and blessed to have been included in the work and that Bill is still here as a strong advocate for surrogacy. He's a Baptist minister with a degree in sexology and has brought sex and religion into a therapeutic model.

Sex Is the Least of It

Tova: A popular misconception is that surrogates only engage in sex, whereas that constitutes a very small part of what they do. So much of the work is focused on building rapport with clients, socialization and teaching clients how to create relationships.

Susan: Exactly. That's why I did my Ph.D. dissertation: to have it recognized as socialization therapy, and not necessarily what people get so concerned about, which is that you're having sex for money or having sex with someone who's not your husband, wife, or lover. But 80% of the clients finish the socialization skills portion, while only 67% progress to actual sexual intercourse with the surrogate partner; and then, when and if you have sex, the sessions are completed. It's not like we hang out and become your sex partner. That part's graduation; it's such a small part of the average fifteen-hour therapeutic program that the work is misrepresented. I believe that's because of our fear, guilt, and shame around how we define sexual connections and sexuality.

I'd like to end with a quote from one of my clients. He said: "Life is an ever-expanding experience." We are born to be curious and to discover. Sexuality is a vital part of this discovery; and yet, many of us stop expanding, maybe due to a bad experience, fear, or embarrassment. Perhaps our lack of knowledge or skill may be in the way, or else our inability to communicate. The rigidity in religious or ethical self-codes, physical or emotional handicaps, or past failures create more failure. The list could go on; everyone has unique problems when it comes to their sexual life. But there is hope; you are not alone. Asking for help is risky, but take the step! Surrogate partner therapy is the beginning of unconditional acceptance.

Contact information:

Email: drsusankaye@gmail.com

Website: www.sacredsexdoc.com

Also see:

Institute for Mind Body Therapy, www.instituteformindbodytherapy.org

Joanne Howell, M.F.C.C.

Photo from istock

"Touch has a memory." —John Keats, poet

Joanne is now a licensed marriage and family counselor.

Tova: What were the early messages that you heard about sexuality growing up in your home?

Joanne: Well, I grew up in the Midwest in the 1950s, and I was taught that sex was reserved for marriage. Everybody knew that. But I think that within my family, the messages were pretty healthy. I remember getting caught with the girl across the street and the boy next door, all of us naked in the outhouse, just exploring one another. We were probably about six years old at the time. And the girl got a beating and the boy got grounded, but I got a comprehensive talk about sex. I remember thinking at the time that my parents were a lot smarter than their parents. So I think it was pretty healthy and there wasn't any shame about nudity. If you came in on your parents and they were undressed, nobody shrieked or anything like that. But it was the 1950s, and I think that was a really formative time. The word went out to the older brothers of the boy who was with us doing the sexual exploration, and nudity was also involved. I remember standing on buckets of differing heights, because somehow we thought that if a boy and a girl put their bellies together, that was "doing it." And I remember going to great lengths to try to figure out the best height for such activity. Nobody knew anything about erections; it was just curiosity. But the older boys heard that the girl across the street and I had participated in this, and that made them pursue us to be sexual with them. So I concluded that girls lost their power if they were sexual, and that then the boys got the power.

Tova: In terms of your relationships, how did that idea influence you as you moved toward high school, puberty, and adolescence?

Joanne: I yearned for a boyfriend, but didn't trust them at all. I had some crushes and dated a little bit in high school, but I never dated anybody that I really cared about. So at that point in my life relationships were really a fantasy.

Tova: You had your fantasy boyfriends.

Joanne: Yes, and that was a lot tidier than any of the poor little fumbling boys who were also trying to figure out how to get through teenage life. The general feeling was that boys would try to get as much as they could from a girl, and your goal as a girl was to keep them around but prevent from getting anything. It wasn't until the summer after I graduated from high school that I had my first real boyfriend, where I experienced being attracted to sex. It was all about power until I found somebody I liked.

Tova: Were there any social or sexual issues that you needed to work out as you moved into adulthood?

Joanne: I married at twenty, and after about three years we agreed to an open marriage. While I was in an open marriage, I fully intended to stay married. I wasn't looking for deep intimacy in my extramarital relationships with men. Rather, I was still working with the power thing, and the feeling of my own sexual potency and a feminist awareness. I also had a fair amount of hostility toward men that I wasn't in touch with at the time.

Tova: How did you first hear about surrogacy?

Joanne: I had a friend who wasn't much into sex, but who was very much into making money, and she commented about my open marriage. I was having sex with men outside of my marriage, and she kept thinking that there should be some way that I could make money from that. I would laugh and say that she didn't understand. She considered that I was a sexual playmate without pay. Then she met Cheryl Cohen Greene, a surrogate partner, so she wrote to me and said, "Joanne, I found the thing that you should do. You should be a sex surrogate. You should call this woman."

My husband and I had bought this old Victorian home and we put all our money and energy into restoring it. One day I was in the basement with sheet rock, hating every minute of it, thinking, "God, I would do anything rather than this."

I didn't want a nine-to-five job, so I became a masseuse. I went to interview at some massage studios in Berkeley and discovered that they were all just a cover for prostitution, and that wasn't for me. Then I interviewed at a place in San Francisco that was much classier but still tawdry. Although I gave a good massage, I was terrible at ripping people off by selling further services.

While I was working there, I met a man who had previously had an arrangement with another young woman there who had been a kind of a mistress to him. She had just moved out of state and he was looking to set up a similar arrangement. He asked me about it and I said no, that wasn't something that I could really see myself doing. He asked me to just think about it, so when I got home, I woke my husband and said, "I have to ask you a question. How would you feel about me having sex for money?" And he said, "Well, I think the question is, how would *you* feel about it?"

I thought about it, then called the gentleman. I went to see him and we were sexual. He was a baker and sent me home with this big box of pastries for my children. That began a two-month period when I'd see him once a week and be paid for having sex with him. I didn't feel good about it because I don't think that he felt good about it. I learned that I could have sex with strangers for money, but the context mattered. Then I remembered Susan writing to me about Cheryl. I tracked down Cheryl's phone number, called her and asked her if she would train me as a surrogate. That's how it all began.

Tova: When did you become a surrogate?

Joanne: I was in my late thirties when I started doing surrogate work and I continued to do so for eight years. I started training with Cheryl Cohen Greene in the fall of 1977. I also received training from other people who were familiar with bodywork exercises. I got a lot of training through the San Francisco Sex Information Hotline as well, where I worked for two and a half years. At that point I had a bachelor's degree in sociology, and Cheryl steered me toward basic sexuality courses at the University of California at Berkeley. I probably started seeing my first client at the beginning of 1979.

Tova: Why do you think you felt so comfortable with your body and your sexuality?

Joanne: I think sex has been very important in my life; there was also the power issue, and the idea of being a valuable woman. I equated that to being sexually attractive and becoming a healer. I really thrive when I'm interacting with a client from a place of healing. I think that was very satisfying to me.

One of the significant things that happened to me as a surrogate was that I shifted away from being a feminist to being a humanist. I think I worked through the bulk of my anger at men as I got to experience being in relationships with men. I used my power to support instead of being a warrior against men. I instead became a warrior of the heart. I was in a safe role as surrogate and I got to experience being desired. I gained insights that were very real for me in terms of the burdens that men struggled with in their lives. I think that the compassion I felt for my clients, and the insecurities stemming from my childhood, combined to form a resolution through surrogacy.

Sex Is the Least of It

Although my work with clients was intimate, it wasn't the kind of intimacy that you seek in a life partner, which can activate a lot of deep, unfinished business from childhood. Coming from a maternal archetype as a surrogate, I got to experience myself as a healer and healed in the process.

Tova: Tell me about some of your client experiences.

Joanne: One experience that comes to mind was a negative one. A man came to me and said he was a pedophile and that he had engaged in sex with children overseas. He had been sexual with a seven-year-old here in the United States and gone to jail for it. I had a sense that he was involved with security, but wasn't a policeman. But this guy was creepy. He didn't come to me through a therapist; I had interviewed him on the phone, but I hadn't gotten all the information I wanted. He contacted me because he wanted to see if he could appreciate sex with an adult rather than with a child. But there was something strange about his energy. It really wasn't believable once I met him and he told me his story. There may have been some truth to what he said, but I got the sense that he was really more interested in a context of prostitution. He was hoping that the interactions with me would take the pressure off him from being with a child, because he knew that if he got arrested, he was going back to jail for a long time. I really didn't think that I could make a difference for him. And I actually felt afraid.

Tova: It's important to point out that not everyone who contacts a therapist is appropriate for the work, and that surrogates are human beings and may have reactions to clients.

Joanne: Oh, absolutely.

Tova: Are there any others that you can recall?

Joanne: Sure, and most of my experiences were positive. Many of the young men who called me were adult virgins and they tended to be students at the University of California at Berkeley. So I felt my work was to teach them the mechanics of sexuality; not just plumbing, but how to give and experience pleasure. I tried to help them improve the quality of their social interactions, and in general they were enthusiastic.

Tova: Enthusiasm goes a long way.

Joanne: The one who I remember best was an English major, and he brought a lot of heart to the process. I didn't usually have to focus too much on setting limits in terms of number of sessions, because students didn't have the money to keep seeing me long-term. So it was more comfortable emotionally having this financial reality set the limits, rather having to set the limits myself.

It's easier for me to talk about patterns rather than individual clients. The other trend that emerged was that I worked almost exclusively with men from cultures that didn't respect women. In the early years, I would get into situations where we would undress and I'd be trying to take him through the sensate focus exercises. At a certain point, when the client became aroused, I guess my boundaries were not strong at that time, and sometimes we would just end up having sex rather than my holding the line and staying within the limits of the exercise. So it became clear to me that I needed to do something different, and that didn't happen until after the first couple years. It had to do with my learning to maintain my authority, and I didn't really know how to do that at the beginning.

Tova: So it was about establishing your boundaries.

Joanne: Yes, boundaries. I think that specifically it was about establishing my authority.

Tova: Through your surrogate experience, what did you learn about yourself?

Joanne: What did I learn about myself? I learned how much I enjoyed that archetypal role, that maternal sex goddess thing. I also learned that my capacity for intimacy wasn't as unlimited as I originally thought it was.

Tova: What do you mean by that?

Joanne: I mean my interactions with my clients had a clear and contained structure, which was a lot cleaner than my personal life with my husband or my lovers. I didn't bring unfinished childhood business into the process. I remember terminating with a client once, and I didn't do this very often, but every once in a while, there was someone who I really enjoyed as a person. And I'd let them come to see me when it wasn't therapeutic anymore. They'd be there for sex, but we also enjoyed each other. Because I didn't need them to be anyone except who they were, they just showed themselves to me as they were.

One of the reasons I stopped doing surrogate work was that it became really boring. I'm the sort of person who looks for patterns in deeper interactions with people, and I could see that often the work wasn't really going to make a difference in the clients' lives. I realized that their being a better sexual machine was not the problem, and I was not very effective at getting the people who really needed therapy to see a therapist.

Tova: So you worked on your own?

Joanne: Mostly, yes. When I first started doing surrogate work, I did the training and put my name out there at the San Francisco Sex Information Hotline. And so I contacted some sex therapists who I had heard about, and I got this casting-couch thing. They wanted to go to bed with me to make sure I was okay. Or they wanted me to take my clothes off. I thought, "These guys needed therapy."

Tova: The therapists?

Joanne: Yes. I was really in a dilemma. When I attended a meeting at BASA, the Bay Area Surrogate Association, a woman who had been doing surrogate work said to me, "You know, Joanne, you don't have to work with a therapist. You could just advertise and you'll get clients." So I began to advertise in Common Ground and Open Exchange, and I did a very professional rather than seductive ad. I had a pretty good sense from a phone conversation whether somebody was a legitimate potential client or not. If they wanted to know what I look like, that was one path. If they want to know what my training was, that was a different path. I didn't often feel like I was out of my element.

Tova: So you didn't feel that anything was lost in the process by not working with a therapist?

Joanne: Oh, I'm sure a great deal was lost. But the guys who were seeing me were not people who were going to see therapists. Over the years, I got a few clients to see therapists. But most of them didn't want to. I would say the bulk of my clients were experiencing premature ejaculation or were men coming out of painful or difficult relationships that had wounded them. They had just gotten stuck in a loop of performance failure. With delayed ejaculation, that was a lot more difficult to treat, of course, because that usually involves a fundamental mistrust of women or sexuality. But, otherwise, the majority of the time I felt that what I had to offer was limited but useful. Most of the guys could assist within the range of what I was offering.

Tova: Tell me about BASA.

Joanne: Well, that was like herding cats, watching a group of individualists and rabble-rousers trying to figure out how to have an organization and how to have rules. The surrogates in the group were from Oakland. Some were from Berkley, some were from Richmond, and some were from San Francisco. The group included two men, including Steven Brown, who worked with both women and men. If you read Cheryl Cohen's book, she talks a lot about her work with Steven. They conducted a lot of trainings together in various schools and classrooms around the Bay area.

Tova: How long did BASA last?

Joanne: We were pretty loosely organized. It was probably 1980 when we started meeting and talking about the purpose of the organization. But more than anything else, we wanted to publicize our work and support one another because it's an isolating career path. Some of the people in BASA who were calling themselves surrogates did not make a very convincing argument for professionalism. And so there was a bit of a struggle with that. We wanted to be inclusive, and yet who were we to say that you had to work with a therapist. I know, for instance, that with the International Professional Surrogates Association (IPSA), working with a therapist was a requirement.

Tova: Was it different for BASA?

Joanne: Sure, because often surrogates do work without therapists. Not all surrogates, but I remember the first time I went to an IPSA conference, sometime around 1980, and I remember feeling like I didn't know whether I belonged there or not, because the group's members would speak very authoritatively about who was worthy of doing the work.

Tova: What do you mean by that?

Joanne: They were talking negatively about surrogates who sometimes did not work with therapists. So I sat through about four hours of this, yearning for support and for a sense of community. But I didn't know if this was possible. So finally I stood up and I said, "Look, I want to be a part of what's happening here, but I don't know if I'm welcome. And I'm not going to be secretive about the way I work. I work on my own more often than not, without a therapist. And I hear you saying that this is an awful thing to do. So am I welcome?" Then there was a long silence.

Tova: And what was the response?

Joanne: Then they sort of said, "Well, we don't know. We don't want people to think that we work without therapists." The IPSA president said, "I don't want you to feel that you can't be a part of us." Then, quietly, during the lunch break and the coffee break, people came up to me and said, "You know, I don't always work with a therapist either." It was the elephant in room, but something that nobody would talk about. That was really an important experience, for me to take that chance of being totally honest, because I noticed that the tone of the conference changed after that. Before I spoke, there had been a lot of professional posturing. But after I spoke up, it became a lot more personal. I wasn't going to leave a conference about helping clients break through lies and tell the truth about sexuality, and at the same time misrepresent myself. By my being willing to be vulnerable, other people began to be more authentic. My speaking out turned out to be a major contribution to the group. And that experience has always stayed with me because it felt really scary.

Tova: And working with a therapist is a prerequisite for a client to work with a surrogate.

Joanne: Well, sure. And then there's what actually happens. And I know that people don't always work with therapists. I would bet that it's the rare surrogate who hasn't seen a client without a therapist.

Tova: Is there anything you'd like to add?

Joanne: Yes, I'm really excited about seeing *The Sessions,* a movie about Cheryl's work with a disabled client. I was surprised at how much of an investment I had in surrogacy when I read about *The Sessions* coming out. I accepted the surrogate experience as being part of my past. But it came alive again through the movie. It has reawakened in me a real enthusiasm for surrogate partner therapy being seen and known again, to let people see how valuable the work is.

Dr. Marilyn Volker

Photo courtesy of Marilyn Volker

"Within my body are all the sacred places of the world,

and the most profound pilgrimage I can ever make is within my own body." —Saraha

Marilyn K. Volker holds an Ed.D. in Human Sexuality from the Institute for Advanced Study of Human Sexuality in California. Dr. Volker was teaching deaf children in St. Louis, Missouri, and was married to a seminarian who was preparing to become a Lutheran minister, when she first became aware of surrogacy.

Tova: How did you first hear about surrogacy?

Marilyn: My husband and I were in St. Louis and he was in a seminary there and I was teaching deaf children. As part of their training, staff from Masters and Johnson came to talk to the seminary students. I think it was 1969 or 1970. They were explaining how the future pastors could address sex problems and bring awareness to their congregations. After the seminarians completed their training, then we'd all be going to our assigned congregations. The M & J, Masters and Johnson, instructors explained how couples seeking help for sexual problems spent two weeks at an intensive Masters and Johnson hands-on program, and then they went back home to implement what they learned. During the seminarians' discussions with the M & J staff, some brave person said, "What if somebody doesn't have a partner but wants help?" I thought that was the most insightful question of all. The instructors then told us about a program they were developing for singles, and that was the first time I heard about surrogacy. I knew about birth surrogates, so this kind of surrogacy made perfect sense to me, that if Plan A didn't work, it is important to have a Plan B, because we always had various educational plans for the deaf children. I thought of it as an educational process, although I didn't want to become a surrogate at the time because I was happy being a teacher. Then we went on our seminary intern year up to Minneapolis, Minnesota.

Tova: Did you learn anything about sexuality in Minneapolis?

Marilyn: Yes, I met Dr. Ted Cole and his wife, Sandra, who were conducting a presentation about sexuality and disabilities. They said if someone did not have a partner, they could work with a surrogate. The Coles were working surrogates who had clients with severe disabilities. Again, it made sense to me with my special education background of using backup plans when something did not work out as expected. I thought "Wow, that's very interesting," but I still didn't want to be a surrogate. Then I started my doctoral studies at the Institute for Advanced Study of Human Sexuality in California, because now the deaf children were asking questions about their bodies and sexuality, and I did not feel qualified to answer them. At a class at the Institute, some surrogates made a presentation, and I realized that, again, it's a step-by-step educational process. Then, when I was being trained as a sexologist and still teaching deaf children, my husband and I went to a party where I overheard a conversation in which a psychiatrist mentioned a patient who could benefit from working with a surrogate. And hearing him, I thought, *I could do this.* I went up to the doctor and expressed interest. I told him about my background and said "I think I can do this, but only if you and a sex therapist will supervise me." I was also really scared; I'd never done this before. I'd always had supervision in my special education jobs. So he contacted a sexologist who became my mentor doctor, Dr. Joan Seif Levy. We worked as a team, and they supervised me at the beginning. It was an amazing experience. Since that time, thirty-seven years ago, at the beginning of my career as a surrogate, the doors just opened. For several years, I worked as a surrogate and as a teacher, while also being a minister's wife.

Tova: What made you feel so comfortable with your body and your sexuality?

Marilyn: I don't know that I was so comfortable. My father was a minister and my parents never really talked about sexuality, but there were some positive messages that did come through. They said there's nothing nasty about your body, and that you would be defaming your Creator if you thought that way. It meant that private parts are not nasty, either. I had scoliosis and had to wear a brace in middle school, so I knew what it meant to be different. And my parents told me, "God loves you just the way you are." Your body is just fine and we are to value all people. And the word was *value*, not *tolerate*. They didn't really talk about gays, lesbians, and transgenderism, issues in which I'm very much involved professionally. But that message of valuing and acceptance was freeing to me. I became interested in learning how could we present sexuality to deaf children. And I wanted to know how people with spinal cord injuries, diabetes, stroke survivors, MS, or MD could deal with sexuality. I was always interested in sexuality for people with disabilities.

Tova: What are the qualities that made you such a good surrogate?

Marilyn: I think I'm a good teacher and I'm also not judgmental. So I didn't judge people around sexuality or their bodies. I also have great empathy and I'm willing to learn. I love to experience differences, so when it came to the surrogate work, I was already primed to look at each client's uniqueness.

Tova: Can you talk about your two or three most memorable surrogacy clients?

Marilyn: With the first one, I was well-supervised by two therapists, particularly Dr. Joan Levi, my first mentor. I so valued the support of my supervisors and their belief in that program. The first client was very successful in business, but he was afraid of the intimacy of touching or connecting. He learned to trust me and I'll never forget him. I was a newcomer in the field, with no experience, and he was still willing to work with me. That's why he was probably the most significant client and the one who had the greatest impact on me as a surrogate.

Tova: Was there anyone else?

Marilyn: My most important client is the one who became my husband, one of my last clients, and this is a real Cinderella story. By that point I was divorced, working part-time as a surrogate, getting my doctorate, and still teaching. I met this client, David Yoblick, on Christmas Eve Day, because a psychiatrist had called with a referral. This was before Viagra and all the other ED drugs. I walked into the waiting room. saw him and I was immediately attracted to him, not just physically, but on some deeper level, that had never happened to me before with a client. I thought: *This is transference, I've read about this.* I also thought, *It can't be good for the process or for the client.*

So we went to the psychiatrist's office to go over the whole program, like we always did with clients. During the consultation, David had the right to say yes or no about working with me. I had never refused to work with a client before this, because I had never experienced that kind of reaction before. I had always felt interest or curiosity, but I felt a powerful attraction to David and thought it would too much of a problem. So after the meeting, I went back to talk to the psychiatrist, not wanting him to think I was being unprofessional in rejecting his patient as my client. I told him, "Look there's something else happening with David and I think its transference. I don't think I'm the best person to work with him because I don't think I can be objective." He told me, "You know, Marilyn, sometimes this happens." I told him, "It's never happened to me and I don't want to mess up somebody's life." He said, "Let's just see what happens." I told him, "I want to find another surrogate for him." I felt I needed to tell David about the situation because we had already met. I said, "I want to provide the best service for all my clients, and when I feel I can't, then I want to be sure you get the best help from someone else." He said, "Why can't you work with me?" I explained, "I feel there's something else going on here." He told me, "We could date!" He had a lot of performance anxiety, and I wanted to find a surrogate who could work with him. But he said, "I'm going to win you."

He wooed me and he won me. We still joke about it thirty-five years later. We got married and had a child who's now thirty years old and married. We talk about transference; we joke about it. We've been on radio and TV together, and we've done many talks where we've revealed how we met, because neither of us is ashamed or want to hide it. David Yoblick, my husband, would be the highlight of the whole surrogate experience for me.

Tova: Did you and David go through the surrogate process together?

Marilyn: Yes, yes. Then I said, "If we're going to date, then we're going to do what couples would do, step-by-step." David always says he thanks God for his limp dick, because without it, we would've never met.

Tova: I know you do a lot of teaching. Is David involved?

Marilyn: David comes to each of the classes that I teach at medical schools and at counseling programs at five universities. He is willing to talk about this process with students and participates with the surrogates on my panel. He talks about how it could help people, even though a whole lot of men don't want to reveal that surrogacy is how they were helped. He's one of the few men who have been willing to talk about it. And I really admire that about him, his great honesty, and his ability to ask for help.

Tova: Did you ever tell your parents about your surrogate work?

Marilyn: Yes, we told my retired minister father and my mother and it was amazing. My father said, "You know, I can understand doing that kind of work, because there were people in the congregations who had big problems and I was never trained to help them deal with it. I didn't know what to do." My mother, God bless her, said, "Couldn't you have just drawn something?" David assured her that he had looked at a lot of pictures and it hadn't helped. My family, especially my parents, were willing to consider this process, and, loved us. They saw into our hearts, which was really important for both of us.

Tova: What did you learn about yourself through your surrogate work?

Marilyn: It really affirmed the parts of me that I knew were there, where I felt so different from other people. In surrogacy, the parts of me that were insecure about feeling different were affirmed in this process. I also learned about the variety of sexual responses that I couldn't have learned about otherwise. I also learned that many men, who were very successful to the outside world, could carry such great sadness and fear of intimacy on the inside. It's helped me tremendously now, as a therapist supervising IPSA-trained surrogates. I also learned about my own sexuality and

149

how it doesn't have to be perfect. That's why David and I have no problem being up front and open about how we met. I learned that when you believe in something, as I believe in really healthy sexuality and intimacy, you go to the mat for it, even if people disagree with you. I have been so honored and humbled to be part of such a unique learning process and clinical caring intervention.

Contact Information:

Email: besafemv@gmail.com

Paul Gethard, MBA, M.A. in Chemistry

Photo courtesy of Paul Gethard

"Some men know that a light touch of the tongue, running from a woman's toes to her ears, lingering in the softest way possible in various places in between, given often enough and sincerely enough, would add immeasurably to world peace."

— *Marianne Williamson*

As a scientist, Paul was involved in pharmaceutical research for Merck, atomic energy research for General Dynamics, and seeking alternative sources of energy for Occidental Petroleum. But for the last thirty years, in addition to being a surrogate, he has worked as a handyman.

Tova: Were you comfortable with nudity growing up?

Paul: No, but as an adult I attended a "clothing-optional" camp in the mountains. Clothing optional is very different from nudity. With nudity gatherings, everyone is usually given one hour to become naked or leave. No physical contact is permitted—not even hugging or hand holding. With clothing-optional gatherings, everyone is permitted to be dressed or undressed as they feel comfortable. Physical contact is okay, but no sexual contact activities are allowed. I had been raised a very strict Catholic, so the nudity was an awakening for me. It was just so fascinating. I didn't take off my bathing suit at the beginning, and it was just amazing to see all these naked people swimming and relaxing. There was absolutely no public sex. By the end of the first week, I finally took off my bathing trunks. What I learned is that not everyone has a perfect body, and so I became much more accepting of my own.

Tova: By this time you had become comfortable with nudity.

Paul: Yes. At that time, someone told me, "If you're now comfortable with this, you might want to try the Clover Patch down in Fountain Valley." So that's what got me involved with the Clover Patch. It took a little time for me to become accustomed to nudity, and I was really shy at first. The gathering's facilitator, Clover, required attendance at an orientation session for folks who were newcomers, where the rules/boundaries of acceptable behavior were explained, e.g., this is not a swing party. After the orientation, I stepped into the living room where there were about sixty people in different stages of dress and undress, all really comfortable. And that's how I met Clover.

Tova: Up until then, what were your feelings about relationships?

Paul: I had been in three prior marriages, and I was the kind of person who really enjoys the totality of sexual contact, not simply intercourse. The sex I'd had in my marriages was always great at first, but later deteriorated within the first year. So I realized that I had some learning to do. I had taken a course after my last divorce called the "Emerging Woman," because I was wondering why things weren't working out for me. There was no equivalent course for men, and this one was geared for women coming out of divorce who wanted to rebuild their lives. I learned what I liked and needed from women. When I met Clover, I thought she was very interesting, but I didn't feel the urge to date her. Over time, I could see qualities in Clover that I really liked. Steadily, I felt romantically drawn to her and we started dating. Life took off from there, and we've been together for over thirty years.

Tova: What got you interested in surrogacy?

Paul: Clover had already been working as a surrogate, and she talked to me about it. She introduced me to Drs. Michel Risken and Anita Banker, a therapeutic team that trained and worked with surrogates. It all sounded really neat. Then I took the training in around 1983 and was an intern; then I became a certified partner. At first, I liked the idea of just taking the training, because not everyone who did that became a surrogate. Some people took it to discover more about who they were in relationships and intimacy. I just loved the idea of getting some training and learning more about surrogacy. By the time I completed my training, I was very comfortable and looked forward to helping people as a surrogate.

Tova: I believe that you and Clover were the only couple in which both of you were working as surrogates at the same time.

Paul: Yes. Over time we discovered that was true.

Tova: Was there any discomfort, and if so, how did you deal with that?

Paul: Clover was very comfortable with herself. And as I mentioned, I'd had three marriages. I knew that, as surrogates, at some point we would be having sex with our clients. But we were very comfortable with each other and with surrogacy.

Tova: So there was no jealousy?

Paul: No. Somehow we just connected and trusted each other.

Tova: What are the qualities that you think made you a good surrogate?

Paul: I was always very attracted to women. I loved being around them and the idea of being close with them, even though I hadn't known much about how to be a good lover. Through the surrogate training, I learned about sensuality, as opposed to getting laid or having penetrative sex. We learned to perform specific touching and caressing exercises that can be more fulfilling than actual intercourse. Clients are directed to relax and experience the sensations that each exercise brings to them. I'm very gentle with women and like making them feel relaxed. Many women grow up feeling like it's their job to satisfy a man, that the pleasure was their responsibility. I wanted to let women know that they were entitled to be sensual and to experience the joy of sex, too; that it wasn't their obligation to make the man feel fulfilled.

Tova: What were your most memorable client experiences?

Paul: I remember a woman who was curious as to whether she was a lesbian, because she had been raised in a convent and had experienced no sensuality, no masturbating, nothing. She told me that many of the women in the convent would sneak into bed with each other and snuggle late at night when the nuns were away. When these women left the convent, they had become used to being with another woman, so she wondered whether she was a lesbian. That's why she entered therapy and wanted to work with a male surrogate. This client was now a police officer, and she was lovely and absolutely gorgeous.

We went through about twelve sessions together, and she thoroughly enjoyed them. By the time she felt ready to end our therapy, she was pretty sure that she was a lesbian and was not interested in intercourse. She enjoyed the sensuality of our time together, but she never got turned on. I felt that I had fulfilled my mission with her, that she had gained clarity about herself. The most fascinating thing was that about six months later, the therapist asked me if I remembered that client. The therapist told me, "Well, she's dating a guy now and she's having a terrific relationship." She said that somehow I just didn't turn her on. The therapist and others were very concerned that I would be deeply hurt for her lack of interest in me. I reminded them that throughout life, as a male, I was quite accustomed to total rejection by some women now and then—no problem. I actually laughed when I heard about her response to me.

Sex Is the Least of It

Tova: Is there anyone else who stands out in your mind?

Paul: One that comes to mind is a forty-five-year-old woman who, most of her life, has not been hugged or touched by a man. A therapist contacted me about helping her to overcome her fear of contact. I told the therapist to inform the client that I was a hug trainer. When that day of our meeting arrived, I came into the office, walked directly to her and, without hesitation, reached out and hugged her. Then we practiced "hug, hug, hug." The original plan was to hug her 100 times, but her goals were accomplished with twenty hugs and one session. From then on, she was fine with touching and hugging men as well as women. The fascinating thing is that there was no sex or sensuality training involved.

Tova: Is there anyone else who comes to mind?

Paul: Many women come into therapy who really need a safe, accepting partner to experiment. That's why working with a male surrogate is so important. One of my clients was a woman whose twenty-year marriage had just ended. The guy she was married to was really self-centered, and she'd worked constantly to entertain him, to give him pleasure, and to give him orgasms. He would just lie there on the bed and she did all the activity. It was never a priority that she should be pleasured. One day she learned that he had a mistress and that he had apparently been active with other women as well. She was absolutely crushed. He blamed her for his failures and that's why she came into therapy. We started working together, and about two thirds along the way, she was able to experience her own sensuality and really break out. In the beginning, she wanted to repeat her usual behavior of pleasing me. But I gently re-focused her attention back to her own sensations. The most important lesson she learned was how to receive pleasure and take it in for herself.

In time, Clover and I took what we learned and started conducting sensuality courses at our church. We would teach people about comfort with their bodies, with nudity, experiencing sensuality, and not rushing into sexuality. As I said before, the camp was clothing-optional, so they could take off their clothes if they wanted to. But no sexual activity was allowed. They could go off into their own rooms to practice the sensate focus exercises we taught them.

Tova: Through your surrogate experience, what did you learn about yourself?

Paul: I guess the most powerful thing was how much I really enjoyed being with women and how wonderful it is to be sensual and contain the urge to be sexual. At a certain point, sensuality and sexuality become equally enjoyable. But touching and caressing are just so wonderful.

Stephanie Wadell, M.A.

Photo Courtesy of Vera

"Love is the secret key; it opens the door to the divine. Laugh, love, be alive, dance, sing, become a hollow bamboo and let His song flow through you."

—*Bhagwan Shree Rajneesh*

Stephanie was born and raised in the Northern Florida panhandle. She was educated and matured in California during the late 1960s and early 1970s at the University of California, Santa Barbara. She received certifications in massage therapy in 1983 in Sydney, Australia, and in 1984 from the Holistic Institute of Massage Therapy in Sacramento, California. Other certifications include Shamanic Hypnotherapy from the Transformative Arts Institute in Marin County, California, in 1986, and in 1988, qualification as a Chuluaqui-Quodoushka Alpha Level 1 Teacher from Phoenix, Arizona. Stephanie completed her Master of Arts degree in Counseling Psychology from the University of San Francisco, California, in 1991. She founded a Shamanic Healing Arts Mystery School from 1998-2010, where she certified people as Métis Medicine Way Light Workers, reflecting her Cherokee lineage.

Tova: What were the early messages you heard in your home growing up regarding sexuality?

Stephanie: My parents were open and affectionate with each other. Every Sunday, we went to a beautiful beach with my brother who was seven years older. We had sugar-white sands and pristine emerald waters. My experiences growing up made me aware of feeling good in my body. I remember my mother telling me secrets about love, such as what her first kiss was like with my father, and how it made her feel, like she was falling away into outer space. The look in her eyes and the sound of her voice were enticing for me.

Tova: You had very positive messages around you.

Stephanie: It was a sensuous, open environment for my body, but in a strict Catholic format. I felt safe about being affectionate, romantic, or sexual with another person when that was under the blessing of the Catholic Church. That's how I grew up and I felt safe. I never felt like rebelling against any of those beliefs until we moved to California.

Tova: Were there any social or sexual issues you needed to work out as you matured toward adulthood?

Stephanie: I was raised in the panhandle of Florida and we moved to northern California when I was seventeen. My whole life was rearranged and confusion flooded me. I tried to make sense of many things in my new environment that were different from the way I was raised in a small town where religion meant something special.

I came to California in 1967, attended UC Santa Barbara in 1968. I lived in Isla Vista during the summer of love in 1969, which propelled me into being as free as I could be. Many issues came up between my parents and me, because now I was in a free environment and at college. There were love-ins and be-ins and "make love, not war" slogans everywhere. The way you got to know somebody was through sexual experiences first. Big conflicts arose for my parents. To me, it seemed natural. I felt fortunate I had been transported to a magical place, once again living on a beautiful beach in Santa Barbara, being sensuous with my body because of the Great Ocean. I felt happy with my body and confident about showing off my body, along with everyone else. We had the freedom of no bras and feeling sexy. Those years created a lot of conflict with my parents.

Tova: How did they deal with the emergence of this new culture?

Stephanie: Not well. I was immersed in the new world of the sexual revolution. Anytime I brought a boyfriend home to meet my parents, my father would say to me, "Why don't you marry that guy?" I felt that he didn't understand me and there was no way we could ever talk it through or work it out, because marriage wasn't on my mind. It caused a big rift between me and my parents. We never returned to being a close family after my years in college.

Tova: How did you first hear about surrogacy?

Stephanie: I began to teach Chuluaqui-Quodoushka, which is a blended Native American (North, South, Central) path of Spiritual Sexuality. I discovered this path when I was around the age of thirty-four. I began to follow the path and I became a teacher. I taught the Quodoushka tradition until I was forty-seven. During one of the workshops, a participant said she was a surrogate partner. I thought, *well, now that's very fascinating; I've never heard of this*. Within the Chuluaqui-Quodoushka tradition from the ancient past, there were sexual rites of passage at puberty. These rites of passage included a vision quest, a new name as an adult re-entering society, and a hands-on sexual educator called a FireWoman or FireMan. A Council of Grandmothers chose the FirePerson, so the young person was matched up with the correct energy wisdom of the FirePerson. I had learned about other sexual rites of passage on the big island of Hawai'i, where I met Professor Milton Diamond, Ph.D., who had researched the Ali'I, the royal Hawaiian people. Those people also went through sexual rites of passage at puberty. If they preferred, they were given a hands-on sexual teacher. When I learned about the FireWoman tradition of the past, I thought, *that's what I want to be*. I was already a massage therapist. I wanted to help people feel better in their bodies. I thought the surrogate partner therapist was a modern-day equivalent of a FireWoman. Perhaps there was a way to become one and help those with problems. Of course, it's against the law to provide any sexual experience for a minor. I wondered how I would pursue this idea, but it didn't go any further for a few years.

At thirty-five, I wanted to complete my bachelor's degree at New College of California in San Francisco. I only needed thirteen units. Their curriculum required me to write a thesis. My thesis was about sex therapy, because at the time I thought the Chuluaqui-Quodoushka teachings were the best sex therapy anybody could ever have. I felt there should be a law that everyone should receive these teachings, including puberty rites of passage, to prevent sexual problems as adults or in marriage. The college required that I do a comparison with other sex therapies or modalities in order to discern which might be the best kind of sex therapy.

I did research and found Dr. Barbara Read living in San Francisco. She had created the Bay Area Surrogate Association (BASA) in the early 1980s. She graduated from the Institute for Advanced Study of Human Sexuality, one of the three places that offered a Ph.D. program in Human Sexuality. On the day I went to visit her, I could see the ocean from her apartment and thought she looked like a jock. "I'm here to learn about the BASA Training for my thesis," I said. She gave me a penetrating look and handed me a questionnaire to fill out. As I began to talk about Quodoushka and show her the manual, she hushed me up. "If I'm to teach you about the BASA Training, then you must be open to learning a direct body approach to sex therapy." She continued, "You're in luck, because I have a man here from Florida who needs a partner to take the training with. You've showed up at the right time." My heart was beating fast, so I stared out at the ocean and thought of where I grew up and began to feel more comfortable. I thought, *when we begin the training, I'm sure she would look sexier than the sweat pants she was wearing*. I took the BASA Training with Larry, which amounted to about 120 hours. Of course, we did most of the Training in the nude, so my sexy outfit didn't matter at all!

Later, I learned that Dr. Read had consulted with the Institute for Advanced Study of Human Sexuality in order to get the BASA Training into the Institute's certification courses. This was not approved at that time due to lack of funds and resources.

Sex Is the Least of It

Tova: Do you recall what year that was?

Stephanie: It was 1985. I was thirty-five at the time. I went through the training never expecting that I would actually do the Work. I had a boyfriend and felt like the Work was way beyond me. I call surrogate partner therapy the Work, in order to honor the whole process as a somatic healing touch experience. I also took the SAR, Sexual Attitude Restructuring, required by Dr. Read. The SAR was taught at the Institute for Advanced Study of Human Sexuality in San Francisco. It was an eight-day course that opened my mind to all kinds of ways of being sexual, uncommon beliefs, and different cultural norms. It was an amazing experience that I could relate to, because it was a lecture series, slide shows, and breakout sessions to discuss each topic. The BASA Training was experiential with full nudity required. Dr. Read critiqued us as we learned relaxation techniques, belly breathing, spooning, sensate focus, and sensual caress of our face, hand, back, and eventually, whole body. We did mirror work for opening up to accepting our bodies as we lived in them. We learned foot bathing, sensual baths, and the importance of hugging and sharing our feelings. Another couple was trained at the same time. After all the body sessions, we drove over to Cheryl Cohen's (Cheryl Cohen-Greene now) house who was working as a surrogate partner in the East Bay. Cheryl showed us her home office and her style of taking notes. Her family lived next door in the other duplex. My mind was now opened in a way I never thought possible. I wondered if I would ever tell my friends about surrogate partner therapy.

It wasn't until 1987 that I actually had my first client, and that was only because Dr. Read said, "This man really needs your help and you have been trained in this work. I don't have any other surrogate partners who can help him. You're the one who can help him." I asked a friend to let me use his apartment in San Francisco, because I was living with my boyfriend and was not set up to work out of my house or work in an office. I worked with this client for ten sessions. My heart opened to his pain and loneliness that he had been living in for so many years. You look around at people and you think they're fine, but oftentimes they're not.

Even when they're married or in a relationship, many people are having issues in their sex life they are not talking about. My first client opened my heart to doing the Work. Dr. Read told me that I did a good job and I helped the client find out what he needed to know about himself. Her program was geared towards changing behaviors, beliefs, and communicating thoughts and feelings openly.

Tova: Was the sensate focus Masters and Johnson's approach part of her training?

Stephanie: Yes. Part of her Training was founded on a combination of the Work of sex researchers Hartman and Fithian from Long Beach, California, who were trained by Masters and Johnson. Theirs was a direct body approach to learn about sex, orgasms, overcoming dysfunctions, and how to communicate with a partner in the bedroom. There were body awareness relaxation techniques that were taught to the client. I developed a method of three different types of touch: therapeutic, sensuous, and erotic. The client could explore how each touch would invoke a different response in me, as his surrogate partner.

Tova: You mentioned that one of the important aspects that Dr. Read emphasized was social sexual skills development. Were there other elements that she integrated into her approach?

Stephanie: Social sexual skills were an essential ingredient in helping clients transition to their lifestyle as they knew it. BASA graduates were taught to be teachers and educators more than relationship partners. We were teaching the client how to change thoughts that were negative and to overcome limiting behaviors while learning the art of communication. I had the great fortune to work with many fantastic, qualified sex therapists that were graduates of the Institute during the mid-1980s to the late 1990s. It was because of them that I was able to do my Work in the best way possible. BASA also met as a support group once a month. Dr. Read helped us review our cases, and we had peer group counseling that she based on Re-evaluation Counseling, or RC, as it was known as in the 1970s. Dr. Read's supervisory skills and capabilities certainly kept me focused on what was important in my Work with each client and each therapist. There were many different personalities to deal with effectively.

She, of course, combined sensate focus with an emphasis on communication. Communicate, communicate, communicate. Helping a client understand the difference between a thought and a feeling was paramount. I think the aspect of her work that involved behavior modification allowed the client to take new skills and apply them to all parts of his life. Certainly there were concerns about sexual dysfunctions, but it was in the beginning phases of relating to me as a teacher and partner that communicating clearly was so important. When a client could identify what he thought and what he felt, then we could create intimacy. Surrogate partners also have to communicate effectively with the verbal therapist. This is just as important as the hands-on sensate focus processes in the bedroom. We built our dynamic work together in the triad of verbal therapist, client, and sexual surrogate partner/educator and teacher.

Tova: Why do you think you felt so comfortable with your body and your sexuality? Where did that come from?

Stephanie: I think my sense of freedom and openness came from growing up in a beach town, spending weekends in a bathing suit since I was five years old. Everyone hung out in bathing suits most of the time. We felt comfortable swimming in the warm Gulf of Mexico waters and feeling good without even thinking about it. We felt natural.

When we were teenagers, we would go skinny dipping at night under a full moon in the warm 88-degree ocean. My sense of body freedom carried on inside of me as I grew older. I was lucky that I was nineteen in 1969, during the sexual revolution that opened the doors to being comfortable with your body and with sexuality. As we used to say; "Oh, you're so uptight," meant you weren't willing to be free with your body or open when there was a sexual attraction.

Sex Is the Least of It

Tova: It was a time of tremendous humanistic change.

Stephanie: It was. I was lucky to be at a young, impressionable age to continue to feel free. My college education was also in a beach town. I believe that's what helped me to feel comfortable and to be willing to expose my body to people I didn't know. I went to nude beaches during that time. There were a lot of people doing this. It was never about how you looked or if you went to a gym. We didn't have gyms back then. Everybody just thought it's natural to be nude on a beach. It's natural to take off your clothes and hang out together around a pool. We loved feeling natural. It wasn't about whether or not you had the perfect body.

Tova: What qualities do you possess that made you such a good surrogate?

Stephanie: I think the Training I experienced from Dr. Read helped me understand how to work with a person's problems: how to listen with empathy rather than sympathy, how to teach social sexual skills, body awareness, and relaxation techniques, and to use sensate focus and modeling ways of being natural in the bedroom, being accepting of one's body image, and establishing rapport. I think it happened because I was working with incredibly qualified sex therapists. Dr. Read was my supervisor with every client. I called her about every case. She advised me and supported me. Oftentimes she would remind me, "Have fun!"

I felt a sense of deep compassion and empathy for clients who were in so much emotional and physical pain around their inability to have satisfying sexual or intimate experiences, whether they'd been shut down or had experienced relationships that broke their heart. I remember one client who was in his early forties. He had gone to see a prostitute in Las Vegas when he was twenty-two. She said something to him that made him feel embarrassed about the size of his penis. From that one experience, he never tried to date a woman for the next twenty years. By forty-two, he was thinking, "I'm not getting anywhere and I'm so lonely. Maybe there's some kind of help for me." I don't know how he found out about sexual surrogate partner work at that time. In 1992, I'm not sure how anyone found out about us before the Internet. Maybe he called a bona fide sex therapist that had been certified by the American Association of Sex Educators, Counselors, and Therapists (AASECT). Somehow he found a qualified sex therapist that knew about surrogate partners. At the time, I was the only person doing this work in the South Bay of Northern California.

Tova: Are there, perhaps, two or three other stories, memorable client experiences, that you would like to share?

Stephanie: One of my most favorite clients was a twenty-seven-year-old man who lived in Honolulu, Hawai'i, in a convalescent home run by his father. He had muscular dystrophy. He knew that he would probably not live to the age of thirty. His family worked very hard to find him a sexual surrogate partner, and not a prostitute, to come and work with him, so that he did not have to pass away as a virgin. He could only move his right thumb and his eyes. This was a difficult

160

emotional and vulnerable situation for him.

Tova: Was he in a wheelchair?

Stephanie: No. He had to stay in a bed. He was on a ventilator. He was beautiful. He had light curly blonde hair and sky-blue eyes. I nicknamed him Delight. He had some kind of glowing light around him. His father was more like the child and he was like the parent. They lived and worked in the convalescent home in Honolulu for many years. He had been there for over ten years. His parents had divorced as a result of the strain over their son's condition. His father had contacted a surrogate partner from Southern California. On her way to the airport, she was killed in a car crash. Delight was never told about her. His father kept looking for two more years for another surrogate partner for his son. They found me in an article in *Men's Health* magazine in the mid-1990s, called "Substitute Teachers." My photo was there, along with photos of a few other sexual surrogate partners.

I traveled to Oahu to work with him. I spent a few days talking with him and getting to know him at the convalescent hospital before we arranged the first body session. He was transported to a nurse's house where we all felt safe. I had to learn about how to control the ventilator in case something went wrong. The nurse and his father were in the living room and we were in the bedroom. I was able to make him feel comfortable and make myself feel comfortable in order to do some basic touching exercises. Remember, he could only move his right thumb. I was very nervous, but I had him use his right thumb to touch parts of my body. He enjoyed our touching exercises!

Tova: Did he have any sensations in his body?

Stephanie: He had sensation but no mobility. He was aware when he could get an erection. He only got a partial erection, maybe forty percent, because there were so many physiological factors going on at the same time. We did achieve penetration and he had an orgasm. Later, we learned that at that very moment, the volcano Pele erupted on the Big Island. He smiled and said he was going to write this in his memoirs, that during his first orgasm with his first woman, Pele was watching over him and erupted at the same time. We all felt that it was not a coincidence and that Pele was looking after him. I went to see him one more time the next year on his birthday. He wanted to have an experience of spending the night with a woman. His father and the nurse rented a hotel. They were in the room next door. Basically I just spent the night with him. There were no erotic sexual experiences exchanged. It was his choice. I spent most of the night crying quietly. This young man had worked so hard to have an intimate experience with a woman, me. I listened to the ventilator all night long. With the early morning sunrise over the palm trees outside the hotel room, we both felt satisfied that he had spent the night with a woman. He had achieved another intimacy goal!

Sex Is the Least of It

Our work together inspired him to go back to college and learn to use a computer. He had a few counseling sessions with me over the phone, and with his physical therapist and psychologist at the hospital. I encouraged him to be brave and ask for what he wanted. He contacted a nurse who'd had a crush on him five years before. She came out to see him and they started dating. They could sit him up and strap him in a wheel chair. They would go on a movie date. We had planned on making videos together, because he was charismatic and articulate about the importance of sexuality for people who are extremely disabled. Unfortunately, something happened one night and his ventilator tube popped out. He passed away before anyone could get to him. I have a lock of his hair and some beautiful photos of us together. I will never forget his strength and courage to make this almost impossible situation happen. I feel privileged to have been the sexual surrogate partner to participate with him.

Tova: We sometimes use words like transformative and life-changing in a very superficial way. But those words truly characterize this experience.

Stephanie: Yes, this is what happened for Delight. He went back to school and took the risk of asking out a woman whom he cared about and was successful. He had tremendous support from his father, the hospital staff, and me! I am fortunate to know what happened with Delight. This was not the case with most of my clients. Today, I still hear from just a few of my former clients as to what happened with their lives and choices when it comes to women and relationships.

We were never taught to track our clients; to check in with them a year later, three years later, five years later. I was taught that this was brief therapy. We help them achieve their goals. Then they continue to work with their verbal therapist. When I was presenting at conferences about sexuality research, that was what every person asked me: "Where's the research?" But we were never trained to track our clients. We were taught to tell them that our door would always be open for them if they needed to have a tune-up, as we cavalierly called it. However, we knew that with every session, whether the client completed the fourteen-session process or half of it, he was a changed man, changed for the better, and more aware and present in his body. Learning about connection, intimacy, and vulnerabilities was always good therapy in this therapy.

I presented at many conferences. I led the special-interest group for surrogate partners for the American Association of Sex Educators, Counselors, and Therapists (AASECT) and the Society for the Scientific Study of Sex (SSSS) from 1989-1997. My first presentation for both conferences was on 'Spiritual Sexuality' and the crossover of the FireWoman Tradition (described in a chapter about me in Ray Stubb's book, *Women of the Light*) to the modern-day sexual surrogate partner body therapist in 1987 in Toronto, Canada.

Tova: And the therapists probably did not monitor them as well, once the therapy was terminated.

Stephanie: That's right. Research was not done to track the client's progress, because it was all so under the radar. It was undercover work, except for a few articles that were written now and then.

There are no laws governing it. People kept it quiet, right up until the recent movie, *The Sessions*, came out in 2012. We did not want to be challenged about whether or not surrogate work was prostitution. We also felt it was important to keep clients' lives very confidential, but the Internet has changed this mindset. It's unfortunate that the movie, *The Sessions*, did not accurately portray surrogate partner work *per se*. Sometimes, sex therapists trained someone to be a surrogate partner and work the way the sex therapist directed.

In the ten years of doing this work, I had one client come in who was an undercover cop. Even though I couldn't prove it, I just knew this person was not a real client, although he had gone through the process of seeing a verbal therapist in order to see me. He only came to see me three times. Of course, in my work, the first five sessions involve hugging, breathing awareness, being aware of the five senses, and touching with clothes on.

The possible-cop client learned the importance of sensate focus, the three touches; breathing together; spooning together; communicating what he was thinking and feeling. I allow the client to feel very comfortable and relaxed in their skin before we ever move into any nudity. There's face caressing and hand caressing, and establishing rapport with me as a person, as a teacher and as a surrogate partner.

Tova: So I imagine that was not what he was expecting?

Stephanie: That was definitely not what he was expecting!

Tova: Are there any other client experiences that you can recall?

Stephanie: I had another client who was unique. He pushed the boundaries of the way I did my Work. I'll call him Robert. He came to me after working for two years with a psychotherapist doing talk therapy dealing with the issue of being non-orgasmic with a partner. We completed all of the steps in my work. At that time, I had fourteen steps in my work. When we started to approach more of the sexual aspects of interacting with each other, I noticed he would shut down. He was fine in terms of being sexual with himself, and he was very knowledgeable about his own sexual fantasies, which are important for anyone to understand themselves as a sexual being. I tried countless ways to help him relax and open up, but he kept shutting down in his body. Finally, after twenty sessions, I told the talk therapist that I felt I could not work with Robert any longer. I was not making any headway. I really did not know where to send him, except maybe to a shyness institute. Maybe he just couldn't communicate what was really going on for him. The talk therapist begged me to keep working with him, so I broke my rule of brief therapy and kept working with him.

What we discovered together is that he needed to be completely in control of a relationship with a woman. This man had it all together. Many women wanted to date him. He was handsome, about six feet tall. He was successful at his job, and you would never suspect he had any problems dating and being with women. He knew how to dress and he drove a sexy car. What we learned is that he needed to say to whomever he dated that he did not want to have sex early on in their relationship. In actuality, he did not want to have any sexual experiences until at least six months had passed.

We did role-playing together. When I flirted with him, he would practice saying the "no sex" dialogue with me over and over. I would dress sexy and would try different approaches to lure him into having sex with me or do petting or erotic touching. He repeated, "I really don't want to have any sexual experiences until we've been dating for six months." It might sound silly, but it worked!

Psychologically, this was fascinating that such a handsome, successful man needed to develop trust and intimacy with a woman before he could be successfully intimate with her. He needed to develop more experiences of sensuality first, which is non-demand touch, just cuddling, touching, massaging, before he ever got into anything erotic. He reported to me later that it took him another nine months to allow himself to have an orgasm with a woman.

Tova: Orgasm is the ultimate act of letting go.

Stephanie: Yes. His issue was control, which is juxtaposed to letting go. A tremendous amount of trust and a sense of security were necessary for him to reach that point. As he came to that awareness and learned to communicate, it was a big step forward. Most clients come in and they want their problem fixed so that they can leap into bed on the third date, because that's standard operating procedure for what is called intimacy in today's world.

I want to tell you about another client who I'll call Dan. He was forty-six and a virgin, overweight at more than 240 pounds, maybe about 5'10", and very shy. I took him through the fourteen sessions of what I had learned in my BASA training. He was able to achieve his sexual rites of passage at forty-six. Then the important work began. I would go over to his house and have him practice having a date with me. This is where the practical social sexual skills came in to play. I would have him cook me a dinner. We would sit on the couch. He would practice getting me from the couch to the bedroom efficiently and effectively.

Tova: So this was real-life training?

Stephanie: Yes, real-life training. I love that term. This was carrying the sexual surrogate partner work from the bedroom into his life. I don't know why I did that with this particular client. You would think I would have done that with every client, and perhaps I should have. Now that I think back on it, I wish I had, just to be sure. Because when I walked into this man's apartment, he was living out of black plastic bags. When he needed a shirt, he would go through a plastic bag to find it. So, the first five visits I sat with him on his bed and we went through everything in the bags.

His mother had died unexpectedly and he just couldn't pull himself together. He thought that his major problem was being a virgin and not knowing how to please a woman. The real problem was how he was living, because no woman was going to feel comfortable in his house with ten black garbage bags around the house. Even in his kitchen, he would get the kitchenware out of a plastic bag and then he would put it back into the plastic bag. As we went through these bags, he cried many times. I did, too. He begged me, "Don't make me throw anything away." I said, "You can keep everything you want, but not in plastic bags." I suggested that he buy a dresser at a thrift store. I said, "I want that dresser to be here on my next visit a week from now." He went to see his talk therapist and discussed our session in his apartment. He processed many feelings and emotions, crying and grieving. The therapist did an outstanding job. Over time, we got everything into dressers and compartments and out of the bags. Hooray!

He was a vegetarian and became an excellent gourmet chef. He also began writing poetry, so he could take his feelings of grief and low self-esteem and write them out. The whole piece of work with him was getting him ready to live with himself. Then he started dating. He was one of those very few and special clients that sent me an invitation to his wedding. He sends me a Christmas card every year and tells me that he's still married. He's writing pieces of his story somewhere on the Internet. He wishes he could write his story of what happened with me and him, but he still feels shy about the whole experience.

Many clients tell me, "I'm never going to tell anyone about you and this work I have to do." It's sad. Our clients need to be proud that they found a hands-on sexual teacher and had the courage to crawl out of their shells. It takes a hero to do this work with us. They—our clients—are unsung heroes and become wonderful men and lovers!

Tova: Through your surrogate experience, what did you learn about yourself?

Stephanie: I learned the ability to see the essence of a person: to see beyond the way a person looked or talked or didn't talk. This was a big experience for me, because I grew up on a beach where almost everybody looked good in their little bathing suits. I can remember throughout my twenties, I thought if a person looked good, then that meant they were smart. It meant that they were a good person, because everyone I grew up with looked good and were smart. In working with my clients, I learned to see beyond the way somebody looked and to get to know the very essence of that person, their fears, and their vulnerabilities. Isn't that what intimacy is? I became a much more expanded person through working with my clients. I see the spiritual aspects of sexuality through my surrogate partner work. Currently, I have been called back to the Work by a few therapists who have been doing psychotherapy with virgins that are around the age of sixty. Marilyn Monroe sang a song called *Specialization*, and I guess she knew what she was talking about! I am now specializing in my surrogate partner therapy work.

I also learned how emotional hardships can shut a person down from their own naturalness, from their sexual freedom, and that a negative emotional experience can be crushing for a person. In these instances, they don't know how to be intimate with someone, without help or practicing hands-on with a surrogate partner. Thank you to all my wonderful clients who worked so hard to make the world a better place by improving their intimate lives, with themselves first, and then others.

Contact information:

Phone: 650-599-5000

Websites: www.mswsacredjourneys.net

www.BayAreaSurrogateAssociation.com

www.GreatTurtleMysterySchool.net

Ray Noonan, Ph.D.

"If fear is the great enemy of intimacy, love is its true friend,"- Henri Nouwen

Dr. Noonan received his Master's degree in Health Education for Specialists in Human Sexuality in 1984 and his Ph.D. in Human Sexuality at New York University in 1998. He is the co-editor with Dr. Robert Francoeur of the *Continuum Complete International Encyclopedia of Sexuality* (2004), and co-editor with Drs. Peter Anderson and Diane de Mauro of *Does Anyone Still Remember When Sex Was Fun? Positive Sexuality in the Age of AIDS* (1996). He currently teaches Human Sexuality, Health, and Stress courses at the Fashion Institute of Technology of the State University of New York (FIT-SUNY) in Manhattan.

Tova: What were the early messages that you heard regarding sexuality in your home?

Ray: I don't think that I really heard a lot of messages about sex growing up. I know my mother was affectionate with us. And we saw that. At one point, when I was a teenager even before I started dating, I remember my mother saying that I'd better never get anybody pregnant. I remember before that when I was about twelve years old that one of my cousins became pregnant and she was not married. Years later, she told me that my mother was the only person who still treated her nicely and with respect. I didn't receive any explicit sex education at all. I don't remember being told where babies come from, but my father said, "You'll find out later," when I asked. I also remember when I was about ten playing "doctor" with a girl, and that didn't go over very well, and I got spanked for that. So that was kind of a negative message. But that was about it. I would look back and write in the acknowledgments to my doctoral dissertation that my parents apparently provided "the environment that gave me the gift of a sexual persona free from the negative emotional tethers that prevent so many people from freely feeling and sharing their sexuality as a healthy part of themselves."

Tova: Were there any social or sexual issues that you needed to work out as you matured toward adulthood?

Ray: I don't think I needed to work through any issues. It was just that I started dating late. We weren't really allowed to date.

Tova: Was that a rule of your parents?

Ray: No. It wasn't a rule; it wasn't for any particular reason except that you need money to date. We were fairly poor. We were working class poor. When you're working and making money you have the resources to date. So it wasn't anything particularly against dating, *per se*. It's just that you can do it when you can afford to.

Tova: How old were you when you started dating?

Ray: I don't think I ever really dated. The only real dates I had were in the eleventh grade. My brother and I were allowed to attend our junior proms and then our senior proms when we were seniors. We were like a year apart in school. Those were formal dates. In college, there was really no formal dating. I was just involved with different people at different times that I would meet at school. At that time, it wasn't easy for me either because I came right out of high school at seventeen and started working at the post office at night while attending college full time in the day. So there wasn't a whole lot of time to date.

Tova: How long did you work at the post office?

Ray: I was there about two or three years. I eventually got fired for not showing up for a few weeks around finals. And I wasn't doing well in school either. It was very hard to do two full-time things at once and getting two hours of sleep a night. So I ended up not doing well in either of them. Then I would take a summer class and it would be great. I'd get an A and then come back to college in the Fall and I would find work-study jobs.

Tova: So you flunked out of college?

Ray: That's right, twice. I was a chemistry major originally at Temple University in Philadelphia. Then I switched majors—too many times for my own good—to philosophy, then psychology, and finally journalism when I figured out I could write. And between going to school full time and working full time, it was just too much.

Tova: What happened?

Ray: I went in and out of Temple for about six years and I eventually never went back. And then I ended up going to Thomas Edison State College in New Jersey about nine years later, which was like a university without walls, for about six months. It's where they transfer your existing credits and then give you a degree, or they evaluate work experience and give you course credit, so you don't actually go there. Now it's expanded beyond what it was then. I actually had enough credits for a fairly quick bachelor's degree, having switched majors so many times across the sciences and humanities. That was about 1981. It was kind of an odd thing, because I had already started as a non-matriculated student in the doctoral program in Human Sexuality at New York University before I actually had my bachelor's degree. But I had to get the bachelor's to actually be accepted, although they wanted me to do the master's first, since it took me so long to get the bachelor's, and they weren't sure I would finish.

Tova: After you graduated, what kind of jobs did you have?

Ray: When I was at Temple University, I got involved with an alternative newspaper, the *Populist*, and found I had a knack for graphic design, editing, and typesetting. Later, I started a popular culture magazine called the *Philadelphia Review*. All of these would later serve me well, because I used these skills to make money for a good part of the time when I was working on my master's and doctorate at NYU.

But during that time at Temple, I did an article for the *Populist* on abortion. This was prior to Roe v. Wade. Then I started doing volunteer work for Planned Parenthood, where I had gone for information for my abortion article, which eventually led to my being hired as a media specialist and their librarian. Soon I was also coordinating the pregnancy testing clinic and doing pregnancy options counseling at Jefferson Hospital in Philadelphia, like I was also doing as a volunteer at Planned Parenthood. Later, after Roe v. Wade, I worked at a private abortion clinic where I ended up becoming a birth control and abortion counselor. I was the first male abortion counselor in Philadelphia, and, apparently, the first male abortion counselor in the country who wasn't a physician, which the EEOC, the Equal Employment Opportunity Commission, helped to facilitate. I counseled the patients before, during, and after their abortions.

At the same time, I became involved with an open marriage group and started an alternative marriage council dealing with non-traditional and non-monogamous marriages and relationships. I also started writing about philosophy and sex in my *Philadelphia Review*. Through these activities, I connected with such luminaries as Albert Ellis, Nena and George O'Neill, Robert Rimmer, Larry and Joan Constantine, Robert Francoeur, and Lester Kirkendall, among others. I created the journal that would become *Alternative Lifestyles*. So that was my pre-doctoral and pre-surrogate life.

Sex Is the Least of It

By the time I got to NYU, we were at the beginning of the AIDS crisis, and, after getting my master's, I spent about a year working for the New York City Department of Health in their Division of AIDS Program Services. Later, while working on my doctorate, I was becoming increasingly concerned with the extreme negativity about sexuality that was being fostered by various authorities, including the media and many health and sex educators. As a result, I got involved with writing a book called, *Does Anyone Still Remember When Sex Was Fun? Positive Sexuality in the Age of AIDS*, with Pete Anderson and Diane de Mauro at NYU. This idea of positive sexuality has been a message that I continue to try to convey to my students today at F.I.T., the Fashion Institute of Technology of the State University of New York in Manhattan. But while I was at NYU, this was one of the reasons one of my advisors said that I was always involved with "fringe" sexuality topics, including my dissertation on sex in outer space, where I connected chaos theory to sexuality, coining the phrase "human sexuality complex," for my Ph.D., and my sex surrogate research for the master's. I would continue to write about "fringe" subjects, such as the sexual roots of terrorism, sexual expression in musical lyrics, heterophobia, and sex and the Internet. I was the first sexologist, best I've been able to establish, to have their own website, with my SexQuest.com. But of all the interesting things that I've done, the most enduring interest has been in my work on surrogates. I still get email inquiring about it.

Tova: What prompted you to write your master's thesis on surrogacy?

Ray: Because I had become a surrogate by that point. I attended an International Professional Surrogates Association (IPSA) conference, perhaps in Nevada or the hills of California. I believe the organization was founded by Barbara Roberts, and Maureen Sullivan was president when I got involved. I decided to do my master's research exploring a survey of surrogates. So Maureen gave me a mailing list she and others had compiled as a part of something called Surrogate Networking, an independent informal network designed to keep surrogates in touch with each other. I mailed out ninety-seven questionnaires and I received fifty-four back completed. I've kept all the questionnaires in a box somewhere. I've often thought it would be interesting to go back to them again and write something for its historical value and to do a new survey to reflect contemporary surrogates. One of the more interesting results that I found was that surrogates at the time were, on average, more highly educated than the general population, including more than 10% of the respondents who had doctorates. My main results, however, clarified that most of the time spent therapeutically with clients was in nonsexual activities, which included experiential, non-erotic exercises; talking, giving sex information and emotional support and reassurance; and focusing on social skills in public settings. Only 13% of the surrogate's time was spent engaging in sexual activities. In the meantime, I've continued to write about surrogates and my original master's thesis can be found online at www.SexQuest.com/surrogat.htm.

Tova: How did you first hear about surrogacy?

Ray: It all started with Planned Parenthood. I got involved with the programs for teens as well as for professionals that they were conducting, along with the pregnancy testing clinic and pregnancy options counseling I was doing, and joined the American Association of Sex Educators, Counselors, and Therapists (AASECT). Planned Parenthood started sending me to various training programs and I started to attend AASECT conferences. At that time, as I mentioned, I was creating my alternative marriage council, which would eventually become the Sex Institute and SexQuest, my website. When I was attending these various conferences, I started meeting healers in the field of human sexuality. Somewhere along the line, I met an experienced surrogate partner and she got me involved with surrogacy, and she became my trainer. That was about 1982, when I became a surrogate. Most of the work I did was from then until 1995, so about fifteen years total.

Tova: I know that this woman became one of the founding mothers of surrogacy on the East Coast. Was there a group of surrogates in the New York area at that time?

Ray: There were a handful of other surrogates that I met through her. It wasn't just the two of us. One of them was a woman named Patricia Pearlman. She and I ended up making a video together for people with disabilities.

Tova: Was there some kind of East Coast organization?

Ray: I got involved with developing ESA, the Eastern Surrogates Association, but not much happened with it.

Tova: Why do you think you felt so comfortable with your body and sexuality?

Ray: I think part of it had to do with the fact that I didn't get any real negative sex messages from my parents. I was comfortable with women and I was able to help them feel comfortable and relaxed. I had a lot of knowledge about sexuality.

Tova: You were a good teacher.

Ray: Yes, I was patient. I didn't push people to perform. I was accepting of where people were in their lives and how they felt. I take people as they are. In terms of sexual functioning, I was good at it and I knew what other people would find pleasurable.

I remember a wonderful song by a well-known singer, Dory Previn, in the 1970s. One song that I really found interesting, *Angels and Devils the Following Day*, was one in which she sang about how the attitudes of different lovers made her feel. She would sing about how one would make her feel ashamed of her body, whereas another would make her feel secure. It's the idea that people respond to how their lovers deal with them sexually. If you think you're doing something shameful, then your lover gets that message. And I never had any shame to transmit to other people. My parents never gave me that negative message about sex when I was young.

Sex Is the Least of It

I remember the song vividly because she says that one lover would "make love" to her and the other would "fuck." It was one of the first songs where I heard that word used and it was very impacting at the time how she arrived at her unexpected conclusion given our common understanding of these words. I was just beginning to explore how sexuality was expressed in music, which expanded my interest in the erotic arts as I explored how sex was portrayed in the visual arts.

Tova: What are the three or four most memorable client experiences that you can recall as a surrogate?

Ray: The first that comes to mind was the first experience of my career. It was a weeklong intensive case. We worked every day for a week in New York. She was a thirty-year-old woman who was anorgasmic, and I believe she was also a virgin. I would describe her as a socially naïve person. She had never gotten involved with anybody because her focus was on her work. However, she wanted to have a relationship. I would meet with her therapist daily who would provide me with guidance. It turned out to be very successful, and inspired me to begin thinking about what would become my master's thesis on the functions of surrogates.

Another therapist referred a woman to me who had a panic disorder. I met with the therapist about how best to work with the client, and then she would have her own individual sessions with the client. I had just one session with this client and it was successful. The problem was dealing with panic disorder, which was triggered when she got into a sexual situation. We both remained clothed; we didn't engage in any sexual activities. I just helped her feel calm in the presence of a man. I taught her how to breathe, which was very important. The strategy was to gradually increase the level of intimacy until we had intercourse. But we only ended up doing the one session.

Later, I heard that this nationally recognized therapist, who had provided me with this referral and was so helpful, stated publicly that she never worked with surrogates and was against surrogacy. Obviously, that was not accurate. Very often, history is rewritten!

It just highlights the fact that sometimes therapists get cold feet regarding the protocol. They may even stop working with surrogates. Sometimes, I think, therapists have a double standard with regard to referring women versus men for surrogate partner therapy. But surrogates usually have great successes. People need to understand that surrogates don't engage in immediate sex; when you meet with a client for the first time, you usually talk and get to know each other. You give them factual information about sex. You participate in social events together to help them refine their dating skills. You do some sensate focus exercises. You do some massage. There are touching experiences and relaxation exercises. Real sexual interaction usually doesn't happen until later, if at all. Interestingly, my research corroborated that this was the experience of surrogates in general.

Tova: Are there any other clients that come to mind for you?

Ray: There was one client I remember. She had been traumatized and raped and cut vaginally with a knife. This was a client that needed great sensitivity and empathy. It stands out in my mind because she told me that the guy who raped her got caught and ended up getting killed in jail. We both felt it was poetic justice. My work with her wasn't just about intimacy or orgasm, but a whole combination of issues. She experienced significant success.

I also remember another case I had with a woman who had a genetic disorder, and with whom I met for a fairly long period of time. When people are born with this particular condition, they are oftentimes severely mentally disabled or have physical deformities. This woman was not physically deformed, nor was she extremely mentally disabled. She had average intelligence. She was sterile.

Tova: Why did she seek you out?

Ray: She knew about sex and she felt she was missing out on something and wanted to be able to experience it. She was basically a virgin when I started working with her. She was never able to have an orgasm, but she was able at least to experience intercourse, some kind of sexual connection.

Ultimately, surrogates work with people so that they can transfer the skills we teach them, and the self-confidence they gain from it, to an outside relationship or develop a real relationship. We don't typically know what happens to them once they leave. But that experience was invaluable for her, and she got to experience intimacy, and then, hopefully, she was able to meet somebody and feel confident enough to be able to enjoy a real romantic relationship.

Tova: Through your surrogate experience, what did you learn about yourself?

Ray: That I had something to offer to people, something that was special. I had some capabilities and unique skills, as well as a certain amount of comfort with sexual interactions and talking about sex. Surrogates deal with sex in a structured and therapeutic manner. It's a different way of looking at sex. It's one thing to have various friends and lovers. Sometimes they turn out great. Sometimes they fall apart and are destructive to a person's pride. But when you are a surrogate, you work in a clinical capacity. You are educated and trained.

I could function analytically at the same time I was functioning subjectively. I was part of the experience, and yet separate enough to handle it in a clinical context. The person I was living with at the time said that being a surrogate was an ideal fit for my personality. She was surprised that it was such a positive thing.

Tova: Tell me about the *International Encyclopedia*. You're one of the pivotal founders of it, aren't you?

Sex Is the Least of It

Ray: Bob Francoeur was the one who originally created it. When I was first involved with it, it was the *International Encyclopedia of Sexuality*. That was the original title. I started working with Bob when I was still a doctoral student because I had the typesetting background that he needed. The publisher wanted the book already typeset. So he got me involved because he knew I had that experience. Eventually, I became associate editor for the fourth volume of the first version and co-editor of the combined, updated single volume. It's now called the *Continuum Complete International Encyclopedia of Sexuality* (CCIES).

Tova: And when was that published?

Ray: The first three volumes came out in 1997 with thirty-three countries. The fourth volume came out in 2001 with seventeen more countries. The most recent version came out in 2004, which received several awards, which was an updated volume combining the first four volumes with twelve additional countries and places, including every continent and outer space. That version was the one that our publisher allowed us to post in its entirety for free and open access on the Kinsey Institute website (KinseyInstititute.org/ccies). I'd like to update that site, because by now it's ten years old. You can go to my website and find links to the *CCIES @ The Kinsey Institute*.

Contact information:

Email: rjnoonan@SexQuest.com

Websites: www.SexQuest.com

www.SexQuest.com/surrogat.htm

www.KinseyInstitute.org/ccies

www.KinseyInstitute.org/ccies/us.php#surrogates

Dr. Barbara Reed

Photo courtesy of Dr Cheryl Cohen Greene

To Surrogate, With Love

by Jason Walsh (*published in the Pacific Sun*)

30 Years Ago

"Direct body work" was what the kids were calling it 30 years ago this week.

It was autumn of 1981–and the age of free love in Marin was officially over. At least it was for clients of local therapist Barbara Reed, the woman who'd placed an ad in the *Sun* classifieds offering her services as a "sex surrogate." The *Sun*, of course, was all over this story like a bad, er, rash.

"Surrogate work is a relatively new approach to sex therapy," wrote *Sun* reporter Catherine Peters. "Surrogates perform 'direct body work' or, less delicately, have sexual intercourse with their clients.

What is the general procedure for therapy?

I see each client for a verbal hour at first. He lays out the issues and problems and I share whatever information I have and what options I see within my context and the context of the Sex Therapy Consortium. I come up with a plan with the client during that initial interview. I give a ballpark number at how long I think it will take, usually set up in a very vague way because until you get into it, you really don't know what the resistances are going to be. Everybody resists change, even if they want it.

Sex Is the Least of It

Sex surrogacy isn't prostitution, Peters pointed out. On the other hand, it wasn't exactly legal either. "I'm operating by precedent," said the 44-year-old Reed. "But I've never been questioned."

Reed had spent 10 years as a personal-growth counselor before taking on sex surrogacy in 1977. Today, the 74-year-old Reed is a licensed sexologist and president of the Institute for Advanced Study of Human Sexuality's alumni association. But when the *Sun* interviewed her about her work in 1981, she was knee deep in this highly controversial method of helping men solve their problems with physical intimacy.

Or, as Reed more bluntly described it: "When their c--- doesn't work."

She charged $60 an hour.

Here are the highlights of the interview:

What happens if the patient needs bodywork?

When we proceed to bodywork, I invite him into the bedroom next door. I don't have him take his clothes off right away; I usually have him sit down on the bed to get used to the room with his clothes on. Then I work the conversation around to the fact that it would be really easier to deal with this with our clothes off, or I would like to take my clothes off to get us used to seeing each other in the nude. I then take off my clothes with what I call an "air of positive expectation." Because at this point, some men get really hung up. That's always the hardest thing—getting him to take off his clothes. If I find a man can't get out of his pants, that's a point of breakdown.

How would you describe your work?

I operate as a coach of sexual behavior. If you wanted to learn to swim you would have a coach who would get in the water and swim with you. You can't learn to swim sitting on the beach and you can't learn to f--k sitting around talking about it. Whether it is swimming, tennis or sex—you need a coach, and that's what I am.

You are not listed in the Yellow Pages.

I advertise in the newspaper. My first ad was in the *Pacific Sun.* I was looking for an upper-class suburban market; I've been doing sex therapy for four years and I assessed that that's where the market is.

Do men who answer the ad in the *Pacific Sun* have different problems than other men?

No, I don't see a lot at difference. Really, people in Marin are the same as everyone else.

The bodywork takes place in bed?

Yes, because that's the easiest place to do it.

Do your clients ever fall in love with you?

Sure. You can't spend long periods of time in intimate body interaction without developing some feeling. I deal with that up front with my clients. I say, "Look, we will be in intimate contact for a long period"—I work in two-hour segments—"and you're bound to develop some feeling for me and I'm bound to develop some feeling for you. That's part of it."

Does that seem to help?

Part of what I do is help men realize that they have feelings and that feelings are an acceptable part of their existence. Men are taught that feelings are not OK and you come up with a lot of sexual dysfunction because of that.

What if you're not somebody's "type"?

I'll ask the man, "How do you feel about doing bodywork with me? Do you feel I am enough of your type that you could potentially feel aroused?" If he says, "God, I really hate redheads; it's a real turn off for me," then I'll look for somebody more his type. I don't think surrogates should be the romantic type. The surrogate is there as a coach—not a potential long-term partner. Most of my clients are professional people—lawyers, physicians, computer people. If I had a problem with a computer, I would hire them because that's their specialty—not to get romantically involved with them. My specialty happens to be sexuality, so when they have a problem they call me. I'm not looking to be the be-all, end-all relationship for the man.

So far you've talked mostly about men. Do women need surrogates?

The percentage of women who seek sex therapy is very, very low…That's not because there isn't a need. In this culture sex is not endorsed for women... If you have a couple and the guy is playing around on the outside, its laughed off—"Well, that's the way it is and isn't he a great cocksman?" If a woman does that she's looked on as a slut.

Hasn't women's lib changed some of that?

I think people's attitudes toward sexuality are the last thing to change. There is an interesting piece of research about the attitudes of daughters and granddaughters of Victorian times. The conclusion was that though women in the youngest generation did lip service to liberated sexuality, in reality the attitudes of the third generation were the same as the grandmother's. There's a lot of talk going on today, but when Suzy shows up pregnant at home, it's a crisis.

Article published in the Pacific Sun, November 11-November 17, 2011.

Therapists Who Work with Surrogates

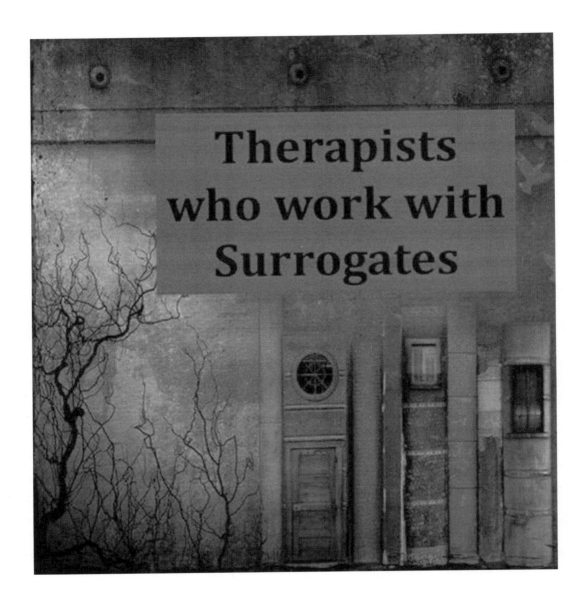

Dr. Ronit Aloni

Photo courtesy of Ronit Aloni

Ronit Aloni earned a master's degree from New York University and a Ph.D. in sexual rehabilitation from the Union Institute in Cincinnati, Ohio. She has taught at Tel Aviv University School of Medicine and is the founder of the Dr. Ronit Aloni Sex Therapy Center in Tel Aviv, Israel, specializing in sex therapy, couples therapy, and sexual rehabilitation.

Tova: What are the criteria that you look for in evaluating whether a client is appropriate for surrogate partner therapy (SPT)?

Ronit: There are only a few criteria. First of all, the client must be single and not have a partner. The client has to have something interfering with his ability to create relationships; perhaps he has tried, but has failed so many times that he is not willing to attempt dating again. A second criterion is that he has never had any relationships, and it's my evaluation that, whether due to physical, mental, or psychological reasons, there is no way he will be able to do that without help. A third criterion is that I have worked with the client in therapy and have tried to move him towards socializing and it didn't work, and the person wants to have a relationship. And the last criterion is that the individual has sexual difficulties that he has tried to overcome with partners in the past and didn't succeed.

Tova: How do you introduce a client to SPT?

Sex Is the Least of It

Ronit: I tell them everything about surrogate partner therapy, and I need to make sure that SPT will not make the client's problems worse. Then I discuss with them the format of the process.

Tova: You have a major sex therapy clinic in which you have many surrogates on your staff. How do you determine which surrogate might be most appropriate for a particular client?

Ronit: I discuss this with the client. And I usually ask him (or her), "What kind of person can you easily get friendly with?" and "What kind of person can you trust?" I do not ask them, "What kind of person are you attracted to?"

Tova: That's an important point. They may not feel physically attracted to the surrogate.

Ronit: I don't think that's an obstacle at all, because most of the clients who come to surrogate therapy may have problems with attraction. They may be attracted to the wrong people, or they don't feel attracted because they are too anxious. So *attraction* is not even a word I discuss with them at that point. And even if the client brings up the issue, I minimize the discussion. I talk about feeling comfortable and relaxed, and I talk about confidence and trust. This is a good foundation to start surrogate therapy, not attraction. What I tell them is that they may have tried relationships with women or men that they were attracted to and it didn't work, so let's try something different. What a client usually discovers is that a surrogate that they may not initially be attracted to will become attractive to them over time as their anxiety level decreases. Or, when they build the relationship, trust, and intimacy, then the attraction develops. I think this is a good lesson for life. I tell them that I am not going to match them with a surrogate who meets their exact preferences. But they may tell me about personal qualities that make them uncomfortable. I say to them, "What are your red flags?" It could be that they couldn't connect with someone who was too fat, too tall, a smoker, too young, too old, or whatever. Then I have a clearer picture from them about whom they might work with best. I can select from among my surrogates to find the ones who would be most suitable. I also tell the client that after the first or second session, if they don't feel comfortable with the surrogate, we can discuss this.

Tova: And if a client still feels uncomfortable by the second or third session?

Ronit: We would talk it through, and I would try to determine whether it's simply anxiety or if there is truly something that doesn't work between them.

Tova: Have you ever changed surrogates?

Ronit: Yes, but that's rarely a problem. On the other hand, the surrogate may not want to continue because she can't feel warmth or empathy for a particular client and it's going to be difficult for her; in that case, then I would make a change. I tell the client beforehand that the surrogate can decline and say, "I don't feel comfortable about this relationship." That makes the match more authentic, because I tell the client that the surrogate doesn't have to accept them, and that he or she needs to feel comfortable with the client, just as the client needs to feel comfortable with the surrogate. To me, this more closely parallels real life, much more so than if the surrogate were to take any client, regardless of what he or she is feeling about the individual.

Tova: It models a real relationship, an authentic connecting.

Ronit: With choices made between two people.

Tova: Do your surrogates and clients, as part of the socialization process, ever meet outside the clinic?

Ronit: At the beginning of the therapy process, they only meet outside. They go out like on a blind date and they meet at a particular place. They introduce themselves to each other, and then they see whether they like each other enough to work together. They continue to socialize outside the clinic and to do whatever they enjoy. So at least two sessions are done out of the clinic, sometimes more. In some cases, that will be the main focus, if the client has problems with social skills and dating.

Tova: Will they go to singles events together?

Ronit: Yes. They will go to singles events, bars, and to the movies, and any other place they would like to go together, such as bowling, the park, the beach, wherever.

Tova: That approach makes sense, because so much of the surrogate's work has to do with building social and dating skills.

Ronit: It's really practical, and I always tell the patient that whatever can happen in your life can happen between you and your surrogate.

Tova: What are the typical clinical issues that may arise during SPT both for the client and for the surrogate? For example, a client may say to the therapist, "I'm not really attracted to this surrogate. Can you get me somebody else?" Or the surrogate may try to create a power situation in which the surrogate may want to consider the client as her client; or perhaps the client may try to play the surrogate against the therapist.

Ronit: Because we conduct all treatment at our clinic, this power-struggle issue is less of an issue than it might be elsewhere. We have monthly meetings for all staff therapists and the surrogates. That's when we discuss surrogate issues as a group. In these meetings, we work out the relationships between the therapist and the surrogate, and sometimes the surrogate or the therapist will bring up a case that we discuss together. We may have group training on different topics or bring in lecturers, so we are always a team at the clinic. If there is a problem between a therapist and a surrogate, it will be brought to me, because I'm the head of the clinic, and then we will address it. There are plenty of opportunities for us to solve problems together.

Sex Is the Least of It

Tova: Do your clients typically ask you about the length of the therapy?

Ronit: Yes. People ask me, "How long do you think therapy is going to take? What direction will the work take?" I cannot answer this, of course, because I look at the therapy from one week to the next, from one session to the one that follows. I want to see what happens, and with that information, I plan the next week's session. Also, I don't want to push my clients too fast, or hold them back if they are capable of doing more. I meet them where they are, and that creates the basis for the upcoming week's work. I cannot know what will be appropriate until the client and surrogate meet and I get the information from both of them.

Tova: Do you follow the Masters and Johnson protocol?

Ronit: No, I don't usually follow any of that. I can say that at least half of the applicants who come to sex therapy don't have any sexual dysfunction. And what Masters and Johnson wrote about was sexual dysfunction. A minimum of fifty percent of my clients have problems with social skills or they have problems with intimacy skills. It doesn't mean that they don't have sexual problems; but they cannot reach the point of dating to find out if they function sexually. The clients are young, maybe in their thirties and forties. They have no diseases and they can masturbate. In other words, they are fine.

Tova: So you don't see erection problems?

Ronit: I do sometimes, but most clients don't have that issue.

Tova: What about delayed or rapid ejaculation?

Ronit: Yes, I see that. But I can tell you that a large percentage of men who have erection problems also have intimacy problems. Once you deal with the intimacy problems and communication issues, deal with how comfortable they feel about themselves, and allow them to discuss their emotions with the surrogate, I don't have to follow any sensate focus exercises. I work with them on how they have approached relationships in the past or what is holding them back. Nowadays, people meet, go straight to bed, and then they don't function. But if they get to know the other person and become more familiar with them so they can talk about their fears or desires, then they don't have any problems.

If I'm dealing with a client who has real sexual dysfunction, I evaluate him. If I determine that he is experiencing sexual problems, then I have the surrogate do the Masters and Johnson sensate focus exercises with him. But that's definitely not the majority of the cases I see.

Tova: I'm sure you deal with situations in which the client or surrogate may fall in love.

Ronit: Absolutely. You cannot prevent a romantic attachment. Many patients fall in love with the surrogate and the surrogate may have real emotional feelings for the patient. That makes it more realistic. This is not sterile work. We want to teach our clients to have intimate relationships with a person they care for. Otherwise, it's just technical, and I don't teach technical sexuality. I talk about relationships, emotions, sharing, empathy, caring for the other person, listening to the other person, being able to give space to the other person, and honor their needs. It's always about emotions. And yet, I've heard from therapists who feel that it's kind of forbidden for a surrogate and client to have those feelings. But I'm not afraid of that. I encourage it. That experience represents real life. When I'm at a conference and someone raises a concern about romantic attachment and separation, I say, "So what if they fall in love? We know that at some point they will separate." I tell the client and the surrogate that the attachment and the separation are important learning experiences. Some of the patients don't know how to separate from a relationship.

Tova: So one of the most important aspects of the relationship is closure.

Ronit: Yes, that's right. They need to learn to separate and to know that they will not be crushed; their lives will go on and they will meet other people.

Tova: How do you present surrogate partner therapy to colleagues? I ask because the therapeutic organizations in the United States and Britain tend to resist SPT.

Ronit: There was research done about 1987 by Zev Wanderer, an American who moved to Israel, and created some of the first research regarding surrogacy. He asked more than a hundred therapists in the United States if they would use surrogate therapy in their practice if it was legal. More than eighty-five percent said yes. And from those therapists who had already worked with surrogates, a hundred percent said they would do it again.

Of course I have colleagues who are not receptive to surrogate therapy. I listen to their objections. Is it about ethics? Is it because they think surrogates are prostitutes? Is it that they feel that intimate problems can only be resolved through talk therapy? Then I respond with information, with research, and with case studies. Some therapists are stuck; and then I cannot do anything. So I just say that there is a place for different ideas and different approaches. When people compare surrogate therapy with prostitution, I say, "I don't see anything that is similar; there is nothing similar about them." Then I come up with ten different comparisons that show how different both professions are. So I say to them, "What is the same? There is nothing that's the same. It's just because surrogacy involves intimacy and it involves money, and those facts blind you."

When I lecture, at the beginning of my presentation, I always start by talking about ethics. If you have a client who can be helped by surrogate partner therapy and you do not refer him for this work, you are not being ethical. This is my definition of ethics; if the therapist has a client in need and will not share information about SPT, especially when talk therapy has not worked, then it's not ethical to withhold choices that could benefit a client.

Sex Is the Least of It

I also say that we all use mentors in various aspects of our lives, because everything we have ever learned, we have usually learned with the guidance of a mentor; somebody showed us how to do something. And we accept that as a valid way to learn. We can accept this concept about anything except when it's about sexuality. When someone raises an objection, which I think is coming from a personal point of view, I will give them feedback, saying, "You have a personal feeling about this, which is okay. But it's a personal feeling, not a professional perspective."

Tova: If someone were to say that SPT doesn't fit with their ethical code, how would you respond?

Ronit: I say, "You are entitled to your own feelings, but our discussion is not about our personal feelings, but about our professional attitudes and approaches. It's about therapeutically serving the best needs of the client. It's not about us or how we feel about it."

Tova: Do you think that one of the elements in the resistance is simply the lack of information and appropriate education for the therapist?

Ronit: I'm sure of that. That's why I always provide complete information to my colleagues. I discuss in detail how surrogate partner therapy works, and that I'm coming from an ethical point of view, which is accepted even by religious parties in this country, by our legal system, and the Minister of Defense. I discuss what traditional talk therapy can and cannot do. I ask, "Is it ethical to keep a person in therapy for three years or five years, while a woman still suffers from vaginismus or a man still experiences rapid ejaculation?" I ask, "Is *that* ethical? What about those five wasted years and what about the cost of therapy during all that time?" So I really get into the little details. I even calculate how much it would cost a person to be in therapy for five years in contrast to being in surrogate therapy for six months. I'm not implying that surrogate therapy doesn't have some weaknesses; of course it does. But let's understand the weaknesses of other therapies; on the scale, SPT comes out very well.

Tova: I wonder if for therapists, SPT may trigger some unresolved sexual feelings that may cause them to shy away from the work.

Ronit: Yes, so I say to them, "Are we talking about attitudes here, personal backgrounds, or are we talking about education? We all have our defenses. We all have our uncomfortable zones. But what does that have to do with the best modality to offer our clients?" I'm dealing with a person's quality of life, and that is my focus.

Tova: There are many psychotherapists in the United States who deal with sexual issues in their practice, but they may not have specialized training in dealing with the broad spectrum of human sexuality, both traditional and non-traditional. Is it similar in Israel?

Ronit: No, it is very different here. Additional training is required in sexuality, including surrogate partner therapy. Since Israel is a very small country, almost every appropriate client is referred to me. But there are cases where other therapists are involved. I encourage them to keep their clients and not transfer them to me. Instead, I instruct them about SPT and help guide them with the surrogate and the client. In this way, I allow the therapist to experience the strength and the power of surrogate therapy. This will help them become my best advocates in the future, because they all have colleagues, and they will, in turn, educate them about SPT.

Years ago, I worked with a therapist from a very traditional psychiatric clinic and she referred a client to me. She had lost all hope and was concerned her client would commit suicide. She said, "I will still be her psychotherapist, but I want to transfer her to you, to see if you can help her." At the end of therapy, the therapist needed to present the case at her conservative staff meeting. "How am I going to say I sent my most hopeless client to surrogate therapy and it succeeded? This woman is alive; she is happy now." This is how I'm educating therapists one by one. We're working in the field of sexuality, rehabilitation, and surrogate therapy in particular, which touches people's vulnerability. SPT goes against everything that we were educated to do. It's a problem we have worked with very slowly. It's not a revolution; it's a gradual evolution.

Tova: How do we best educate our therapists in the United States?

Ronit: I train surrogates and therapists at the same time. This is my model. This makes a huge difference, because therapists have the opportunity to deeply understand how the process works.

Tova: Our main therapeutic organization here is the American Association of Sex Educators, Counselors, and Therapists (AASECT). Over the last thirty years, very articulate surrogates have presented numerous papers at conferences, as well as case studies and seminars explaining SPT, and still there seems to be little movement. What do you think would be the best way to educate our therapeutic community?

Ronit: Every therapist in my clinic has to go through the SPT training along with our new surrogates. This is the way we do things in Israel. I don't know much about the American culture; I just lived in New York for three years while I was studying. I can tell you that I think it should be the therapists advocating for surrogate partner therapy, not the surrogates themselves. This would have more power. Therapists need to take the lead. SPT also needs to be introduced in a highly visible way, such as in the recent movie, *The Sessions*. The movie depicts surrogacy from the perspective of the field of rehabilitation. We see how the life of a disabled man was meaningfully changed by his contact with a trained surrogate. I think that therapists and the American public can understand this, they can accept it, that providing intimate contact to the disabled can be life-changing.

I've found that when you introduce surrogacy into the field of rehabilitation, people are more tolerant; they don't react by being critical. They can empathize and shift from being judgmental to being humanistic. From this point of view, they understand that this is an ethical practice, and that it's about helping people.

Tova: When did you start using SPT?

Ronit: Since 1989, so about twenty-four years ago.

Tova: From your experience, what is the effectiveness of SPT and how do you evaluate that?

Ronit: What I can tell you is that the complaints clients present are usually resolved at a much higher percentage than from other modes of therapy. Half of our clients are not appropriate for SPT, but those who work with surrogates have good results. The other thing that I think is more important is that it's not only about sexuality. SPT affects all aspects of their life, their self-esteem, their confidence, and the way they look at themselves. After working with a surrogate, clients often take action in their lives. They will change their apartment to make it more comfortable for dating, or they may move out of their parents' house. Or they will have better relationships. People will notice that they're more open, more social. Surrogate therapy affects all aspects of a client's life because sexuality may have interfered with their social interactions. It's not only about their sexual life or relationships, it's about everything.

Tova: I would like to ask you about Patricia Pearlman, a late surrogate who worked in New York. How did you meet her, what did she teach you, and what are your recollections of her?

Ronit: She was introduced to me as someone who dealt with the disabled, and this was my field of interest. At that point, I was studying at NYU in the Human Sexuality program and was seeking someone who had experience in this area. I lived in New York and Patricia lived in New Jersey.

Tova: How did the relationship develop?

Ronit: I called her and she was very open; she invited me to her house. I ended up using her experience as the basis for my master's thesis and we remained friends. She educated me from her experience, teaching me about her clients, her techniques, and her approach to the work—she gave me all the fundamentals of surrogate therapy and rehabilitation. In my training program with my new surrogates, I still use videos that she recorded with her clients. She introduced me to a client with cerebral palsy who lived in New Jersey, making an appointment for me to speak with him. We met and we talked for several hours, and then I wrote a seminar about him. Patricia introduced me to another man who was very articulate, but he was deaf and had no experience. He was a virgin in his forties and she did surrogate therapy with him. She introduced us, and I wrote a case study about him as well.

When I returned to Israel, I stayed in contact with her. She visited me in 1990 for an international conference in Bethlehem about sexual rehabilitation. Then she trained my second group of surrogates, and some surrogates from my first group joined in too. She trained them and she had trained me as well. At the Bethlehem conference, she talked about SPT for people with disabilities. Then I presented the first group of surrogates and discussed surrogate partner therapy.

Tova: It sounds like she had a tremendous influence on your life.

Ronit: Patricia's spirit, her openness, and her ability to perceive every person as having sexual rights was really part of her DNA. She passed that legacy onto me, and I've passed that on to all the people I've trained. I feel her spirit is alive in me. In fact, one of the protocols we use when working with the disabled is called the Patricia Protocol, and it's named in her honor. She was very warm, caring, and open. She had a big heart and didn't withhold anything from me. She shared everything with me that I needed to learn. And she was also very funny, with a great laugh, and a truly good person.

Contact information:

Email: dr_aloni@netvision.net.il

Dr. Seth Prosterman

Photo courtesy of Dr. Seth Prosterman

Seth Prosterman has a Ph.D. in human sexuality from the Institute for Advanced Study of Human Sexuality, an M.S. in Counseling (MFT), marriage and family therapist, San Francisco State University. He is a licensed marriage and family therapist and a Board-Certified sex therapist in private practice in San Francisco since 1984.

Dr. Prosterman first heard about surrogate partner therapy when he went to San Francisco to begin his master's/doctoral program. He met surrogates who were preparing a presentation for the Institute in 1980 and learned about what surrogates do and the treatment methodology involved. As part of the surrogates' presentation, he played the role of a patient, which was an important step for him in understanding SPT and how powerful it can be.

Tova: What is the role of the therapist in surrogate partner therapy (SPT)?

Seth: The therapist is ultimately responsible for determining the course of treatment and ensuring that plan is adhered to in the best interest of the client. There are also a number of other responsibilities, especially the initial evaluation of the client to determine his eligibility for the process. I evaluate the client's psychological, physiological, and medical information to determine if he or she may be helped most efficiently by working with a surrogate partner. If I deem that the client is appropriate and working with a surrogate will be beneficial, I present SPT as an option to him.

Tova: How do you evaluate whether a client is appropriate for SPT?

Seth: I consider the patient's diagnosis and mental state to assess whether a client has a mental health issue that might impair the work or create safety issues. In addition, I need to feel comfortable that SPT is a beneficial treatment option as opposed to some other treatment methodology.

I think the therapist is also responsible for choosing the surrogate partner that he or she thinks will be the best fit for the client; this is done by knowing the various surrogates who are in practice. They each have their particular strengths, and this would influence whom I select.

Tova: Describe the role of communication in the therapist/surrogate/client triad.

Seth: First I get a signed, written release from the client with an expiration date so that I can share confidential information with the surrogate partner regarding the client's physical and mental health history. That allows ongoing dialogue during the course of therapy.

Second, I obtain a written agreement signed by the client, the surrogate partner, and myself outlining treatment goals, expectations, STDs, transference, boundary issues, emotional issues that may come up during therapy, and the right to terminate at any time, which is a right for each of the three participants.

I inform my clients about the rules of sexual contact in the course of therapy. Sex is often a part of surrogate partner therapy, but may not be the main focus, depending upon the needs of the client.

Tova: What are some of the clinical issues which may arise during surrogate therapy?

Seth: There are issues regarding client expectations about the pace of therapy. Sometimes clients complain that things are moving too slowly. I need to understand what the client means, and whether speeding up or slowing things down would be in their best interest, with input from the surrogate partner. I think another clinical issue is attraction to the surrogate. Many clients wonder about whether age difference or physical attractiveness matter in treatment. I find that these concerns are often not much of an issue. I have surrogates working with men or women who are either older or younger than they are, and these are issues that we talk about with the client. These questions could be part of a clinical picture of avoidance, or something that keeps the client from making more intimate contact with somebody. The therapist always has to be aware of such clinical issues and whether they may represent a behavioral pattern.

Tova: We talk about the needs of the client, but what about the needs of the surrogate?

Seth: I think the boundaries, the range of experience, and comfort level of the surrogate play a huge role in the process. If a surrogate is uncomfortable with a client interaction, it's important for the surrogate to be able to say, "Okay, let's talk about this; what were you thinking when you said this or did this?" The communication between the two of them is essential. A surrogate uses her clinical intuition all the time. They use it to figure out where the client is, and they ask appropriate questions if they're picking up anxiety. Those are all important aspects of treatment. If the surrogate felt he or she had a boundary around a particular behavior, this becomes an issue for the surrogate partner to handle with the therapist. It's up to the surrogate to say, "I felt this way, what do you think about that?" and "How should I handle that?" and "Was that the best way to handle it?" The surrogate and therapist need to continually talk about the progress of the treatment plan, the course of therapy, and to deal with feelings the surrogate may be experiencing. There are many opportunities to express what's going on for everyone.

Tova: How do you present surrogate partner therapy to your colleagues who are resistant to or uncomfortable with the concept?

Seth: I tell colleagues that surrogate partner clients represent a small number of cases in my practice, but when I do work with surrogate partners, it is one of the most efficient ways to help specific clients reach their goals. I let colleagues know that surrogate partners work to assist an un-partnered individual who's either physically incapable, such as someone who's disabled or socially unskilled, or lacking confidence because they can't find someone to work with. Then I let them know that surrogate partners are capable of helping clients develop competence in a wide range of areas, including social skills development, sexual skills development, sex education, anatomy, and physiology, areas that are all related to interpersonal relationships or the repression of social and sexual anxiety or fears.

I emphasize that the intention is always to help the client develop the skills they'll need to generalize to the real world once they have completed their surrogate partner therapy. I use an analogy with other clinicians of a patient who'd had knee surgery. The orthopedic surgeon refers that patient to a physical therapist to help them regain strength and range of motion by doing a series of physical exercises and other strategies that help the client recover. And once that treatment plan is complete, the patient is able to return to normal activities. In the same way, a sex therapist refers a client who is un-partnered to a specialist who is an outside specialist—a surrogate partner—and that surrogate partner carries out the physical experiential aspect of the treatment plan to help the client reach their goals. I also work with specially trained pelvic floor physical therapists who work specifically with women and/or couples on specific issues, such as dyspareunia, which is pain with intercourse, and vaginismus, which is clamping of the vaginal muscles when penetration is attempted. It's the same kind of collaborative effort that I use with surrogate partners, and there are a number of physical therapists who do sexual work. So surrogates are not the only type of collaboration that a sex therapist might use. We also collaborate with gynecologists and urologists to get feedback or information on the physical aspects of what may be going on for a client.

Tova: How do you handle it if someone tells you that, as a clinician, they don't find SPT ethical, and even though you say that these surrogates have special training, how is this different from referring a client to a sophisticated escort? Has anyone put it in those terms?

Seth: Well, you're talking about two things: an ethical concern and comparing surrogates to an escort or a prostitute. The latter doesn't come up very often; I can think of only once when it explicitly came up during a small group lecture I was doing at a hospital. It was a podiatrist who asked about the difference between surrogacy and prostitution, because he couldn't make the distinction. I made a very clear distinction between the two.

I think ethical issues come up for clinicians without the training or the understanding of sexuality and sex therapy. They don't understand the value of a surrogate providing human contact to an individual, and that having a trained partner as a resource is essential to carry out many treatment plans where clients need to be physical. So, if you have an ethical issue with something, don't do that type of therapy. I would respect someone who doesn't want to do that. I sometimes get referrals from therapists who are not well versed in sex therapy. I would have more of an ethical issue with someone who is trying to work outside of their area of expertise without getting the proper training to do that type of work. I wouldn't attempt to do knee surgery without proper training, or try to be a physical therapist without being schooled in it. Therapists need to be trained and licensed within their specialty, or in the process of getting that training. If they are doing so, then I think the ethical issue doesn't exist, because they are obviously interested in broadening and expanding their view. I think a lot of ethical concerns might be dispelled if therapists and other practitioners had a proper understanding of the value of surrogate partner therapy.

Tova: What about when a therapist feels like they might be losing their client to a surrogate?

Seth: The main thing to understand is that this is the therapist's case and there is collaboration between the therapist and the surrogate partner. In that collaborative effort, the therapist is ultimately responsible for making the decisions that are in the best interest of the client, and they should also be comfortable working in a clinical format. The collaboration includes listening to suggestions offered by the surrogate partner and mutually developing a treatment plan, before beginning and during the course of therapy. The therapist is responsible for making decisions, yet it is a collaborative and team effort. If clinicians are concerned about the relationship aspects of surrogacy, they may not be sufficiently trained to understand that the intention is that the surrogate partner establishes a more intimate relationship with the client. That will enable him to develop social and sexual skills and to generalize his experiences when he is ready to leave therapy and develop his own relationships.

Tova: Can you address the concern about malpractice and malpractice insurance?

Seth: It's a good, valid concern, and I'll have to give a multilevel answer. First of all, malpractice insurance covers sex therapy and relationship therapy. For a licensed marriage and family therapist

(LMFT), for instance, malpractice insurance would not cover the surrogate partner part of that kind of therapy, because you're referring to someone who is usually not licensed; they're typically certified, but some are not. This means that malpractice insurance does not cover the surrogate partner part of that therapy. I've never heard of any lawsuits, so I don't know how that would actually work. I have contacted the legal department of the California Association of Marriage and Family Therapists and talked about surrogate partner therapy, and whether working with surrogates was ethical and grounds for any kind of action by the board. I was told that you have to be a sex therapist, and that sex therapy has to be a part of your scope of practice; if it is, then working with surrogate partners should not be a legal or ethical issue as far as the board is concerned. There also are legal issues: I've asked lawyers about this point and was informed that there's never been a case that's been prosecuted. I've been advised that it would be highly unlikely to prosecute a surrogate partner for any type of sexual interaction with a client.

Tova: How do you describe the difference between surrogates and prostitutes?

Seth: On the comparisons with prostitutes, I make a really clear distinction that there's no relationship between surrogacy and prostitution; prostitution is defined as the act of sex for money and usually occurs in a single interaction. On the other hand, when it's part of a therapeutic treatment plan, sexual interactions between clients and surrogate partners often occur at some point in the process. It may not be the main focus of the work, especially when things like social skills development, anxiety reduction, overcoming fears, sex education, etc., are part of the overall plan. A therapeutic sexualized interaction may be a significant, but smaller part of a treatment plan, along with other issues that are also being dealt with.

Tova: Another difference is that it may take months before that level of intimacy occurs in SPT.

Seth: That's possible; it depends on the case. I agree that most of the time, sex and sexual interaction happen later in the process. You start off with a three-way meeting with the therapist, the client, and the surrogate partner. The surrogate has an interview-style meeting with a client alone to talk about goals and history, and they do that in the first session. There may be some clothed interaction. But there's a process going on the whole time, and sex, while it can be a significant portion of the process, may not happen until a number of sessions have taken place.

Tova: Could it be possible that for some therapists, surrogate partner therapy may trigger unresolved sexual feelings that cause them to shy away from using this process?

Seth: I'm sure that's the case. I believe unresolved issues about a therapist's own sexual development or sexual history may interfere with or trigger feelings regarding surrogate partner therapy that inhibit them from using it. But, I think the sex negativity and judgmental attitudes around sexuality that are rampant in our culture have more to do with therapists who haven't gone through the process of acceptance of sexuality, sexual orientation, and lifestyles. And they'd benefit from some kind of educational or desensitization process in which they get a chance to speak openly about their own issues. That would be an important part of a therapist's training.

Tova: Could you explain what you mean when you use the word *desensitization*?

Seth: It means being exposed to, through some education process, the breadth of human sexual behavior in a way that helps a person to not be judgmental about any consensual sexual act that people may engage in and or want to do. So desensitization is a process of becoming more comfortable with sexuality, sexual terminology, and the variety of sexual expression.

Tova: That's the same as many surrogates go through in training: the Sexual Attitude Reassessment (SAR). Would that also mean it might be valuable for a therapist to undergo their own personal therapy?

Seth: In general, it's important for therapists to have gone through some therapeutic process of their own to get an understanding of how therapy works and actually see how it feels. If a client goes to a sex therapist that has not done work around their sexuality, the client probably will not be talking about sexuality unless he/she brings it up. And even when clients and/or therapists were to bring up sexual issues, a number of therapists are not comfortable or well-trained enough to competently talk about sexual topics. That, again, speaks to the need for specialized training to help sex therapists become more comfortable with their own sexuality and sexuality in general.

Tova: What would be the best ways to educate the therapeutic community about surrogacy?

Seth: Well, I think the best way is to have people who are familiar with the process of surrogate partner therapy present it in a positive light and talk about the benefits of using surrogates. And that could be collaboration between a therapist and the surrogate, where you go out into the community and give some lectures. The important thing is that surrogate partner therapy is presented in a favorable manner which conveys its value as a helpful treatment option that is very efficient and successful.

We, as clinicians in the sex field, must come together and talk about the process of surrogate partner therapy and ways that we might further educate the public and create new strategies. Change takes time; it often takes years, but we just have to keep chipping away at it.

Tova: From your personal experience, how do you assess the effectiveness of surrogate partner therapy and how do you evaluate it?

Seth: In the majority of cases where I've used surrogate partner therapy, it's been one of the most efficient ways of helping a specific group of clients reach their goals. I would say that the effectiveness rate is in the eighty or ninety percent range, like most sex therapy. I usually evaluate this by continuing to do therapy with the individual after the surrogate-client interaction ends. I want to see them begin to generalize what they've learned in the real world.

Sex Is the Least of It

Tova: Can you explain what you mean when you use the word *generalize*?

Seth: It means having them go out into the world and actually do the things and use the skills they've learned, to actualize their confidence and newfound abilities in terms of developing relationships. That doesn't happen all the time, and sometimes I have a follow up with a phone call to see how they're doing. I always ask clients to give me feedback, call me and let me know how things are going.

Tova: So, might an evaluation of success be: 1) the client says they feel better, more confident, more at ease; however, when you check in with them six months later, their social behavior may not have changed, or 2) you check in with the client in six months and their social behavior has changed, and their sexual comfort and interaction have improved, and their relational interaction has changed. Or would both be appropriate ways of defining success?

Seth: Both would be a way of determining success; the client's evaluation of how successful things are is very important. Coming up with some way of measuring that, and having a set of standard questions that therapists might ask and notate, would be valuable data to include in an evaluation.

I would like to mention that sexual interaction and sexual contact as part of the surrogate therapy often happens somewhere down the line in the therapeutic process. However, sometimes there are cases where sexual interaction has happened earlier in the process for a specific purpose or an assessment. The process is a shorter one and that happens in a small number of cases, where I'm trying to gain specific information or carry out a certain treatment plan where that would be in the best interest of the client. While sex never happens on the first session, it may be a shorter process and more sexually focused some of the time. That has been very effective for specific clients, but as I said, the numbers of surrogate collaborations that I supervise represent a small percent of cases in my practice. But I don't want to give the impression that sex only happens in the twelve-session order; it could happen earlier in the process if it's in the best interest of the client, as determined by the supervising therapist in collaboration with the surrogate partner. There needs to be some flexibility in the treatment plan that accounts for different situations.

Contact information:

Email: sethphd@sbcglobal.net or sethphdmft@gmail.com

Website: www.sextherapy.org

Phone: (415) 948-9590 cell

Mailing Address:

2918 Webster Street, San Francisco, CA 94123

Dr. Joshua Golden

Photo by Jack Goldsmith

Joshua S. Golden is a clinical professor of psychiatry at the David Geffen School of Medicine. He is the former Director of the UCLA Human Sexuality Program and the former Assistant Dean for Student Affairs in the Geffen School of Medicine. Currently, he is retired.

Tova: What do you see as the role and responsibilities of a therapist in Surrogate Partner Therapy (SPT)?

Joshua: I think the therapist has to be sufficiently aware of the value and limitations of surrogate partner use to be able to make an intelligent and appropriate choice. There are a lot of people who don't really understand what surrogates are all about and who might use surrogates inappropriately. A good example is a relatively inexperienced therapist who gets a client with a sexual problem, doesn't know what to do, and finds a surrogate who is perhaps more knowledgeable about these things than the therapist is, and basically turns over the treatment of the client to the surrogate. That wouldn't necessarily be a good thing to do. It's conceivable that you may have a very experienced and capable surrogate who would do well in that situation. However, the surrogate is working under the supervision and direction of the therapist, so you must have a therapist who knows what he or she is doing.

Sex Is the Least of It

Tova: What criteria do you use to evaluate whether a client is appropriate for surrogate partner therapy?

Joshua: Obviously it depends on the case. One criterion would be that the client could learn things about himself from a surrogate partner. If they don't have a sexual partner and have demonstrated a difficulty or inability to get one, then a surrogate could be very useful in certain beginning phases of successful treatment. If the client has a relationship with a partner—let's say a wife or someone with whom they're in a relationship, and for whatever reason, that person is not willing to participate in the sexual therapy program, it's clear that a surrogate could be helpful. That's a loaded circumstance; because if a male client has a wife who's unwilling to participate in sex therapy and the man begins to have success with the surrogate, the wife becomes jealous and resentful. So the therapist needs a fairly broad understanding of the dynamics of the couples' conflicts, and the therapist must be flexible and in charge of what's going on with the surrogate and the client. That is why it is safer and more efficacious for a surrogate to work with a single client that does not have a partner.

Tova: In such a case of working with a client who is married, do you think that it would be beneficial to have that partner sign an agreement, because that could be a situation fraught with potential problems?

Joshua: Yes, it would be useful to have them sign an agreement. But that's no guarantee that, as the situation progresses, feelings won't develop; the non-participating partner may become jealous or resentful, or may not want a sexual relationship with the partner who's in surrogate therapy in the first place. You cannot solve all problems with releases or written documents. You may be able to protect yourself against the possibility of a lawsuit with a signed agreement, but in terms of solving the problems between the couple, it wouldn't necessarily help.

Tova: Yes, that's why I believe most male and female surrogates work with single individuals.

Joshua: That's true. And even though most surrogates work with heterosexual partners, the same kinds of problems will occur with same-sex surrogates and partners. The issues are the same, although the gender preferences may be different.

Tova: What criteria would you use to evaluate and select a surrogate for a patient if there were three or four surrogates available?

Joshua: For me, it would be a question of how well I know the surrogate, and if I've been fortunate enough to have previous opportunities to work with them. I'd have some sense that they're experienced and scrupulous about doing what I direct them to do. I've found that some surrogates tend to be very mechanically engaged in what they've learned to do, and in those cases, they have a hard time being flexible and working in a way different from their training protocol. One of the problems is that many therapists who have heard of surrogates might not seek out one because they don't really have a lot of experience doing sex therapy. They essentially turn the case over to the surrogate. Then that places the success or failure of the treatment plan in the hands of the surrogate, and that can be a real problem.

Tova: What are the typical clinical issues or problems that may arise for both the client and the surrogate during the course of surrogate partner therapy?

Joshua: Clients generally enter the course of surrogate therapy without a very clear understanding of its limitations; for example, it may take longer than they anticipate. It's not necessarily going to immediately involve having sexual intercourse. A lot depends on both the therapist and the surrogate being adequately prepared, so that they have realistic expectations of what's going to happen. And the costs can be a concern. Also, sexual problems are very symptomatic of other serious emotional or psychological problems. So even if you do something about the sexual symptoms, you're still dealing with the residue of other problems, perhaps major psychological or emotional problems that surrogates aren't necessarily in a position to fix any more than therapists are.

Tova: In a situation like that, where the client has a sexual problem, but the therapist discovers, as things progress, that there are many other significant issues going on that need therapeutic intervention, is it still beneficial to address the sexual issue?

Joshua: It depends on the circumstances and the individual case. Ideally, the therapist would continue to work with the patient while that patient is working with the surrogate partner. There should be regular, consistent contact and feedback between the directing therapist and the surrogate about what's happening in the sessions and the problems that are occurring. However, in practice, that's a little harder to maintain than it is in theory. Sometimes experienced surrogates who do good work and know what they're doing don't want to be "supervised," so to speak. There could be some potential conflicts with that, although it's rarely been a problem in my experience with surrogates. The ones I've worked with I know fairly well. They seem knowledgeable, confident, and good collaborators.

Tova: In your supervisory experience, what other problems have you seen that might arise for surrogates?

Joshua: I think it's important to keep the lines clearly drawn, and if you can't work comfortably with a surrogate, you have to find another surrogate with whom you can work well. I can't think of any instance over many years where I have stopped working with any surrogate. Sometimes the work with a surrogate stops of its own accord, or the patient or the surrogate feel that they've accomplished the goals they originally set out to accomplish. But I don't think I've ever had an experience where things worked so badly that I've had to say, "Stop, don't see this client anymore." Of course, the issue of feelings that develop toward the patient or the therapist can exist with surrogates as well. That's the nature of what we do in therapy, whether it involves surrogates or not. It makes you vulnerable to developing feelings. A good professional knows that and understands how to keep those things separate and out of the therapy, because that would be potentially disastrous on many levels.

Tova: How important is initial physical attraction? Such as if the client says, "You know, I feel really comfortable with her, but I'm just not attracted to her."

Joshua: I think that it is definitely an issue, and if you can engage a client with a surrogate they don't initially find sexually attractive, it often works well, because initial sexual attractiveness is not crucial to solving many problems. But sometimes it's difficult to get past the client's initial reaction to a lack of attraction. The therapist can talk about the benefits of working with that surrogate and offer some reassurance that it may be much less of a problem as they get to know one another. But it definitely can be a problem for many potential surrogate partner clients.

Tova: How do you present SPT to other therapists who may be resistant to the concept?

Joshua: We made it part of their education in the Human Sexuality program at UCLA. We would invite surrogates to do presentations for therapists, and there would be discussions of when surrogates might be useful, what they do, and what their training encompasses. Yes, we educated therapists in somewhat formal ways. Informally, I had a number of therapists contact me when they wanted to find a surrogate for a client. I would routinely ask them what they're trying to accomplish, and then advise them whether resolution of a sexual problem could be accomplished with a surrogate. It isn't advisable or realistic to work with a surrogate in all cases. But the point is that it's necessary to educate your colleagues.

Tova: When you're speaking with therapist colleagues about SPT, what do you say if they bring up the often heard comparison between surrogacy and prostitution, even if they acknowledge that there is training for the surrogate partner?

Joshua: I would explain the differences. There is one similarity, in that both the prostitute and the surrogate are getting paid for sexual contact with a client. But the intention of the sexual activity is different, and beyond that, the differences are quite extensive and dramatic. The most significant differences are in the motivation, the treatment plan, and the development of a relationship between the two. A person who goes to a prostitute is not looking for the same kind of experience that they would gain when working with a surrogate partner.

Tova: So would you emphasize the difference in a surrogate's specific training protocol or in the intention of the sexual activities?

Joshua: It has a lot to do with the attitudes of the therapist raising the question. If they're very moralistic and think that any kind of sexual contact with someone who isn't the client's committed partner or spouse is wrong, that therapist might have difficulty with the idea of working with a surrogate, no matter how well you explain the differences. Someone who's primarily interested in helping a client solve a problem with which a surrogate could be helpful, is going to be amenable to learning about the SPT process, differences, and motivations. I don't think there are a whole lot of prostitutes who are in that line of work because they want to help people; they do it for the money. In comparison, I have been impressed that many surrogates approach this work out of a genuine motivation to help people.

Tova: It occurred to me that whether or not therapists are familiar with surrogate partner therapy, they may not have gone through Sexual Attitude Reassessment (SAR), or done a great deal of introspection. Perhaps they haven't worked through some of their own sexual issues. Do you think that surrogate partner therapy could trigger unresolved sexual feelings that might influence a therapist to shy away from the process?

Joshua: That is certainly a possibility. That hasn't been an issue that I've experienced with people. Usually, if a therapist gets to the point of consulting with me about working with a surrogate, he or she is comfortable with the idea of recommending one to a client. They may not have a good idea of what a surrogate does, and they may be somewhat naive and inexperienced about this, but I don't think they have too many moral reservations.

Tova: The lead article in the February 2013 issue of *Contemporary Sexuality* is titled "Sexual Surrogacy Revisited." It didn't appear that the organized therapeutic community, such as AASECT, was more open about acknowledging surrogate therapy. I'm wondering if you have any thoughts about that.

Joshua: I don't know how familiar you are with organizations like AASECT. The training is inconsistent and there's no uniformity to it. There's no guarantee that if you get your sex therapist certification, you're going to be competent, or that the people who trained you are competent. And the requirements are sort of arbitrary. In the years when I was more active in that organization, there were some who were trying to divide their attention between the financial survival of the organization and the quality of training that was made available to members who qualified for certification. Good quality programs regarding human sexuality were disappearing across the country. There used to be a number of them, including our own at UCLA. But as a result of the loss of these programs, it's very hard to get any kind of meaningful training today. Meaningful training would include supervision of the therapist in working most effectively with clients. It's expensive, it's cumbersome, and it's often done long distance, because therapists and qualified trainers don't exist in the same location. The result is that you have a very heterogeneous group of people who are supposedly qualified because they got their certifications, but the quality of training may vary. I think the best we can do is to make information about human sexuality and surrogacy widely available in a variety of forums.

Sex Is the Least of It

Tova: Many people are concerned about the quality of the surrogate's training. But the other concern is how well trained is the therapist to deal with a broad spectrum of human sexuality issues? To the best of my knowledge, the curriculum required to train mental health practitioners includes only one course in human sexuality. Many of these people are going to be seeing clients who present with sexual problems, and even though they may not be "sex therapists," they will probably address those issues. And so what if you have a thoughtful, articulate, client who has read ten books on sexuality? What if that client has read more than the therapist about variations in sexual behavior? Should there be additional required education on human sexuality for any kind of practicing therapist?

Joshua: Yes, I agree with you. But then the realities are that people are always competing for time and curriculum, and issues have their own time when they're in fashion. Human sexuality was a popular topic in the 1970s and 1980s, and even into the 1990s. Now it's almost disappeared. And when Jerry Brown was governor in the 1970s, a law was passed requiring at least a ten-hour course on human sexuality for any licensed therapists, physicians, psychologists, MFTs, etcetera. But all those courses are superficial survey courses. There's no uniformity; there's no policing of the content. There's no testing of the results to verify whether people have learned anything useful.

Tova: In your experience, what is the effectiveness of surrogate partner therapy and how do you evaluate that?

Joshua: Well, it really depends on what kind of problem you're trying to address. Let's say you've got somebody who's a virgin. You work with them and they've had no sexual experience, whether it's due to shyness, lack of access, or some other reason. Those are people who can significantly benefit from working with a surrogate who can teach them social and intimacy skills. Whereas, for a client who's having an erection problem who's in a relationship with a partner, SPT is going to be a lot less successful, because the issues in the relationship are not necessarily going to be addressed by working with a surrogate.

Tova: When a client has a spouse or partner, wouldn't that be more appropriately handled in couples' therapy?

Joshua: Yes, because issues such as erectile dysfunction are not necessarily the problem of the identified client. It may be the problems of the partner. So, success depends on whether you can identify clear goals that can be achieved by the conclusion of therapy. Being clear about what you can accomplish, and realistic about what you can do, helps to clarify the treatment goals. But obviously, surrogate therapy can be helpful for some things and not for others.

Tova: So on the occasions when you have worked with surrogates, what kind of impact do you feel that surrogate therapy has had on the client?

Joshua: When I have chosen to use surrogate therapy with clear-cut, achievable goals, mostly the clients have benefitted by accomplishing most of their goals. I think the things that complicate the work are not being clear about the goals, or having decided on goals that are probably impossible to reach. Occasionally, things emerge in the course of work with therapists and surrogates that you cannot anticipate, but they're human beings and it is a dynamic process. The therapist, the surrogate, or the client may change in time; there are all kinds of variables that may come into it. It's like anything else in medicine; even penicillin doesn't cure every infection. Some bugs are resistant to treatment and sometimes people are allergic to the medicine. But, if you have designed clear goals, generally things work out favorably, in my experience.

Tova: The last question is, what do you tell colleagues who have legal concerns about working with surrogates?

Joshua: I have certainly run into colleagues who have had legal concerns about it. I have never known of anybody who's been sued for working with a surrogate, so it seems to me that if there are any legal constraints, they're not being enforced. A couple of my more careful colleagues have gone to lawyers and asked, "What's the risk?" Their lawyers have gone through the books and said this, that, and the other could happen. But I've never known of anybody who's been sued. Personally, it doesn't seem to be a realistic concern.

Dr. William R. Stayton

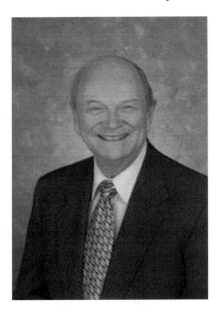

Photo courtesy of Dr. William Stayton

Dr. Stayton has a Master of Divinity degree from Andover Newton Theological School, has a Doctor of Theology in Psychology degree from Boston University, and a Ph.D. from the Institute for Advanced Study of Human Sexuality.

Tova: What is the role and responsibilities of a therapist involved in surrogate partner therapy (SPT)?

Bill: I do a very thorough evaluation of a client before even suggesting surrogate partner therapy. To me, it's essential to establish the appropriateness of a potential client to work with a surrogate. I know of other therapists who do not adhere to this guideline and have endangered a surrogate in some way. I think I would never be able to forgive myself if I made a wrong referral to a surrogate partner that ended up endangering her.

Tova: What criteria do you use to evaluate the appropriateness of a prospective client for SPT?

Bill: Two important criteria would be that I had worked with this client for a period of time and felt comfortable with his/her emotional stability, and also felt that he/she would benefit from working with a surrogate. If, when I am discussing working with a surrogate, the first thing a client says is, "What does she look like?" or "Do we get to have intercourse right away?" that's a danger signal. Because surrogate partner therapy is for the purpose of socializing a client, helping him to develop social skills and move toward dating, not for the purpose of having sexual intercourse. I want to stress very much that this is a socialization process, and this is one of its major contributions. We teach them the sensuality process and lead them through a series of exercises that helps them become more confident about themselves and their ability to be with a partner. In addition, the surrogate partner gives a lot of homework exercises: how to call a woman, how to approach a woman in a social situation, how to initiate a conversation, and how to set up a date. All of this is in the service of readying the client for participating in society and being able to make healthy choices for dating partners. If a client and surrogate end up having intercourse, it's an additional opportunity to practice; but many clients choose not to do so, because they want to save this particular intimate activity for a partner of their own choice.

Tova: That's an important point, intercourse does not always happen. People don't often understand that intercourse is not always a part of the surrogate process.

Bill: Right. And if it does happen, it usually means that the person is ready to graduate from SPT and move on with their life. If intercourse does occur, surrogates have a lot to teach. They instruct clients about safe sex, how to properly use a condom, how to introduce using a condom to their partner, and explain their responsibilities as a sexually active man or woman.

That's why, in many ways, a person who is a prostitute is not a good candidate to become a surrogate. The intention is completely different. They have a financial motivation, whereas a surrogate provides her services out of a genuine desire to help people, just as a therapist does.

Tova: What are the typical clinical issues that may arise for both the client and the surrogate during SPT?

Bill: One of the things I've found in working with surrogate partners is they often get information that does not come out in talk therapy. I think clients feel so safe with their surrogate that they often reveal deep secrets and experiences, ones they have not told the therapist. For this reason, I ensure the client clearly knows I am in constant communication with the surrogate, and she with me, and we exchange suggestions to help the client advance. For example, the surrogate might say: "This is where I am. What do you think might be the best way to go from here?" and then I would make suggestions from a therapist's perspective. On the other hand, in therapy, I might get clues from the client that would help the surrogate in her work with the client.

If the client seemed to be holding back in order to have more sessions with the surrogate, then that's an important issue to talk over. Or if the client expresses feelings of falling in love, this is an issue I would work through with the client. I would tell him that yes, you are going to care deeply for a surrogate and she will have feelings for you. But the purpose of this process is to help you be able to find a partner of your choice. If a surrogate approached me and said, "I am feeling too much attraction for this client and I may not be appropriate to work with him," then I would refer that client to another surrogate. It is natural for a client and surrogate to have feelings for one another, but the surrogate must always know when it is time to bring this issue to the therapist to keep their work on track.

Tova: How do you present surrogate partner therapy to your colleagues who are resistant or uninformed about the concept of SPT?

Bill: I share the miraculous changes that I've seen take place through doing this work with surrogate partners. I explain that my own hesitancies were overcome when I actually saw what happened, and the progress a client could make with SPT. I make the case that we are helping the client to become a better communicator, a better lover, more confident, and more open about their sexuality. I wish we could teach these skills to young people before they become sexually active; teaching these relationship skills is so important and I think therapists would agree. But therapists get skittish when the process becomes sexual, and this may be a reflection of their own judgments and attitudes about sexuality. Again, this is why I think it's so important for therapists to go through a Sexual Attitude Reassessment (SAR) program. I am a firm believer that it is essential for all people to have the opportunity to reassess their attitudes and beliefs about sexuality, and even more so for therapists. It is critical for a therapist working with a client to go through SAR, to help them get in touch with their own values and opinions.

Tova: If you told a therapist about your positive experiences with SPT and the therapist said, "You're working with a woman who's going to have sex with your client and is going to be paid for it. What differentiates her from a prostitute?" How would you respond?

Bill: It's something that we hear a lot. A prostitute has a whole different motivation, and the client pays a fee for a particular sexual service or practice. For example, if you want to have intercourse, here's the price; if you want oral sex, it's this much; if you want something else, it will cost this amount. But surrogate work has nothing to do with that kind of fee for a menu of services. With SPT, the motivation is to help the client become more functional and to help them to develop. In truth, sex is fairly easy to teach. The challenge of SPT is to teach the socialization part of the process, which I think is the most important aspect. It's teaching the client how to communicate. It's teaching relational skills. All of these skills are really important to develop and take a long time for the surrogate to teach.

Tova: So how do you address the legal and malpractice concerns that a colleague may raise when considering working with a surrogate?

Bill: There is nothing illegal about surrogate partner work. The laws therapists are concerned about have to do with procuring, so it's really important that the lines are drawn clearly. The client pays the therapist separately from the surrogate, and that's an important distinction. There's never been a legal case in which SPT has been challenged. I have consulted with a family lawyer and she has attended my classes. She has reviewed the different laws, and does not see any specific language that would indicate that surrogacy is illegal. But it is always viewed as a gray area, and it's true in every state I know of, although I am not a legal authority. However, I have not been able to work in the surrogate process for some time now.

Tova: Was that the result of a guideline from the American Association of Sex Educators, Counselors, and Therapists (AASECT)?

Bill: It came from the licensing board of the Pennsylvania Psychological Association, an affiliate of the American Psychological Association, which forbade any psychologist from working with surrogates.

Tova: Is that PPA rule still enforced?

Bill: As far as I know, I haven't been told differently.

Tova: Have you ever heard a therapist say, "I'm afraid that during the course of SPT, I could lose my client, because we're introducing a third person who's going to have a very different relationship with my client."

Bill: Yes, I have heard people express that concern, but I have never experienced that situation.

Tova: I think that concern is really an illusion, because the client does belong to the therapist. And if the work is done properly, with all three parties communicating openly, there's really no opportunity for the client to be lost.

Bill: That's right, and it's always seen that way.

Tova: Is it possible that among some therapists, the use of SPT could trigger unresolved feelings to surface that would cause them to shy away from using the process?

Bill: I would not introduce working with a surrogate partner to an inexperienced or new social worker or therapist. The only people I work with are those who have been in the field for a number of years. A true professional is aware of their "own stuff" and keeps it away from their work as a therapist. That doesn't mean that it couldn't happen. But new therapists participate with supervision and can work out their issues under the aegis of an experienced clinician.

Tova: What do you think would be the best ways to educate the therapeutic community? The reluctance of the therapeutic community appears to remain strong, even after forty years of SPT practice, and despite the many papers presented to AASECT and to other esteemed professional bodies, and a great deal of public speaking by many of the senior surrogates.

Bill: Yes, I agree that there is still some reluctance in the therapeutic community. One of the things we need to be aware of is that the field of sex therapy, in many ways, is still run on a sex-negative attitude system. That even though they think that they're positive, when you begin discussing issues like surrogate partner therapy, then some of the sex-negative attitudes come up that really are based upon mythology. And, as we know, these myths are not true. One, for example, is that monogamy is natural to human beings; it's not. And when it comes to sexuality, you're dealing with deeply held belief systems verses what is nature's intention. That's why I think it is so important for all professionals to evaluate their attitudes and values regarding sexuality; because they may think they have a positive view, but when they reassess it, their attitude really is based upon a negative view of sexuality. We need to keep reassessing and reeducating ourselves as professionals. Also, we've become a much more litigious society, so almost anyone can get sued for anything, and that the more vulnerable the issue, the greater the fear of being sued. We've become such a fear-driven society.

Tova: In your personal experience, how effective is surrogate partner therapy?

Bill: I measure the effectiveness of SPT in terms of the success of the treatment and the client's subjective assessment that he has met his goals.

Tova: So is it enough that a client says they feel better, more confident, and happier? What if, in six months, their actual behavior has not changed, they are not dating, and they are not socializing significantly more? Is it enough that a client feels better, or are you looking for a change in behavior?

Bill: Well, one consideration is their original intention. What was their original purpose in coming into therapy? What were their goals? How did they feel about their original goals and then at the end of therapy? So if a client says, "I wanted to feel better about sexuality; I wanted to feel more confident in sexual relations," and six months later they say, "I don't have a new partner, but I do feel confident and I do feel that I'm happier." Then I think that's a success. Success is rated not only on behavior, but on the client's perception of where they are. The client has to progress at their own rate; so if, at the end of six months, they do not have a new partner, but they do feel more confidence, then I consider that a success.

Tova: Do you think that therapists who want to specialize as sex therapists are adequately trained?

Bill: First of all, my only experience in the training of other therapists is on the graduate level. When I was at the University of Pennsylvania, we developed a Ph.D. program in Human Sexuality though the Graduate School of Education. In that program, I introduced working with a surrogate partner to people who were going into the field with a specialization in sexuality. They were taught the full scope of what it means to be a therapist and what it means to be a sex therapist. That was also true in 1998 when the program moved from Penn to Widener University in Chester, Pennsylvania, where I served as the director of the doctoral program in Human Sexuality. We developed dual-degree programs with the School of Clinical Social Work and the School of Clinical Psychology. So a person could actually get a dual degree, like a Master's in Social Work (M.S.W.) and a Ph.D. or Ed. D. in human sexuality. With the clinical psychology program, they would get a Psy.D., along with a Master's in Human Sexuality; this meant that our students had full, comprehensive training.

I want to end by saying that working with a surrogate partner, I have seen miraculous changes take place with people who had given up all hope, or who were late-life virgins and fearful of performance, or who had a chronic illness or disability. I have story after story of successes through SPT, and I think it's a shame and really inhumane to discourage this work. That's why I'm such a strong proponent of continuing SPT, because I've seen such incredible progress as a result of the work.

Contact information:

Email: wmstayton@cs.com

Trainers of Surrogates

Dr. Ronit Aloni

Photo courtesy of Dr. Ronit Aloni

Ronit Aloni earned a master's degree from New York University and a Ph.D. in sexual rehabilitation from the Union Institute in Cincinnati, Ohio. She has taught at Tel Aviv University School of Medicine and has her own private practice in the center of Tel Aviv focusing on sex therapy, couples therapy, and sexual rehabilitation. She is the founder of the Dr. Ronit Aloni Sex Therapy Center, Tel Aviv, Israel.

Tova: My questions for you break down into three categories: First, how you personally became involved in therapy and why you chose to specialize in sex therapy; second, why you created your center and what motivated you to start working in the field of surrogate-assisted therapy; third, what's involved in your surrogate partner training programs.

Ronit: I'm pleased to discuss all of this. I'm really happy you are creating this book because there is very little written about surrogacy. The fact that you are writing such a comprehensive work is very important.

Tova: What attracted you to the field of sex therapy?

Ronit: I was a teacher and my students asked me questions about sexuality. So I became a sex educator. Then I moved to the United States and decided to enroll in NYU's Human Sexuality program. At first I wasn't really sure what I wanted to do. But then I took a class about sexuality and disability and was immediately drawn to the subject. That's when I knew that this was going to be my field of expertise. And the more I understood people with disabilities, the more I knew that I couldn't treat them without working with surrogates.

Tova: How did you first hear about surrogate partner therapy?

Ronit: I knew about SPT because I'd read a book written in the sixties called *Surrogate Wife* by Valerie X. Scott, a surrogate who had worked with Masters and Johnson. In it, she described a few cases she had treated, working as a surrogate. I was looking for a surrogate who worked with the disabled, and somehow I got the name of Patricia Pearlman, a surrogate who practiced in New Jersey. I met her and we became friends. Patricia was very generous about sharing her experiences with me, and she taught me practically everything. Then, when I moved back to Israel, I invited her to train the second group of surrogates in my clinic, and some of the surrogates from my second group joined in too.

Before I came back to Israel, when I was still a student, there was a conference in 1985 about sex education for children with disabilities. I introduced surrogate partner therapy as a mode of sex education for children who could not reach their genitals, who were blind, or who may have had significant communication problems.

Tova: What happened after you returned to Israel?

Ronit: In the summer of 1986, upon my return to Israel, I started to work in the Lowenstein Rehab Center, which is a rehabilitation hospital owned by the Israeli national health care insurance. I was approached by Nira Dangur, a Ph.D. from another rehabilitation center affiliated with the kibbutz movement, and I started working with them. So my first jobs were at rehabilitation centers.

By 1989, I had established a program at the kibbutz center for rehabilitation, and we put together the first training for surrogates, but which also included the rehabilitation counselors and the social workers. They all went through the same training, because I felt it was important that we all knew about each other's work. I started with three surrogates who worked with the disabled, but we didn't disclose this fact: it was a secret. And that's how we added surrogate therapy to the program. In 1991, I published the results of our work at the World Association for Sexology (WAS) Conference in Amsterdam. After that, we went public and talked openly about surrogate therapy, which was picked up in our major newspapers. That was the first time surrogate therapy was introduced to the public here in Israel. Here, from the beginning, SPT was coordinated among the therapist, surrogate, and client.

Tova: Did you find that over the years you were able to encourage receptivity among therapists for SPT?

Ronit: I know that is a problem in the United States. I started in 1991, at the time when we came out openly about our surrogate program, it was only conducted at the rehabilitation center. That is where I introduced it. By starting in the Kibbutz Center, we had to get permission from the religious Kibbutz Rabbis. So we applied to the Rabbis, who gave us permission to conduct our surrogate program with only one restriction: that the female surrogates could not be married. We then applied the same rules for male surrogates as well.

Tova: And the Orthodox Rabbis agreed to the surrogate program?

Ronit: Yes, they accepted it. In fact, the very Orthodox community recently requested that we work with them to help their patients. So we have never had any problem with the Rabbis or the religious groups. I think this is because we introduced SPT from the rehabilitation point of view. After six years, the surrogate program at the Kibbutz Rehabilitation Center closed because most of the applicants were not disabled. After that, I worked with private clients, many of whom were people with disabilities, mental retardation, and psychiatric problems, as well as regular clients without disabilities.

Tova: How did people find you?

Ronit: After 1991, when we went public, people knew about us because we were all over the newspapers, television, and the Internet. I presented case studies at conferences in Israel and abroad, so more and more people became educated about surrogate therapy. Now I have quite a big Internet website, so people contact me through that.

Tova: What is the legal status of surrogates in Israel?

Ronit: In Israel, the law says that in order to commit a crime, you must have criminal intent. In surrogacy, there's no intention to commit a crime. Israeli law enforcement doesn't interfere with us, and we have never had a problem.

Tova: So, you've never had to go to court?

Ronit: Never. The only challenge has been gaining acceptance in the academic and professional arenas. We've been gaining recognition slowly over the years. I encourage outside therapists who want to work with a surrogate to do so, and I instruct the therapists. Now there are quite a number of outside therapists who have experience working with surrogates, and they share their experiences with other professionals. SPT gains more and more acceptance here, although there are always those who are negative about it.

Tova: So you still encounter some resistance?

Ronit: It's never easy. You know some people don't like the concept on a personal level, or they will raise moral or ethical issues. But when I present at conferences and people bring up moral issues, I find that easy to deal with, because it truly is moral to offer surrogate therapy. Three years ago, we had a conference about ethical issues in sex therapy. I presented a paper about ethics and

Sex Is the Least of It

SPT because this issue was raised. And it was very interesting to see that people who were initially negative, gradually change their minds after I fully explained SPT with all the details. It's really about educating people. We also got permission to conduct SPT from the Minister of Defense, and they have sent patients to us. This is also a sign of recognition of SPT's legitimacy.

Tova: What goes into your surrogate training program?

Ronit: Our training consists of two weekends. We talk about ethics and professional conduct. We have a full day of Sexual Attitude Reassessment (SAR), which is conducted for trainees to promote their awareness of their attitudes and values related to sexuality. We also do a half-day of touching exercises. We teach them about sex therapy and what sex therapy with a surrogate includes. But, I don't want my surrogates to be therapists. I want them to be good partners.

What I want them to take away from the training are the basic core words, the concept of therapy, and an understanding of sensate focus exercises. They need to understand the language of sex therapy so they can communicate effectively with the therapist. They also need to know about social skills, because many of our patients come to us because they lack social skills, rather than because they have sexual problems. They have intimacy problems which can be helped through their relationship with the surrogate.

Tova: How did you select surrogates to work with?

At the beginning, when I was looking for surrogates, I wanted people who had some background in the helping professions. But then I found out that it's not really needed, and it's not even the best way. Now I have only one surrogate who came from the helping professions. All the rest of them bring different backgrounds to their work. I have three surrogates who are actors, and they are doing great jobs. They know how to get into the role and how to get out of it.

Tova: Why do you think people from the helping professions have not worked well as surrogates?

Ronit: Because they were trying to be the therapist. They didn't recognize the limitations of their role, and they became more therapists to the patient than partners. Surrogates need to be partners to the patients as much as possible, and to be as real as they can with the patient.

Tova: Do you teach the traditional Masters and Johnson protocol, with the progression of sensate focus exercises, starting with the face caress, through the front caress?

Ronit: No, I don't teach that in the training. When a surrogate has a client, we may work similarly to the Masters and Jonson approach. When there is a patient who has a sexual dysfunction, then I will more closely follow the M & J step-by-step protocol. But, if a patient has intimacy problems or anxiety problems, I don't stick to those steps. I want them to learn more about relationships and building social skills with the surrogate. In those cases they don't have the interpersonal skills, so the SPT focus is different.

Tova: Do you use elements from other modalities?

Ronit: Yes, we take some things from Tantra. We did a Tantra course for our staff here in the clinic, and we used some breathing and relaxation techniques. We don't incorporate this in the surrogate training, but each therapist can instruct the surrogate about these techniques. Also, some of our surrogates have come from different fields, so they've had experience in yoga and meditation. Our surrogates need to consult with their therapist beforehand and receive permission to use these other techniques.

Tova: It sounds as if the surrogate is closely guided and instructed by the therapist, who also serves as a teacher.

Ronit: They are completely guided by the therapists. The responsibility of the therapy is completely on the shoulders of the therapist. Then the therapist introduces the surrogate into therapy when the therapist thinks the patient is ready. From that time forward, there is a weekly instructional session between the therapist and the surrogate, so it is very structured.

Tova: In the classic model, the surrogate and the client meet with the therapist to prepare them for the session; then they have their first session on the premises, and afterwards they have an assessment with the therapist. Unfortunately, in the U.S., we don't have centralized sex therapy clinics such as yours. Here, surrogates work on their own in conjunction with licensed therapists, but for the most part, they are left to be their own advocates.

Ronit: You cannot do that ethically.

Tova: Surrogates can't advocate?

Ronit: No, they should not advocate for themselves because it exposes them to the public, meaning clients could approach them directly, and that's a problem. So what we do here is completely different. The surrogate is part of the clinic, and there is no contact between the patient and the surrogate beforehand. Here, the patient comes to the clinic, starts therapy with a therapist, and the therapist introduces the surrogate to the patient. We also change the surrogates' names, because it would be too easy to locate them on the Internet. In the past, they were introduced by their first name only, but now we don't even do that. I instruct the surrogate before she meets the patient, and between sessions, I speak with the surrogate and give her feedback on what I think is the next step. After the session, the surrogate writes a report. So I get both points of view, that of the patient and that of the surrogate. That helps me decide how to move forward. Here, surrogates gain credibility by working with therapists who provide them with "roofing." What I mean by *roofing* is that the surrogate is protected by the therapist, who should advocate for him or her.

Tova: Do the surrogates that you employ typically hide their profession in their personal lives?

Ronit: That depends on the individual. In the past, they were more secretive about it. But now, more and more surrogates tell their families and friends about what they are doing. I think the main problem is when they are in a relationship. In that case, they do the work for a certain period of time, but when they are ready to create their own family, then they usually quit. As I mentioned before, the rabbis stipulated the surrogates be single and I accept that.

Tova: Typically, how many surrogates do you have on staff?

Ronit: Sometimes I have between eight and fifteen surrogates at any time, with more women than men.

Tova: What is the age range?

Ronit: I usually try not to employ a surrogate younger than age thirty. That gives me confidence that they will stay with us, maybe into their forties and fifties.

Tova: What would be the best way for surrogates to gain recognition in the United States?

Ronit: I would say they should start by focusing on the rehabilitation field, which was our origin. It's much easier to accept it morally and ethically when it is introduced in this way.

I saw the movie *The Sessions* in New York and watched the people around me in the theater. They were all in tears, and I think the story really touched their hearts. When there is somebody with a disability, the public can understand why they would need a surrogate. Once they understand the value of a surrogate in that situation, it is easier to shift from the field of rehabilitation to the mainstream. Professionals working in rehabilitation are more likely to support surrogates.

Contact information:

Email: dr_aloni@netvision.net.il

Ronit Aloni, Ph.D.

Sexual Therapy & Rehabilitation

& Surrogate Therapy Ltd.

Surrogate Partner Training Schedule Posted Below

Friday	
8:15 – 8:45	Introduction
8:45 – 18:00	S.A.R. - Full Day (Sexual Awareness Reassessment)
Saturday	
9:00 – 10:30	Anatomy and Physiology of men and women
10:40 – 12:10	Human Sexual Response and Sexual Dysfunction
12:10 – 13:40	Meeting with a Male Surrogate
14:40 – 16:10	Sexuality and Disability
16:20 – 17:50	Clinical Procedures
18:30 – 20:30	Movie "The Sessions" + Discussion
Friday	
8:30 – 13:00	Sensate Focus Touch Workshop
14:00 – 15:30	Basic Terminology of Sex Therapy II
15:40 – 17:30	Sex therapy for women Sex therapy for women who underwent sexual abuse
17:30 – 19:00	Meeting with a female surrogate

Saturday	
9:30 – 11:00	Sex Therapy for Men
11:10 – 12:40	Meeting with a former surrogate specializing with disability - case studies + a video with Patricia
12:40 – 14:10	Social Skills training in Surrogate therapy From a surrogate perspective
15:10 – 16:40	The triangle: patient, sex therapist, surrogate IPSA Code of Ethics
16:50 – 18:30	Closure – getting prepared for work

Dr. William R. Stayton

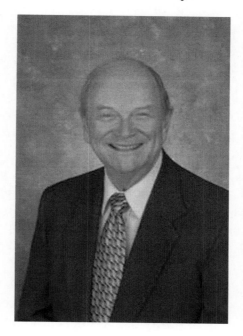

Photo courtesy of Dr. William R Stayton

Dr. Stayton has a Master of Divinity degree from Andover Newton Theological School, a Doctor of Theology degree in Psychology from Boston University, and a Ph.D. from the Institute for Advanced Study of Human Sexuality.

Tova: What criteria do you use to select a person for your surrogate training program?

Bill: When I was training a prospective trainee, we went through three separate interviews: First, I used my own assessment of the candidate using my skills as a psychologist. Second, I asked a professional surrogate from the International Professional Surrogates Association (IPSA) to interview the surrogate partner candidates. Third, I asked an outside therapist to interview the candidate. Through this multi-level screening, a lot of people were disqualified from going through the process.

Tova: What were the specific qualities you were looking for?

Bill: One was that the candidate was a stable person. I considered their intentions and reasons for wanting to do the training. I wanted to know if they were in a stable relationship, and if they were, they needed written permission from their partner to do this work. It was essential for me to understand their motives and to determine that they weren't going into this to meet their own personal needs. In many ways, they had to have exactly the same motives I had for becoming a therapist, that's simply a sense of caring and compassion for people.

Tova: Was your training program strictly the Masters and Johnson's Sensate Focus Sequence?

Bill: To answer that question, let me first tell you about how I got into surrogate training. The sex therapists in the Philadelphia area invited a sex surrogate to spend a day with them to talk about what being a sex surrogate was and what they did in their professional capacity. She taught us about sensate focus and the Masters and Johnson program. I had never known about this before; I knew Masters and Johnson had started working with surrogates, and I found out the head of my department at the University of Pennsylvania had worked with a surrogate. It was only hearsay that attracted me to her presentation, but I was very excited about the potential for surrogate partner therapy. At that time, I already had a client who I thought would be perfect for working with a surrogate. I talked it over with the surrogate who presented, and I referred the client to her.

That was my introduction to surrogate partner therapy, and it was incredible. I told the trainer, "We really need to train some new surrogates in our area of the country." So, she and I developed a training program together that took up two full weekends, from Friday through Sunday. She served as a mentor to the new trainees, which was so important for their skills and professional development.

Tova: What were the primary skills that you taught during your training program?

Bill: The female trainer and I would do a demonstration, and then the trainees would do it together with partners. We always gave the theory behind what we were teaching, explaining why we were doing what we did. In addition, I showed a wonderful training film called *The Dimensions of Surrogate Therapy*. The prospective surrogates needed to have as much information as I could give them on the nature of sexual function and dysfunction. And they also needed to learn how to interview a client and how to make a decision on whether an individual was an appropriate candidate for surrogate partner work.

In addition, we talked about the three-way arrangement of therapist, client, and surrogate partner, often referred to as the triadic relationship. I gave a lot of information about human sexuality, the variety of lifestyles, and sexual dysfunction in both men and women. The trainer and I conducted a body image exercise, and then let the trainees try it as well. We also taught trainees how to help clients with body image issues.

In our body image process, we had trainees start at the top of their heads and work all the way down to their feet; they talked about how they felt about their hair, about their face, about their shoulders, their chest, abdominal area, legs, thighs, feet, hands, and their genitals. And then we had them work with a mirror so that they could see how they felt about their back, shoulders, bottom area, and the backs of their legs. This exercise enabled the trainees to see how a client might feel vulnerable and embarrassed. Then we went into sensuality and sexuality exercises.

Tova: Did you try to keep a balance between male and female trainees?

Bill: Yes, we tried to do it so that a female trainee could go through the exercises with a male partner, and a male trainee had the opportunity to work with a female partner. Afterwards, they gave us their feedback. They talked about what they felt and what they noticed. We talked about the PLISSIT Model.

Tova: What does PLISSIT stand for?

Bill: The PLISSIT model was created by Jack Annon of the University of Hawaii. The "P" stands for *P*ermission, meaning that a lot of people need permission to experience pleasure. "L-I" stand for the *L*imited *I*nformation that we wanted to educate them about, whatever their issue was. "S-S" stands for *S*imple *S*uggestions, and these were sensate focus suggestions. The "IT," if none of this worked, meant they would refer out to a therapist, or "I-T" for Intensive Therapy. That's the PLISSIT model.

Tova: What else was included in your training program?

Bill: We had the candidates practice spoon breathing for relaxation, and sculpting.

Tova: What is sculpting?

Bill: That is an exercise where they would go over their partner's body and outline or draw it with their hands without touching it. This was done with the hands just slightly over the body. As they were going over the body and outlining it with their hands, they talked about the experience, giving positive feedback. From there, we went into the sexological, where we had the opportunity to talk in depth about anatomy. So we talked about Kegel exercises, hygiene, menstruation, birth control issues, and safe sex. All surrogate-client activity was done using safer-sex techniques, and this was about the time that the HIV scare was starting. We felt that one of the real benefits of surrogate training was for the surrogates to be able to train their clients in safe-sex practices and to help them to eroticize those practices. This meant that instead of a man wearing a condom and it detracting from the experience, the surrogate would show him how to make using the condom fun and sexy.

We talked about masturbation and showed a film about it. We encouraged trainees to talk about their own masturbatory practices. This led into a discussion about genital pleasuring. This pleasure was not for the purpose of either arousal or orgasm, but to teach clients how to enjoy sensual energy. Moving on, we talked about oral-genital pleasuring, where we talked about appropriate hygiene, which could also be appealing and sensual. And we discussed intercourse, different positions, what worked best for various body types and for people with physical limitations. Our trainees were always very excited, enthusiastic, and energized by the training. And I really appreciated, not only the information we shared in the training, but also the superb follow-up by the supervising surrogates. This was important because I had an opportunity to work with the Veteran's Administration in the Pennsylvania area to help some of their patients, especially those with spinal cord and brain injuries, to develop their sexual potential. We did a lot of work on how we could help them connect with a therapist and understand how SPT could benefit them.

Tova: Is there anything else you'd like to mention about your training program?

Bill: Yes, I want to add a few more things about my training. Most important was having them learn how to lead a client in developing social skills. We did a section on history-taking and talked about their work atmosphere. Sometimes a work environment could generate a tremendous amount of stress that could overlap into surrogates' personal lives. We talked about music and relaxation; record keeping, starting s practice, and finances and bookkeeping. I required that every trainee go through a SAR, Sexual Attitude Reassessment, to help them better understand their own sexual attitudes and judgments. I've been conducting SARs for more than forty years and I'm very familiar with them. I encouraged trainees to join the American Association of Sex Educators, Counselors, and Therapists (AASECT) and the Society for the Scientific Study of Sexuality (SSSS) so that they could be in the loop about what was going on in the field of sexuality, and also for networking purposes. From 1982 onward, in many of the ASSECT meetings, there was always a surrogates section with an open house to introduce therapists to the concept of SPT.

Tova: Could you tell me more about the involvement of AASECT within the community?

Bill: AASECT stands for the American Association of Sex Educators, Counselors, and Therapists. And SSSS was the Society for the Scientific Study of Sexuality. It was at their conference in San Francisco in 1982, we led a workshop called, "So You Want to Work with a Surrogate: Practical Aspects of Surrogate Sex Therapy," where we discussed issues for therapists to consider in working with surrogates. We described the role of the supervising therapist, that of the surrogate, and of the client. We had a lawyer speak to us about potential legal issues involved in surrogate partner therapy.

Dr. Bill Stayton's Training Program

Module 1

Pre-training

- Fill out an extensive questionnaire

- Interview by three skilled professionals

- Participate in a SAR (Sexual Attitude Reassessment)

Module 2

Overview of physiological and psychological issues

- Presentation: "Dimensions of Surrogate Therapy"

- Physiological anatomy and functioning

- Sexual functioning and dysfunctions for men and women

- How to interview a client

- Effective listening and communication skills

Module 3

Masters and Johnson - Sensate focus exercises

- Learning about the purpose of a caress

- Hands

- Feet

- Foot

- Spoon breathing

- Sculpting

- Body Image and discussion

- Back caress

Sex Is the Least of It

- Front caress without genitals

- Full front caress including genitals

- Sexological examination

- Genital touch

- Subsequent work depending on the needs of the client as determined by the supervising therapist

Module 4

Discussion of the PLISSIT Model

- P permission

- L-I limited information

- S-S simple suggestions

- I-T intensive therapy

Module 5

Other Issues

- Teaching social skills

- Use of music

- Record keeping

- Building a private practice

- Finances and bookkeeping

- Professional conduct

- Personal ethics

- Networking opportunities

Dr. Michael Perry

Photo Courtesy of Dr. Michael Perry

Michael Perry, Ph.D., is a California-licensed marriage and family therapist. His doctorate is in psychology, with a specialization in human sexuality. He began training sexual surrogate partners in 1983 in San Diego, California. Previously, he had been trained as a surrogate at the Institute for Advanced Study of Human Sexuality, San Francisco. Dr. Perry has produced four films and numerous instructional videos dealing with surrogate work.

Tova: You've trained surrogates for many years. What qualities did you use to select a surrogate?

Michael: When I advertise that I'm conducting a surrogate training, I get responses from curious people from all over. I attempt to weed out the inappropriate applicants via a pretest and interview.

The main quality I look for in a prospective surrogate is empathy. I look for someone who is caring and compassionate, someone who can deal with a variety of sexual problems, social issues, and personalities that they might encounter while working as a surrogate. Surrogacy is a helping profession. A trainee would have to be accepting and nonjudgmental, because they will be working with people from a variety of backgrounds and lifestyles.

Sex Is the Least of It

I require a balanced male-female ratio in the training classes that I teach. Nevertheless, I tell the women attending the training that they can, potentially, expect a good number of client referrals, but not the men. Back in the 1980s, a woman could make a living doing surrogate work full time. I tell the men that they should take the training for their own interest, and to enhance their own sex lives, but there wouldn't be enough referrals to make a full-time living.

Tova: How long did your surrogate partner training program take?

Michael: The time frame for the course depends in part on the schedules of the people in the class. This means my training could take three, four, or five months to complete. It is a sixty-hour in-class course, plus hours of outside reading, homework, and video viewing. And that doesn't even include the internship.

Tova: What was included in your training program?

Michael: The first part of the training includes the SAR process which stands for Sexual Attitude Restructuring or Reassessment. It's a twenty-hour course that typically runs Friday evening and all day Saturday and Sunday. The SAR process helps the participants re-evaluate and, if necessary, restructure their sexual attitudes and conditioning. The class provides a safe space for a person to look at their own sexuality and various sexual lifestyles and behaviors found in contemporary society. This challenges the participant's ability to be open and accepting. The format consists of visual material, some explicit, along with lecture presentations and group processes. One of the objectives here is to allow the participant to become thoroughly aware of, and comfortable with, his or her own sexuality, and to appreciate the diversity of sexual experiences of others.

The next aspect of the training is what I call the Clinical Issues Seminar and is a minimum of forty hours. Ideally, it consists of one weeknight per week for five weeks, one Saturday, and one full weekend. We focus on various types of sexual dysfunction and treatment modalities, behavioral modification theory, sensate focus theory, and basic counseling skills. A surrogate is not a licensed therapist, but I want him or her to have at least a passing knowledge of the therapeutic process, behavioral therapy, sex therapy, and hands-on surrogate therapy. The main objective here is for the participants to gain a thorough knowledge of sexual dysfunction and the appropriate direct therapy treatment approaches. In addition, I believe it is necessary that a competent surrogate be able to at least recognize pertinent therapeutic issues and confer with the supervising therapist.

I teach prospective surrogates about the work of some early pioneers in therapy, sex therapy, and research, including Sigmund Freud and Alfred Kinsey and, of course, the work of Masters and Johnson, who created the surrogate process, as well as the contributions of Hartman and Fithian, Jack Annon, Lonnie Barbach, Bernie Zilbergeld, and Helen Singer Kaplan.

The final part of the training is the Supervised Clinical Internship. This part may take an additional six months, depending on the number of clients with which a surrogate has worked. This segment is made up of forty to fifty hours working with actual clients who are experiencing some form of social skills inadequacy and/or sexual dysfunction. The surrogate intern is closely supervised by the licensed therapist. If I'm training them, I'd be providing the psychological talk therapy with the client. The intern will gain direct experience with various sexual dysfunctions within the traditional client-surrogate-therapist relationship.

My training differs from others in that I want participants to have some understanding of cognitive behavioral therapy and sex therapy, as well as surrogate therapy, even though they do not function as clinicians. I want the surrogate to be cognizant of the role of the therapist and the therapeutic process. This helps them understand deeper issues that may underlie sexual dysfunction and certain psychological issues that could arise between them and the client. The surrogate and therapist must communicate effectively using a common vocabulary.

A surrogate partner needs to be informed, direct, and nonjudgmental. They have to be permission-giving and have a sex-positive attitude. Being able to use appropriate language with clients is essential. Each client speaks in a certain sociocultural style of language. They may be college educated, or they may have barely gotten out of the eighth grade. It's important that a surrogate be able to speak to each client on a level that's appropriate for them. It's also important for the surrogate to be able to listen without interrupting or jumping to conclusions.

Among the techniques that I emphasize, I include Kegel exercises for both men and women. This exercise was developed by Dr. Arnold Kegel to teach people how to strengthen their pubococcygeus, or PC muscles, which make up the bands of muscles that stretch from the pubic bone to the coccyx. Kegels used to be taught only to women so they could be more comfortable in the birthing process and heal more quickly afterwards because their muscles were more elastic. Research has shown that women who have strong PC muscles are more reliably orgasmic, and men have better control over their ejaculation. There is a real correlation between having strong PC muscles and healthy sexuality.

Tova: In terms of the Masters and Johnson protocol, starting with the hand caress and moving forward, did you find it valuable to teach that "as is," honoring the classic approach, or did you change it in some way?

Michael: I follow the classic Masters and Johnson model with some modifications and updates. As an example, I have added in a whole component of social skills—what happens way before the "sex" begins. The surrogate and client may start off with just looking at each other's faces and learn to relax in the presence of another person. This is the first step in learning to have a conversation. I emphasize the distinction between a caress and a massage. Massage is used to relax a person, to let their muscles become looser. In contrast, a caress wakes up the nerve endings and makes a person become more aware of their own sensations via a much lighter touch. I tell clients: "You're going to experience a sensate focus caress. Focus on *your* senses and touch lightly. Most importantly, when you touch, do it for yourself, not for the other person. When you're caressing, I want you to focus on what the touch feels like to *you*." I emphasize this because, so many people initiate lovemaking while being so uptight, and so concerned about their performance, that they put their full focus on pleasuring their partner and lose the sense of relaxed pleasure for themselves.

Tova: Can you go through the list of all the steps, from the hand caress all the way to intercourse, as you have taught them?

Michael: I use the classical Masters and Johnson process with embellishments. The client, surrogate, and therapist meet for the first time in the therapist's office. The next time the surrogate and client meet, it may even be on a "date" out in the world. Then most all subsequent sessions are held at the surrogate's "office" (often her home).

Here is an outline of my typical modified female-surrogate/male-client exercises:

Sensate Focus Exercises

Take Pleasure for Yourself

- Hand Caress [Getting to Know You]

- Foot Caress

- Face Caress [Increased Intimacy]

- Back Caress [Nude to Waist] [Staring Exercise]

- Back Caress [Fully Nude]

    o   Full Body Staring Exercise

    o   Mirror Exercise [Look, Feel, Function]

- Communication Games

    o   "May I…, Will you…"

    o   Erotic Mapping Game [Likes, Dislikes, Numeric Rating]

    o   Sexological Exam [Name Parts. Describe Function. Use Speculum]

- Front Caress [Without Genital Contact]

- Front Caress [Incidental Genital Contact]

- Front Caress [With Genital Contact]

- Genital Caress

- Oral/Genital Stimulation [Optional or During "Various Positions," Below]

Mutuality: Give and Take Simultaneously

- Sensuous Shower

- Genital Juxtaposition (closeness)

[Woman on Top for subsequent Exercises]

- Quiet Vagina [Stuffing Option/non-erect penis]

- One Partner [Surrogate] Thrusting

- Other Partner [Client] Thrusting

- Both Partners Thrusting

- Various Positions [Other Than Woman on Top]

This is the typical progression of exercises, one each session, that a female surrogate would follow with a male client. Between each surrogate/client session, there is a follow-up conversation between the therapist and surrogate. Written notes are also given to the therapist from the surrogate. They include:

- Session Goal

- Tasks [Exercises]

- Results

- Observations

- Homeplay [Homework]

The client then sees the therapist. The client/surrogate session is discussed; therapy proceeds. There is a follow-up conversation between the surrogate and therapist. A new exercise is devised for the next client/surrogate encounter. I emphasize with my trainees that when you're with a client, and you and the therapist have agreed upon a lesson for that day, if the client becomes excessively nervous or some other obstacle arises, you can make a change midstream. For example, if the scheduled lesson that day is the back caress and that triggers his anxiety, the surrogate may say: "Okay, rather than do the back caress today, let's do the face caress again. Or let's try something different." I want the surrogate to realize they have the ability to make decisions on their own as appropriate to best serve the needs of the client.

Tova: How did you handle the body image exercise?

Michael: Body image work is very important and can trigger a number of psychological issues. A body image exercise: The client and the surrogate disrobe. They stare silently at each other starting with the top of their partner's head and work their way down to the feet. They then talk about the various parts of their bodies, including the genitals, and describe how they feel about their own and partner's parts, how it feels being stared at and staring unabashedly at another nude body. Barriers slowly come down. Within this process, they may include touch in a shower or a hot tub together depending on the facility the surrogate might have. A variation could include an eyes-closed experience while your partner touches your face or hand or penis or vagina. Sometimes people are better able to focus on sensation when they are not distracted by sight.

Tova: Did you ever do an evaluation of a surrogate trainee after the conclusion of the training, and decide that he or she might not be appropriate.

Michael: Before the training even starts, I give them an elaborate questionnaire. The questionnaire asks about their feelings, judgments, and opinions regarding various sexual practices and behaviors. There is a sexual information segment and a comprehensive sexual history. I based my questionnaire, with some modifications, on the one I used when I was doing my internship at UC Medical Center, San Francisco, Sex Counseling Unit. I tell my trainees: "I want you to do your best with the informational segment of the questionnaire, and when you are retested at the end of the training, you can see how much you've learned." Throughout the training, I want them to discover the answers to the questions posed on the questionnaire. That's the knowledge part. As the training progresses, I observe them to determine whether they are mastering the sensate focus exercises, acquiring the ability to speak and listen effectively, and are able to comfortably ask and answer questions regarding sexuality. That's the empathy part.

Tova: Once a surrogate is in her supervised internship, is it a judgment call when you feel a surrogate is ready to go out on her own and work with you or another licensed psychotherapist?

Michael: Yes, it is. They complete the process with a closely supervised internship of several months and/or a specified number of client hours (forty to sixty). Their goal is to demonstrate that they are sufficiently prepared to work with both clients and therapists. If, in the course of training, I find a prospective trainee who is really inappropriate, I would excuse them from the training.

Tova: What kind of communication do you expect from a surrogate?

Michael: Let's say we are talking about a female surrogate working with a male client. First I make sure that the client is appropriate and ready to take on the surrogate process. The client and I confirm that he is ready to start. Then I speak to the surrogate about this person, giving her a brief history and an outline of his concerns. I advise the surrogate as to how I think we can best work together. The next step is that the surrogate comes to my office to be introduced to the client. This is the beginning of the triadic relationship: client-therapist-surrogate. They agree to meet at the surrogate's office (home) for all subsequent sessions. However, I would see them together in my office if some difficulty warranted it. The next time we would all meet together would be at the termination of the surrogate process.

My preference is that the client meets with the surrogate once a week and also sees me once a week. The surrogate and I speak by phone after each surrogate session and after each therapy session. I ask the surrogate how the session went, including, "What exercises did you do? How would you characterize the client's reactions and emotions?" I don't tell the client in advance what exercises he may be doing with the surrogate. That information could trigger unnecessary anxiety on the part of the client before meeting with the surrogate. And, for good reason, the surrogate may decide to alter the lesson plan. The surrogate then fills out a report, which she sends to me. Then I see the client and I ask, "How did it go?" Hopefully, the two versions mesh, that what the surrogate told me and what the client told me are congruent. But sometimes they're not: the surrogate reports that the client was so nervous, he could hardly sit still, and when I see the client, he informs me that he was completely relaxed and there was no problem at all.

I would tend to believe the surrogate more than the client, because the surrogate's trained to observe behavior and body language. After I see the client, I call the surrogate and tell her what I learned from the client, and then we decide what is most appropriate for her to do next. Sometimes a client will try to push for an activity that the surrogate and the therapist have not agreed to, particularly intercourse. Or, the client may say to the surrogate: "Okay, this will just be our little secret. Let me tell you something, but please don't tell the therapist." I'm very upfront with clients that there are no secrets, and I'm very clear with the surrogate that the process is completely transparent, and she cannot hold onto information and not share with me.

Tova: What if a client falls in love with a surrogate?

Michael: During the surrogate therapy, I encourage the development of a relationship. If they do not create a real relationship, the process will not work well. Although this is a time-limited relationship: one hour a week for twenty weeks, there will be real feelings involved, and at some point this relationship will end. I encourage a relationship that may even be intense and the first one the client has ever had, if it is in accordance with the parameters of the therapeutic process. However, after the termination of the surrogate process, the client and surrogate will observe a six-month moratorium during which there will be no communication between them.

Tova: That models a real relationship in which there's a beginning, a courting period where deep feelings may develop, and then the relationship may end. So the surrogate-client process goes full circle in reflecting what may happen in a real-life relationship.

Michael: The surrogate process is really about learning how to have a relationship, about how to fully communicate verbally and sexually with another person, and about experiencing both joyful and sad emotions. This isn't just about technique or how to have an orgasm. Surrogate therapy is about how to *love!* It really is a very powerful, life-altering process. And people have literally had their lives changed by going through this therapy.

Another unexpected aspect of the surrogate therapy training is learning how to end a relationship well. In our society, it seems relationships have to end badly. How about parting on good terms? That's how the surrogate relationship ends and may serve as a model to end any relationship nicely.

Tova: There appears to be a diminishing number of trained surrogates. Looking ahead, what do you see as the future of surrogate partner therapy?

Michael: Back in its heyday, in the '70s, '80s, and '90s, there were lots of properly trained surrogates… at least on the two coasts. And at the time, I had many male and female clients who worked with surrogates. I don't know whether there is going to be a resurgence of the work. I wish I could say that there will once again be a flourishing profession like it once was; but I rather doubt it, with the flood of information on the Internet about therapy and sexuality. I think there may be fewer people seeking sex therapy, let alone the services of a surrogate.

However, "surrogacy" may take newer, different forms: video surrogacy (see my *Virtual Sex Surrogate* film); Internet surrogacy; surrogate partner "coaching" (as opposed to "Therapy"); dating coaching; social media apps.

Tova: In your experience, what has been the value of surrogate partner therapy?

Michael: To me, the surrogate process is invaluable when it is called for. I can do all the depth talk therapy, provide all the books and films, but that falls short of the direct hands-on surrogate experience. Talk therapy is necessary, especially to uncover underlying causation, but sometimes it is not sufficient. Effective surrogate partner therapy is always a meld of cognitive behavioral psychotherapy and the intimate touch of a well-trained surrogate. Surrogate partner therapy is a wonderful, superb process and I wish it would flourish. I'd like it to evolve, grow, and expand.

Contact information:

Email: MepSexDoc@aol.com

Websites: www.sexualintimacy.com and www.MichaelPerryPhotography.com

Barbara Roberts, M.S.W.

The Early Years of Sensual Enrichment Training

The Sexual Enrichment Experience (SEE) was designed in the 1970's by Barbara Roberts, psychotherapist and founder of the Center for Social and Sensory Learning in Tarzana, California. In the following pages, you read about the sexual training program that was offered to the general community and to prospective surrogates. Several surrogates in the book refer to the SEE class as being a foundational part of their learning. Although not designated as a surrogate training program, per se, its touching exercises, communication techniques, and emphasis on body awareness bear a striking resemblance to contemporary surrogate training programs.

Its value is as a historical antecedent to the various training programs provided in New York, Los Angeles, London, and Texas.

Sexual Enrichment Experience Overview

by Barbara Roberts, circa 1980

At The Center for Social and Sensory Learning, Tarzana, CA

This is a small experiential class designed for people who want to learn more about themselves as sexual beings and to improve their sexual relationships. This class is not for the treatment of sexual dysfunction.

Our premise is that in our society we are taught almost nothing about our sexual potential or the art of intimacy.

What we have learned from parents, school and church is basically negative and inhibiting. The information we gained from childhood friends or through our own experimentation is limited and often misinformation. Therefore we tend to have a narrow and rigid view of sexuality and relationships. The SEE Class provides basic information about ourselves as sexual beings, but more importantly it provides a safe and supportive atmosphere for guided experimentation with new attitudes about sexuality and new interpersonal behavior.

Participants learn to regard sexuality as a respected and integral part of their lives and are provided with new options through which they can fulfill their optimum potential for sexual pleasure and satisfaction as an enriching facet of their lives.

Sex Is the Least of It

The method we have developed is called The Sensory Integration Process™—a series of structured touching and communication exercises which provide the basis for fundamentally new attitudes and behaviors regarding sexuality and relationships. These new attitudes and behaviors are often in direct opposition to traditional Puritan values which are strongly negative and repressive with regard to the acceptance of the body, touching and pleasure.

Our process is based on our belief that all learning utilizes the five senses for information gathering and particularly the sense of touch with respect to sexuality and intimacy. Therefore class members participate in touching and communication exercises first. They discuss the significance or meaning of that interaction second. In this process old beliefs and behaviors are challenged, creating an opportunity for the development of new beliefs and behaviors.

SEE Class Structure

Each of the twelve sessions follows a general pattern consisting of three parts.

A. Review of homework assignments. Leader's introduction and demonstration of new subjects and exercises

B. Group or couple interaction. Leader's instructions for the exercises, interspersed with the exercises when done by the group; given in full for couples to follow in private.

C. Share feedback and conclusions through a lively interchange with participants and leaders, insights and conclusions are drawn from interaction experiences

#1 Tuning into Oneself – Introduction to Group Nudity, Body/Self Image with Mirrors, Hand Caress, Saying Goodbye

#2 The Nurturing Touch - Body/Self-Image with Mirrors, Pelvic Thrusts, Grooming, Face Caress and Foot Caress

#3 Sensuality, Total Body Awareness – Couple Shower, Group Hot Tub, Back Caress, Spoon Breathing (Cuddling)

#4 Taking Turns: Giving and Receiving – Couple Shower, Group Hot Tub, Pelvic Thrusts, Non-Genital Front Caress, Touch Memory, Touch Anticipation, Spoon Breathing

#5 Respecting Personal Space – Hygiene (tooth brushing), Personal Space Demonstration, Kissing and Hug Lessons, Front Caress with Casual Genital Touching, Containment and Dispersal of Sexual Energy, Face to Face Cuddling

#6 Playing Doctor – Adult Style – Sexological Examination of Male and Female Genitalia, Demonstration for Group, Couples in Private Examine and Explore Genitals, Exercises for PC Muscle

#7 Peaks and Valleys: Surrendering to the Flow – Breathing with Noise, Non-Demand Couple Genital Caressing, Group Pelvic Undulations

#8 Overcoming Pleasure Anxiety: Sex Can be Fun – Romping and Horseplay, Handling Bloopers and Distractions, Touch Focus, Quiet Penetration, PC Muscle More Code

#9 Getting and Giving Permission: Developing Trust – Pelvic Undulations and Breathing with Noise, May I? Exercise, Group Touch, Progressive Penetration, Discussion and Masturbation

#10 Being in Charge of Your Own Sexuality – Breaking Old Habit Patterns, Containment and Dispersal of Sexual Energy, Love-Making Positions

#11 Mutuality – Pelvic Undulations with Shaking and Noise, Will You? Exercise, Hand Dance,

Sex Is the Least of It

Touch Focus, Mutual Free Flow Integration

#12 Completion - Group Hot Tab, Sensuous Feast, Kindling and Channeling Sexual Energy Through Chanting, Wrap Up Discussion, Goodbyes

SEE Class Home Assignments

1 Hand Sanitization

2 Hand Game

3 Hand – Face

4 Self-body Caress

5 Belly Breathing

6 Belly Breathing – Knees Bent

7 Foot Sanitization

8 Pubococcygeus Muscle

9 Limb Flops

10 Mirror Locking

11 Sensuous Bath or Shower

12 Pelvic Thrusts

13 Progressive Relaxation

14 Feel Clothes

15 Bellying Breathing with Noise

16 Genital Exploration

17 Word List

18 Outrageous

19

A. Pelvic Undulations

B. Pelvic Undulations with PC Muscles

C. Pelvic Undulations with Sound

20 Descriptive Words

21 Use of Speculum

22 Asking for What You Want

23 Genital Self Pleasuring with Mirror

24 Genital Peaking and Detumescence

25 Genital Peaking and Detumescence with PC Muscles

26 Panting/Undulations

27 Shaking

28 Switch Focus

29 Closure

SEE Home Assignment Details

1 Hand Sanitization

Touch many things—animate and inanimate objects, fabrics, plants, etc. Spend some time with the touching and become aware of such aspects as their texture, contour, temperature, weight, tone and any other sensory aspects that your hands register.

2 Hand Game

1. Put the back of one hand in the palm of your other hand. Let the palm be the active hand and the other be the receptive hand.

2. Imagine the receptive hand belongs to someone else. Focus on your active hand caressing and exploring the receptive hand. Register the sensations and feelings in your active hand as it caresses the other hand.

3. Switch focus and let the receptive hand be your while imagining that the active hand belongs to someone else. Become aware of what your receptive hand feels like when it is being caressed by someone else's active hand.

4. Change hands. For instance, if the left hand was the receptive hand, make it the active hand. Repeat the above steps.

5. Have both hands caressing each other mutually and become aware of the sensations in both hands simultaneously.

3 Hand – Face

Caress your face slowly, tenderly, exploringly. Imagine that the face belongs to someone else. Focus on the feelings in your hands, touching the face. Discover the skin, texture, the bone structure, the contours, the fine holes etc and how this all feels in your hands. Switch focus... Let the hands belong to someone else and become aware of how your face feels when it is being touched by the hands.

4 Self-Body Caress

*   Slowly caress your body from the top of your head to your feet, touching as many parts of your body as you can reach. Merely register sensations while using a variety of touches...

*   Discover places on your body that feel good when touched.

*   Switch focus between your hand touching your body and your body touching your hand.

*   Touch genitals casually as merely another place on your body.

*   Take your time, perhaps as long as half an hour, but stop if you get bored or feel you have touched long enough.

5 Belly Breathing

Lie on your back in a comfortable manner.

Slowly inhale through the nose and slowly exhale through the mouth.

Let the abdomen rise with the inhalation and collapse with the exhalation.

Imagine the air is actually filling the belly, not only the chest. Be aware of the feelings in your total body as you slowly inhale.

Be aware of the stop & hold place at the end of your exhalation.

6 Belly Breathing – Knees Bent

Continue belly breathing, as described above, but with knees bent. On exhalation let breath be audible. Perceive the rocking sensation.

7 Foot Sanitization

Walk about in bare feet. As with the hand sanitization, let your feet be aware of the sensations produced by what they tough. Be aware of textures, contours, temperatures and whatever other aspects you can register. Experiment with having your bare feet coming into contact with not only the usual surfaces, but try having your feet come in contact with new and different surfaces for you (sand, glass, appliances, etc).

8 Pubococcygeus Muscle (PC Muscle)

Exercise muscle by tensing three seconds and then concentrating on full relaxation of muscle. Begin with thirty/three second tensing and relaxing, and thirty fast flicks. Do exercises at three separate times of day—dividing total holds and relaxations and 200 fast flicks per day. Then, back off to 100 times a day for the rest of your life. At first use cues to remind you. Such as at red lights, stop signs, phone ringing, when the alarm clock rings in the morning etc. Do not overdo. The PC muscle will get sore like any other muscle you have not exercised regularly.

9 Limb Flops

Raise opposite arm and leg slightly off the ground, and let it flop back down. Alternate with raising the other opposite arm and leg. Breathe in as you raise arms and legs; breathe out as you let them flop. Do this with as little effort as possible. Time to comfortable breathing pattern. Be equally aware of lift tension and letting get of tension.

10 Mirror Locking

Stand nude in front of a full length mirror. Touch and examine all parts of your body, assessing what parts you like or dislike. Pay attention not only to form but also to feeling and function. If there is a part of your body you particularly dislike, give it special touching attention as often as possible.

11 Sensuous Bath or Shower

Use water, soap and atmosphere you create (candles, incense, warmed touch, etc.) for a sensuous experience. Take lots of time and focus on your bodily sensations. Pamper self-use variety of touch. This is not for focus on cleanliness but rather is another medium of self-caressing.

12 Pelvic Thrusts

Sex Is the Least of It

Standing with knees slightly bent, thrust pelvis back and forward. Keep rest of body in stationary position. No need to use muscles other than those to move the pelvis. Kneeling, supporting weight on hands and knees and/or elbows and knees. Move pelvis toward ceiling and forward toward bed. Note as you bring pelvis upward or backward, your back will arch, pelvis moves forward, making the back round and shoulders hunched.

13 Progressive Relaxation

Breath in, hold, tense face and neck. Release tension as you breath out. Repeat, tensing face, neck, shoulders, arms and hands. Repeat, adding to the above, chest and abdomen. Repeat, adding buttocks. Repeat, adding thighs, calves, feet. Repeat—total body.

14 Feel Clothes on your body as you dress, undress, walk, etc.

15 Bellying Breathing with Noise: add vocalization (sound) to release your breath.

16 Genital Exploration: Look at genitals with a hand mirror. Touch genitals for sensation only, not for purposes of arousal.

17 Fill Out Word List

List as many term for parts of the body and sexual functions as you can think of. Decide on which terms you feel comfortable saying.

18 Outrageous

Do something which extends your normal boundaries and yet is safe for you and for whoever else may be involved in doing it with you. Risk. Break your pattern. Find new options.

19

A. **Pelvic Undulations** – Lie on your back with your knees bent. Raise your pelvis upwards until there is a slight tension in your thighs, then lower, rolling your buttocks under you. There will be a slight arch to your back as you roll under. This is a slow flowing, undulating motion. Breathe in, as you lower your pelvis, and breath out as you raise your pelvis.

B. **Pelvic Undulations with PC Muscles** – Lie on the floor or bed – breath out as you raise your hips – squeeze your PC muscles when your hips are raised. Breathe in, relax muscle as you lower your hips to the floor and roll your buttocks under.

C. **With noise on exhalation** – Listen to your sounds.

20 Descriptive Words

Use as many words as possible to describe sensory experiences as you have had during the week, using the senses of sight, sound, taste, smell, touch and being touched.

21 Use of Speculum

- Women – Practice insertion with speculum for self-exploration

- Men – Practice insertion with speculum for female partner

22 Asking for What You Want – Can be in a sexual or non-sexual way

23 Genital Self-Pleasure with Mirror – Look for body changes

24 Genital Peaking and Detumescence

Women – Touch genitals to a peak of arousal, then detumescence by cupping hand over vulva, exerting firmer pressure on clitoris, or your own method for reducing arousal. Experiment… repeat several times. If orgasm occurs despite attempts to reduce arousal – enjoy!

Men – Touch genitals to peak of arousal. Step before point of ejaculatory inevitability. Squeeze head of penis until urge to ejaculate or arousal subsides. Repeat. Do not try to control by taking focus on attention away from sensations. Use physical means only for detumescing and reducing arousal. If orgasm occurs… enjoy!

25 Genital Peaking and Detumescence with PC Muscles

Tense PC muscles at point of detumescence (women). (Men) Tense PC muscle at the same time as external squeeze. Experiment with 1 - pulling PC muscle in and 2 - pushing PC muscle out.

26 Panting/Undulations

Lie on your back with knees bent, take short panting breathe with pelvic raise. Use short breaths and short pelvis lift coordinating them.

27 Shaking

Lie on your back with knees bent and separated. Slowly, about ½" at a time, drop knees toward the floor. When legs start to quiver, keep them at that place and let tension build until the entire body is shaking. Allow yourself to go with the shaking.

(Alternative to the above.)

1. Drop legs down and start up slowly about ½" at a time until legs begin to shake.

2. Press soles of feet together, knees bent and apart, raise knees keeping soles of feet together

      to a point where the shaking begins.

3. Stand with knees slightly bent – begin shaking legs, let the shake travel up to your torso, down into arms, into neck and head. (Like a rag doll with an internal vibrator.)

28 Switch Focus

Repeat: Hand Game (#2), Hand-Face (#3), and Self-Body Caress (#4) with emphasis upon switching focus.

Touch two objects at once, touch yourself and an object, touch another person and yourself, touch another person while being touched. In all these touching exercises switch your focus back and forth between the two points of touch.

29 Closure

During each class at the completion of an exercise have a verbal or non-verbal "Goodbye" which indicates recognition of the experience you had with your partner.

At the end of each session do the same with members of the group being leaving.

If something is unfinished or incomplete about your "hear and now" interaction, complete it.

Be aware of what you can now incorporate into your own being from your experience. What is now part of you which you can take away with you?

In Memoriam

Adele Kennedy

Adele P. Kennedy blazed a trail very early in the infancy of the surrogate community, starting in the mid-1970s. She worked with many different medical pioneers, including Masters and Johnson, where she was a fellow of their institute.

Over a career spanning more than twenty-five years, she taught many people to have richer lives, both as couples and as individuals, including those with profound disabilities. She taught them confidence in sexual and sensual skills, as well as helped them to improve their overall social skills. Her clients always were referred by a licensed therapist who worked closely with her throughout the course of treatment.

In addition to her work with clients, Adele Kennedy ran numerous workshops for sex therapists, surrogate trainees, and women's groups, based on her book, *Touching for Pleasure*. She was a founding member of the International Professional Surrogates Association (IPSA), and a member of the American Association of Sex Educators, Counselors, and Therapists, as well as the Society for the Scientific Study of Sex.

She appeared on numerous television programs, including Dinah!, Geraldo, and Playboy Channel

interviews, and was featured in a documentary *Sex Surrogates: Intimate Profiles*, by producer/director Arnold Shapiro, best known for the popular documentary *Scared Straight*.

After retirement, Adele Kennedy remained active in the medical community, acting as a surrogate patient in the geriatrics departments of the large medical schools in the Los Angeles area. A trooper until the end, she allowed her doctors to try several experimental therapies to advance the learning of the medical community, and to help others. Her husband of fifty years and two adult children supported her completely throughout her long career.

Many thanks to Jo Kennedy for providing this information.

Jerry De Haan

Jerry De Haan made an invaluable contribution to the field of sex surrogacy as a teacher, surrogate, and researcher. He is the author of the ground breaking book, *Reaching Intimacy: A Male Sex Surrogate's Perspective.* It was the first book written by a male surrogate. Jerry also worked with the legendary sex researcher, Beverly Whipple, in her cutting-edge research on the discovery and photographing of the female G-Spot.

In his book, Jerry describes his work as a surrogate as follows: "I feel the need to talk about my work because I know many couples suffer in silence, longing to communicate but unable to get beyond the barrier of words. I work with women who need to experience intimacy, with someone—a husband or lover—but who find that, when they reach out for love, all they get is sex. Being a surrogate allows me to provide intimacy with a few select women."

He went on to say, "I learned about myself and my masculinity—about the difference between being macho and being male. I became conscious of my feminine side and its characteristics. And I learned the difference between sexuality and sensuality. I truly experienced what I'd known only intellectually before—that the brain, not the genitals, is the center of sexual sensations." Jerry concluded with this: "Through intimacy, we relive our hurts and pains and, through sharing and love, find healing. We expose our needs and desires, and find them reflected in the longings of our partners. We learn to show love because we feel it, to embrace because we want to have our partner near us, to caress because touching gives us pleasure. And because we trust our partners to feel as we do, we can take pleasure in being loved, embraced and caressed."

Patricia Pearlman

Patricia Pearlman was a surrogate partner who lived in New Jersey and specialized in working with the disabled. She was introduced to Ronit Aloni, a budding student of sex therapy, who also was drawn to working with the disabled; she, too, was living in New Jersey, and was studying at NYU in the Human Sexuality program.

Ronit Aloni had heard about Patricia's work. She recalls, "I called her and she was very open. She invited me to her house and I ended up using her experience as the basis for my master's thesis. She educated me about her surrogate practice, about her clients, and what she did. She gave me all the fundamentals of surrogate therapy and sexual rehabilitation for the disabled."

Patricia introduced Ronit to one of her clients, a man who had cerebral palsy. Ronit spoke with him for several hours and wrote a seminar presentation about him. She was also introduced to another client of Patricia's who was deaf and had no previous intimate or sexual experience. He was a virgin in his forties and she did surrogate therapy with him. Ronit ultimately wrote a case study about him.

Later, Dr. Ronit Aloni returned to Israel and ultimately opened her own sex therapy clinic. Patricia visited her in 1990 for an international conference about sexual rehabilitation held in Beth-Halochem Afeka. At that conference, Patricia talked about surrogate partner therapy for people with disabilities, and Dr. Aloni presented her first group of surrogates and discussed surrogate partner therapy (SPT).

Patricia trained Dr. Aloni's second group of surrogates, and Dr. Aloni said, "She trained them and basically she trained me as well."

In describing Patricia, Dr. Aloni said: "Patricia's spirit, her openness, and her ability to perceive every person as having sexual rights was really part of her DNA. She passed that legacy onto me, and I've passed that on to all the people that I've trained. I feel her spirit alive in me. In fact, one of the positions we use when working with the disabled is called the 'Patricia Position.' We have named it in her honor. She was very warm, caring, and open. She had a big heart. She didn't withhold anything from me. She shared everything with me that I needed to learn. And she was also very funny, with a great laugh, and a truly good person."

Epilogue—What Is It About Sex?

Epilogue—What Is It About Sex?

In a way, surrogacy partner therapy is not about sex, although, of course, it is. But it's also about communicating and interacting in other healthy, social ways, as the lives of the individuals in this book clearly show. At the same time, in the stories we've just read, we see a virtual history of the development of surrogate partner therapy, and the experiments done by some surrogates, therapists, and clients over the years to discover or reawaken their sexual selves and to develop the profession. Back when I first became a surrogate, I did what was apparently the first study of what "sex surrogates" actually did with their time with clients. The present study takes that study thirty years ago light years further, and begins the process of telling us what the lives of surrogate partners were like at a certain point in time, when they are or were practicing, as well as the journeys that brought them to that point. In the process, what can we learn from reading pieces of their stories that we can apply to our own sex lives to make our relationships more fulfilling?

To begin with, we learn that it's not just about technique, although that's important at some level. Leonore Tiefer tells us that "Sex is not a natural act," by which she means we—humans—have to learn it, in the broadest sense: It is not something we automatically know how to do innately or instinctively. We need to contextualize it and frame it in the various cultures we inhabit or interact with—often with contradictory and confusing messages. And we need to look inside ourselves and see how we connect to others and they to us. I always say that most of what I know about sexual touch I learned from the people with whom I've connected. It's those connections that most people are seeking. Still, it's surprising when recent studies show that anywhere from ten to thirty percent or more of people check their cell phones or social media during or right after sex. Thus, the need for sexual surrogate partner therapy in the future is likely to increase, rather than decrease, because pharmaceutical therapies are not designed to correct social sexual dysfunction.

While all of this is happening, there is the real possibility that the profession of sexual surrogate partner is disappearing—just as we see the need for them increasing. Pharmaceutical interventions can only solve some of the problems. When there is a true physiological problem, certainly they can help. But we know that most sexual dysfunctions are not strictly physiological. Sexologists speak of sexuality in a biopsychosocial context, and what I call the *human sexuality complex*, to describe the diverse aspects of its constituent components as a unified interconnected whole that resembles complex, chaotic systems, which I derived from my doctoral dissertation on sex in space. Intimacy for many is as distant as the edge of the galaxy.

People are often in emotional pain, although it's not always obvious. And they are often afraid, although they won't sometimes admit it, even to themselves. The sexual surrogate partner brings the listening and accepting aspects of the practice to the therapeutic encounter to facilitate the change that is sought by the client by acknowledging the pain and allaying the fears. As an adjunctive experiential therapy, it allows the client to strongly reinforce behaviors that are only discussed in the talk sessions with the therapist, wherein lies the strength of the surrogate partner therapy. It's also about self-empowerment and expectations, both as sexual actors and teachers. What is gained is confidence and self-acceptance, which is a big part of what it is about sex that nourishes us emotionally and physically. In addition, we seek to foster a comfort with one's own body, comfort with one's femininity and masculinity, comfort with one's weaknesses and strengths, and comfort with confronting one's traumas and disappointments with relationships and self.

These surrogates—*we* surrogates—are helping people with one of the most sensitive intimate areas of their lives. We are not special people; we are like you. Yet we *are* special people in that we may have some key skills that we can help share with others. These are not even unique skills—others have them too—but we have perhaps honed these skills and developed the capacity to analyze and control those skills to help others find their hidden, damaged, broken, or vandalized sexual selves. We help to undo some of the negative effects of media representations of sex that too often reinforce the conundrum that Love has built its temple in the place of excrement, to paraphrase Yeats.

If we looked at the intimate relationships of social/sexual/sensual partner surrogates, would we find the perfect relationships? We wish! Relationships are always dynamic, with needs and wants often requiring negotiation and complex dances. An interesting study would be one exploring the intimate relationships of surrogates—and for that matter, therapists!

I am reminded of an incredible insight by Igor Kon, the pioneer in Russian sexology who wrote the chapter on his country in my *International Encyclopedia of Sexuality*, that I only discovered while reading some remembrances of him after he died in 2011. Regarding some of the contemporary tenets of celebrating diversity and promoting tolerance with respect to LGBT individuals being fully accepted in a given society, he asked, "Which is better: tolerance or indifference?" His answer was indifference. He said that LGBT people would be fully accepted when society's attitude toward them was one of indifference. Why? Because it doesn't—shouldn't—matter most of the time, just like it doesn't matter if one is heterosexual. It doesn't matter until either you become sexually interested in them or they become sexually interested in you. Then it matters what your respective sexual orientation is vis-à-vis the other and whether they match.

The same could be said of surrogates. It doesn't matter that they exist, until we need them. Sex heals, and sexuality is our complex toolkit to help make it happen.

Raymond J. Noonan, Ph.D.

Co-Editor, *Continuum Complete International Encyclopedia of Sexuality* (CCIES).

rjnoonan@SexQuest.com

Brief Bibliography

Noonan, R. J. (1998). *A Philosophical Inquiry into the Role of Sexology in Space Life Sciences Research and Human Factors Considerations for Extended Spaceflight.* New York University. (UMI publication number: 9832759)

Appendices

Appendix A: Research and Clinical Studies

Literature Summary

There are fourteen studies reviewed in this document, each one taking a slightly different approach to the effectiveness of surrogate therapy.

Some of the studies were not efficacy studies of any population. Malamuth, et al. (1976) looked at the willingness of psychologists and various professionals to use surrogates, and Johnston (1978) looked at the role and practice of sexual surrogacy, not its effectiveness. Similarly, Aloni and Katz (2003) looked only at the possible application of surrogacy techniques to patients with brain damage. No efficacy assessment is undertaken.

Studies that did assess efficacy, but not at a population-wide level, include the Benton & Cotter (2007), Aloni, et al. (2007), and Roberts (1978). All of these papers involved case studies of individual surrogate-patient pairs and found improvement. However, such limited studies are not good grounds for the generalization about the effectiveness of surrogacy at large.

The remaining eight studies attempted a wider level analysis of surrogate effectiveness.

Ben-Zion (2007) is the only study to look exclusively at the sexual health of women. They found that in a study of 16 women, surrogate therapy was 100% effective in helping the patient achieve penetrative sex, but only 75% effective in a couple's therapy setting. The paper cites the cost of surrogates.

Zilbergeld (1975) looked at men, but did not look at the effectiveness of surrogacy, *per se*, but rather the effectiveness of small groups. Treatment was deemed to have resulted in the achievement of patients' goals in two-thirds of the cases. Sommers (1978) also looked at a relatively small sample ($n=12$) and found complete relief for 75% of his patients, as evaluated subjectively on a 7-point scale. The findings remained upon follow up.

Five studies looked at a wider data set with more rigor. Kaye (2000) looked at 151 cases, and found the cessation of problems in 69% of cases, with no follow-up confirmation. However, Apfelbaum (1984) found a similar result when looking at a sample size of $n=407$ with 6-month and one-year follow ups: 69% of patients experienced completely or largely successful treatment as rated by therapists upon reading a patient's evaluations. Many types of disorders were assessed and the evaluation criteria were in the hands of therapists combined with the subjective evaluation of the patients themselves.

The three best studies remedy some of the difficulties with the preceding studies. Cole (1985) uses an objective 5-point scale with a 6-month follow up (though only a small percentage of patients were followed up) and a sample size of $n=128$. This study found that the average improvement for both men and women was 1.59, a modest improvement. Cole (1988) uses a larger sample size, $n=316$, and found an improvement of 1.88. However, the study dropped analysis of those who quit treatment. Also, the follow-up procedure in this study was not recorded.

Last, Dauw (1988) looked at a sample size of $n=489$ using an objective criterion of when a sexual dysfunction had been resolved (e.g., penetrative sex in 75% of attempts). The success rate across the various disorders was 89%. However, the therapeutic course was complex, making it hard to ascribe the gains exclusively to surrogacy. Additionally, follow ups were only three months after treatment and were self-reported.

None of the studies compared the efficacy of surrogate therapy to a control group with no intervention or to an alternative treatment. As a result, the studies provided here suggest that surrogacy has a positive effect on patients, but without controls and more objective criteria, it's hard to know how much confidence to ascribe to the statistics.

Aloni, R. and Katz, S. (2003). Sexual Difficulties after Traumatic Brain Injury and Ways to Deal with It

Ronit Aloni and Schlomo Katz

Methods: Chapter 9 does not report an inquiry into the efficacy of sexual surrogate therapy. Rather this is a literature review and summary of surrogate practices.

Key Results: Studies have shown that sexual surrogacy is effective and practitioners who use sexual therapy for brain-injury survivors recommend it for use with those with mental disabilities.

Aloni, R., Keren, O., and Katz, S. (2007). Sex Therapy Surrogate Partners for Individuals with Very Limited Functional Ability Following Traumatic Brain Injury

Ronit Aloni, O. Keren, and Schlomo Katz

Methods:

TBI=Traumatic Brain Injury

VLFA=Very Limited Functional Ability

This paper is a presentation of a case study of G., a person who suffered a TBI. He was able to move only a fraction of his body with effort and could not walk or switch sleeping positions by himself. He displayed inappropriate sexual advances to female caretakers, visitors, and his sister. It was suggested that he undergo sexual surrogate therapy as a way to reconnect with his sexuality as well as to deepen his understanding of what it was to be a sexual creature.

Key Results: G. was able to achieve a series of cognitive, emotional, and sexual successes. He was able to concentrate for 90 minutes at a time, a large increase over his previous concentration time-frame. He was able to express his desires and emotions, and he was able to learn to masturbate as well as to pleasure the surrogate working with him.

Big Picture: Working with a sexual surrogate can have significant benefits, even for someone with TBI.

Apfelbaum, B. (1984). The Ego-Analytic Approach to Individual Body-Work Sex Therapy: Five Case Examples

Bernard Apfelbaum

Methods: The data in this study were taken from the treatment records of 407 patients treated between 1971 and 1981. Outcome ratings were a number from 1-5 (1=completely successful, 2=largely successful, 3=moderately successful, 4=no change, 5=worse) assigned by the treating co-therapists after reading a post-treatment questionnaire filled out by the patient.

Some patients (n=268) responded to a follow-up survey at six months, and some (n=244) responded to a follow-up survey at one year. The overall distribution of success ratings for those cases with follow ups were not different from the original ratings.

Population

Age range is 19-83 with roughly even frequencies spread through the decades of the 20s through the 60s. Most patients live in the U.S. or Canada. About a third have not been in psychotherapy and do not consider themselves to have psychiatric problems.

Key Results: These results are hard to parse because the following percentages include many types of pathologies.

Of all the patients that were treated (n=407), for all sorts of problems, the ego-centric treatment was:

Completely Successful in 119 patients (29% of the cases)

Largely Successful in 172 patients (40% of the cases)

Moderately Successful in 86 patients (21% of the cases)

No change in 27 patients (7% of the cases)

Worse in 3 patients (1% of the cases)

Big Picture: Subject to the caveats offered by Apfelbaum (see the quote below), it appears that Apfelbaum's body work treatment modality achieved high success in almost 70% (69%) of patients. The treatment made the problem worse or had no impact in only 8% of cases.

Other Notes:

This study evaluates the surrogate "body work" approach of Apfelbaum, which is importantly different than other more traditional surrogate modalities.

Apfelbaum explains, "The term 'bodywork' sex therapy refers to a subfield of the larger field of sex therapy in which paraprofessionals take a variety of roles, from surrogate partner to sensory guide to body work co-therapist, working from a variety of therapeutic models."

Caution from Apfelbaum:

> Outcome ratings collected in one setting should not be compared with outcome ratings collected in another setting unless these are blind ratings done by independent raters using specifiable criteria, corrected for rater bias, and based on adequate information. Our ratings, although typical of those found in the literature, meet none of these criteria. The immediate-outcome ratings are entirely subjective and uncorrected, and are done by the two therapists who treated the case. The follow-up reports consist of self-ratings and brief written comments by the patients. The criteria they are to use is not specified, and there is no opportunity for independent verification or even for inter-views. It is our view that such material can only be evaluated by the therapists who treated the patient. They can decide whether their immediate-outcome ratings should be adjusted on the basis of this new information. These judgments are, of course, no less idiosyncratic than are the immediate-outcome ratings.

Benton, K. and Cotter, S. (2007). It's in the Touch: ... Tantratouch Therapy ... to Assist an Anorgasmic Middle-Aged Male

Kim Benton & Shauna Cotter, 18th Congress of the World Association of Sexual Health.

Method: A single case study of a man suffering from anorgasmia and masturbation incompetence. Data came from the man's self-report.

The patient sought assistance at a Melbourne, Australia sex therapy clinic. A three-month program was devised using two therapists, a psychologist, and a tantra touch therapist. The psychologist used rational emotive behavioral therapy and the tantra therapist provided hands-on therapy.

Key Results: The client reported reaching orgasm during intercourse. He also reported increased sexual enjoyment and masturbation competence.

Big Picture: This is an individual situation where participation with a hands-on sex expert produced improvement in a patient's condition.

Ben-Zion, I., Rothschild, S., Chudakov, B., and Aloni, R. (2007). *Surrogate versus Couple Therapy in Vaginismus*

Itzhak Ben-Zion, Shelly Rothschild, Bella Chudakov, and Ronit Aloni

Method: Data were collected from the records of 16 patients with vaginismus treated with male surrogate therapy and from the records of 16 patients with vaginismus treated with couples therapy.

Success criterion was successful pain-free intercourse upon completion of therapy.

Sample details of the two groups are exhaustive and available in the chart on pg. 730.

Key Results: 100% of the women who were treated with surrogate therapy succeeded in penile-vaginal intercourse. Only 75% of the women treated with couples therapy were able to achieve successful penile-vaginal intercourse.

100% of the women who were treated with surrogate therapy discontinued therapy because it was fully successful. Only 69% of the women in the couples' group opted to discontinue therapy because it was fully successful.

A more precise breakdown of all results is presented on pg. 731.

Big Picture: Surrogate therapy appeared to be much more effective than couples' therapy. This may be for several reasons. (see pg. 732)

1. Surrogates have no sexual dysfunction whereas the partners of the coupled women were affected.

2. Surrogates are more involved in treatment whereas the partners of the coupled women were not as involved.

3. Surrogates do not introduce as much interpersonal tension. Some of the partners of the coupled women left after unsuccessful treatment.

The authors cite surrogacy's high cost as one of its disadvantages.

Cole, M. (1985). Surrogate Sex Therapy. In W. Dryden (Eds.), *Marital Therapy in Britain* (Ch. 5)

Martin Cole

Case Studies: Cole presents two case studies from his practice.

The first involves David and Pauline. They are both virgins after 11 years of marriage, partially owing to their Catholic upbringings. Pauline is afraid to touch David's penis and David doesn't know enough about the vagina to achieve penetration. David works five sessions with a surrogate named Jane with Pauline's consent. Progress is made and David and Pauline are able to have a son.

Michael and Erica were the second couple. They had an unsatisfactory sex life for a while, though they had two children together. Erica had an affair, which devastated Michael's confidence. She gave her consent for Michael to meet with a surrogate, Penny. Michael improved over the course of two months, but the sex life of Michael and Erica, though better, was still not satisfactory.

Methods for Quantitative Study:

Cole used a sample of 128 patients treated by his institute (no time frame given). These 128 patients were subdivided into A, B, and C groups.

A group: Patients who sought care with knowledge and consent of partner; often this resulted in both partners undergoing simultaneous therapy. (I believe Cole is interpreting "partner" narrowly to only include spouses in a marriage.

B group: Patients who sought care without the knowledge and consent of their spouse.

C group: Patients who sought care and were without a partner (divorced, widowed, or separated)

Presenting Problems by subgroup (from pg. 102 of Cole)

	Problem	A group n=37	B group n=59	C group n=32	Total n=128
Male	Erectile Dysfunction	6	24	17	47
	Premature Ejaculation	9	14	5	28
	Retarded Ejaculation	2	1	1	4
	Drive Dysfunction	4	12	1	17
	Sex variation	-	1	-	1
	Physical handicap	-	1	-	1
	Non-consummation	2	1	-	3
	Organogenic	1	1	1	3
	Other	1	2	-	3
Female	Vaginismus / Dyspareunia	2	–	1	3
	Orgasmic Dysfunction	3	2	3	8
	General sex dysfunction	5	-	3	8
	Non-consummation	2	-	-	2

Age and number of treatment sessions, by subgroup

	Group A (n=37)		Group B (n=59)		Group C (n=32)	
	M n=25	F n=12	M n=57	F n=2	M n=25	F n=7
Mean Age (whole sample)	41.7	36.3	44.7	30.0	47.3	34.2
Mean No. of Sessions (whole sample)	4.4	2.6	3.2	9.0	5.7	2.3
Mean no. sessions (excluding drop outs)	4.9 (n=2)	3.0 (n=11)	3.8 (n=47)	9.0 (n=2)	6.9 (n=16)	3.3 (n=4)
Range of program length (treatment sessions)	1-13	1-6	1-14	3-15	1-32	1-7

Key Results:

Cole measures outcome results on a scale of 0-4 for each particular dysfunction. For example, the outcome scale for erectile dysfunction looks like this (pg. 117):

0 – Absolute block to intercourse…

1 – Poor performance, intercourse possible only rarely… High levels of anxiety. Erection never firm but penetration possible occasionally.

2 – Sexual behavior precarious… Sudden loss of erection after penetration not unusual.

3 – Sexual performance adequate but elements remain which reflect the patient's inadequacy.

4 – Sexual performance good, falling within normal range of behavior.

Follow up scores were obtained at least 6 months after treatment.

Sex Is the Least of It

Outcome results by Subgroup

Patient Category	Patient drop out	Mean patient score (excluding drop outs)			
		Presenting	Outcome	Therapeutic Gain	Follow-up
A (25M and 12F)	4M and 1 F	M .43 F .64	M 2.3 F 2.6	1.87 1.96	2.4 (n=10) 2.5 (n=4)
B (57M and 2F)	10M and 0F	M .72 F 1.00	M 2.4 F 1.5	1.68 .5	2.4 (n=12) 0.0 (n=1)
C (25M and 7F)	9M and 3F	M 1.06 F 0.00	M 2.7 F 1.8	1.64 1.80	3.3 (n=6) 2.0 (n=4)
N=128	N=27	N=101			N=37

Big Picture:

Cole found significant improvement in a large number of the patients included in this study. Unfortunately, follow-up numbers are biased and assessments at the time of termination of therapy are likely to decay over time.

Cole, M. (1988). Sex Therapy for Individuals. In M. Cole, and W. Dryden (Eds.), *Sex Therapy in Britain* (Ch. 16)

Martin Cole

Methods: Study data were collected from the participants at the Institute for Sex Education and Research (ISER) who were patients from 1970 to Fall 1986. In this time, there were 425 patients, 390 of which were male. However, only 316 of the patients underwent treatment for long enough to justify including this efficacy. [Note, this decision is questionable as the reason that some people left treatment might have been that the treatment was not working.]

Key Results: The 316 patients (men and women but mostly men) who were included in the final data table had a mean presenting score (i.e., a rating of their symptoms) of 0.44. The final mean outcome score for the group was 2.32, meaning that the average improvement was 1.88. This improvement score comes on a score of a 5-point scale (from 0-4) that Cole tailored for individual symptoms (see the next entry).

Sex Is the Least of It

The complete data results are here for Men:

Presenting Problem	Total sample size n=390	Treatment sample size (n=289)	Percent of total sample	Mean presenting score	Mean outcome score	Therapeutic gain
ED 1 biogenic	7	6	2.1	0	1.3	1.3
ED 1 psychogenic	1	1	<1	0	0	0
ED 1 idiopathic	36	27	9.3	.4	1.6	1.2
ED 2 biogenic	7	6	2.1	.3	1.8	1.5
ED 2 psychogenic	12	10	3.5	.5	3.2	2.7
ED 2 idiopathic	65	46	15.9	.5	1.8	1.3
Premature Ejaculation	47	30	10.4	.6	2.9	2.3
Retarded ejaculation absolute	1	1	<1	0	2.0	2.0
Retarded ejaculation coital	19	17	5.9	.3	1.6	1.3
Heterophobia absolute	95	74	25.6	.2	2.7	2.5
Heterophobia partial	36	28	9.7	.5	2.3	1.8
Low sex drive	1	1	<1	0	0	0
Heterophobe / homophile	12	8	2.8	.3	2.6	2.3
Gender identity role conflicts	1	1	<1	0	0	0
Sexual variation	9	5	1.7	1.0	1.4	.4

ED and PE co-presenting	5	4	1.4	0	1.5	1.5
Desire dysfunction	15	9	3.1	1.0	3.9	2.9
Handicapped	7	5	1.7	.2	2.6	2.4
Medical indication	5	3	1	0	2.0	2.0
Non-consummation	4	4	1.4	0	2.3	2.3
Medical, psychiatric	3	2	<1	0	0	0
Other	2	1	<1	0	0	0
Mean Scores (all men)				.46	2.26	1.80
Total sample both sexes	425	316		.44	2.32	1.88

Big Picture: Cole measured an average improvement of 1.88, since the entire scale is just a 5-point scale, an average improvement of almost 2 points is modest. The number of sampled patients is also one of the larger samples in our collection.

Dauw, D. (1988). Evaluating the Effectiveness of the SECS' Surrogate-Assisted Sex Therapy Model

Dean C. Dauw

Method: 501 cases involving the use of a female sexual surrogate in a Chicago clinic during the years from 1970 to 1980 were evaluated. Surrogacy was used in tandem with traditional psychotherapy. Treatment included self-disclosure and sensate focus exercises.

Surrogacy at this clinic was reserved for only those without partners.

Rigorous home study, cassette tapes, and book reading were employed.

Each case report was generated by the surrogate to the supervising psychologist after each session with the client. The next surrogacy session was planned as these reports were generated.

Sessions were roughly one per week.

Professional Breakdown

95% were professionals of some kind and so had high levels of educational attainment

Religious Breakdown

45% Catholic

40% Jewish

12% Protestant

3% No religious affiliation

Additional Psychiatric Disorders

86% had no additional or previous psychiatric disorders.

Major Dysfunctions that were treated

53% Temporary erectile dysfunction of a psychogenic origin

26% Premature ejaculation

11% Primary impotence

6% Inhibited sexual desire

4% Disturbances of ejaculatory function

Surrogates

Twenty-four surrogates were used, and each one worked on an average of 20.9 cases. Each one had more than 100 hours of training and a master's degree.

Definitions of Success

Successful treatment of erectile dysfunction = ability to maintain erection to orgasm in at least 75% of attempts at intercourse.

Successful treatment of premature ejaculation = ability to maintain an erection for 10 minutes during intercourse.

Successful treatment of inhibited sexual desire = client experiences "normal" sexual desire for partner at least once a week.

Successful treatment of disturbed ejaculation = ejaculation in more than 50% of attempts at intercourse.

Key Results: Success rates were determined by classification according to the above success definitions when the follow up *self-reports* three months after treatment were consistent with the surrogate reports at the end of treatment.

Attrition left 489 cases for the results.

Condition	N	Failures	Successes	Success Rate
Primary Impotence	55	1	54	98.2%
Secondary Impotence	256	39	217	84.8%
Premature Ejaculation	127	5	122	96.0%
Ejaculatory Dysfunction	20	3	17	85.0%
Inhibited Sexual Desire	31	2	29	93.5%
Total	489	50	439	89.77%

Big Picture: Surrogacy-assisted therapy seems to be very effective. Dauw cautions two things. First, success rates may be exaggerated because post therapy self-reports may be biased toward success (people want to think they've been successful). Second, since a cluster of therapies were tested, it's difficult to judge how much each therapy contributed to success.

Dauw compares his clinic's surrogacy therapy to other types of therapy and finds that surrogacy-inclusive therapy is much more effective.

Johnston, D. R. (1978). Some Current Practices in Sex Therapy with Surrogates

David Ross Johnston

Methods: The data for this study were collected by interviewing a total of 28 people: 13 therapists, 13 surrogates, and two clients of surrogates.

Definitions, pg. 14

Tables 1-5 have good comparisons of the major sex therapy practitioners.

Discussion of Masters and Johnson, pg. 48

Discussion of the demographics of all participants, pg. 104-122

Structure of the interviews, pg. 127

Key Results: Three basic approaches were studies, cognitive/behaviorial approach, the holistic/experiential approach, and the adjunctive approach.

Ch. 4 – Ch. 8: Various questions were asked: a range of questions about their attitude toward client type, preferred therapy structure. There was almost nothing about the effectiveness of surrogate therapy. The questions were concerned with what various practitioners thought about SPT therapy. Johnston writes:

> Also, what is the most effective treatment for the client is strictly a value judgment at this point. The most effective treatment structure is simply not known. The data shows there isn't even consensus regarding what constitutes success, let alone procedures to evaluate success. (pg. 292)

On pg. 289, Johnston discusses the issue of role modeling for a few pages, and has some interesting points, one of which is that though a client may "model" future relationships based upon his or her relationship with the surrogate, he may also model his relationship on that between surrogate and therapist, making the character of this relationship important.

Johnston (starting pg. 296) found evidence of sexist attitudes in therapists and surrogates.

Big Picture: This dissertation does not address the effectiveness of surrogacy and echoes practitioners at the time who questioned the results being proffered by sex therapists working with surrogates. The dissertation is designed to give a range of information about how surrogates and therapists approach their work.

Sex Is the Least of It

1. Johnston concludes that cognitive/behavior therapy is risky and relies on a certain degree of emotional maturity to be present in the client. See pg. 306

2. Johnston concludes that holistic/experiential depends on the therapist's ability to differentiate resistance on the part of the client from resistance on the part of the surrogate. See pg. 313

3. Johnston concludes that the adjunctive method is vulnerable to collusion between various parties in the treatment and must be used by a therapist who will take supervision very seriously. See pg. 322

Further conclusions are listed on pgs. 340-343.

Kaye, S. (2000). Surrogate Treatment: A Case Study of 151 Male Clients and Surrogacy Coaching

Susan Kaye

Methods: This was a retrospective, case-based, quantitative study. The data for this study were collected from the archives of three professional surrogates (she calls them surrogate coaches). 151 studies (see table 10 on pg. 96) of Caucasian males from the eastern portion of the United States were used. They participated in surrogate coaching between the years of 1977 to 1992. Long term follow ups were either not available or not conducted and so benefits reported may have been temporary.

Presented problems:

1) late life virginity, 2) erectile dysfunction, 3) premature ejaculation, 4) sexual orientation uncertainty, 5) avoidant personality, 6) orgasmic dysfunction, 7) social phobia, 8) aversion disorder, and 9) significant mental or physical challenges, such as bipolar, autism, and mental retardation.

Surrogate data

Three surrogates, A, B, and C, along their records were used for this study. Details about them are found starting on pg. 68. One was married and one was divorced, all were white, and all were from the east coast.

Client data

151 cases were submitted, all white males. The range of ages was 19 to 71 years old. The median age was 33 and the average age was 35.5 (exhaustive data in Ch. 4)

Key Results:

85% (129/151) of those studied were able to complete sensate focus socialization techniques.

Effectiveness

Of the patients that were able to complete the sensate focus stage of treatment, a majority of participants within each problem category were able to completely solve their problem. The average across all presenting problems was 68%.

271

Sex Is the Least of It

For instance, 8 of those who had an avoidant personality were able to finish sensate focus. Thus, 100% of them resolved their problem of social avoidance.

Of those who finished sensate focus and had a problem with premature ejaculation, 81% were able to solve their premature ejaculation. (complete table on pg. 95)

Big Picture: Of those participants who were able to complete sensate focus therapy, 68% saw the resolution of their problem.

Malamuth, N., Wanderer, Z.W., Sayner, R. B., and Durrell, D. (1976). *Utilization of Surrogate Partners: A Survey of Health Professionals*

Neil Malamuth, Zev W. Wanderer, Richard B. Sayner, and Doris Durrell

Method: Survey mailed out to various professional publications. 111 participants

Professional Breakdown

72% Licensed psychologists

9% Psychiatrists

8% Licensed social workers

11% Including physicians and marriage counselors

Sex Breakdown

78% Male

22% Female

Prior Use of Surrogacy

28% of the respondents indicated that they had referred a client to a surrogate.

Key Results: 87% of the respondents (~96), said that if it were legal, they would refer a client to a surrogate partner. Previous use of a surrogate was correlated with willingness to refer (everyone who had previously referred to a surrogate would do so again), but even so, 78% of those who had not referred to a surrogate before would be willing to do so.

Big Picture: Most professionals working in mental health/overall wellness would be willing to give surrogacy a chance.

Roberts, B. (1978). Utilization of a Surrogate Couple in the Treatment of a Sexually Dysfunctional Couple

Barbara Roberts

Method: Study of "Jack," late 50s, and his wife "Jill." Jack initiated therapy due to his anxiety about sex along with his belief that he suffered from premature ejaculation.

This paper contains a verbatim report from Cecily Green, the surrogate who worked with Jack.

There is also a verbatim report from Bill Lyon, the sexual surrogate for Jill. Jill's use of a surrogate came after Cecily Green treated Jack. Jill reported 30 years of painful sex, lack of trust in a man, and emotional withdrawal.

Key Results:

The data presented in this paper was not qualitative. Rather it was based on the reports of the two surrogates. As such, distilling this paper is tricky.

Jack worked first with a surrogate and made complete, total improvement. It's not clear what happened when he returned home to his wife, as she soon enrolled for treatment. She worked with a surrogate. The work was effective and exposed that she had lesions on her labia that needed to be repaired before she could have sex that was pleasant and not painful.

After conjoint surrogacy failed to repair the sexual trust between Jack and Jill, they both came in together to work simultaneously with a surrogate couple. Jack and Jill worked jointly with two surrogates (I presume Bill and Cecily) and they were briefly separated so that Jack could have his previous learning reinforced.

Big Picture: The therapy was deemed successful, though it appeared that there was a risk of both partners backsliding and thus the recommendation that Jack and Jill continue with marriage counseling.

Sommers, F. (1978). Treatment of Male Sexual Dysfunction in a Psychiatric Practice Integrating the Sexual Therapy Practitioner

Frank G. Sommers

Method:

Df. STPs = Sexual Therapy Practitioners

Study of a group of 12 patients undergoing "sexual therapy." Data collection includes psychiatric interviews, socioeconomic data, presence or absence of nonsexual pathologies, and responses to questionnaires and MPI's.

The course of treatment takes place over 10-15 sessions over about four months (average client received 10 sessions with a range of 6 sessions to 14 sessions). The STP works with an overseeing therapist and the client, STP, and therapist meet to discuss treatment. At this point, the article goes into great detail about how candidates are selected and the tests that take place before sessions with the STP begin.

All SPT sessions take place at the client's home.

Composition of 12 Clients

Age

Average age: 32

Age range: 21-50

Religions at Birth

Jewish: 3

Roman Catholic: 5

Eastern Orthodox: 1

Greek Orthodox: 1

Anglican: 1

Agnostic: 1

Sex Is the Least of It

<u>Presenting Complaint</u>

Erectile dysfunction: 9

Ejaculatory control: 3

<u>Complete Breakdown of Diagnoses</u>

Primary Impotence: 4

Secondary Impotence: 5

Premature Ejaculation: 3

<u>Other Psychiatric Diagnoses</u>

Depressive neurosis: 3

Secondary depression with anxiety: 4

Secondary depression: 2

Secondary anxiety: 1

No psychiatric diagnosis: 2

Key Results:

Outcome results were operationalized using the responses to a questionnaire along a 7-point scale. Questions were things like: "Being able to anticipate having intercourse without fear, anxiety, or resentment."

<u>Results</u>

Complete relief of presenting complaint: 75% (9 clients)

Improvement: 17% (2 clients)

Equivocal improvement: 8% (1 client)

These results held after an average follow-up period of 17 months

Big Picture:

STP therapy was completely effective at remedying a large majority of patient complains.

Zilbergeld, B. (1975). Group Treatment of Sexual Dysfunction in Men Without Partners

Bernie Zilbergeld

Method: This study focused on groups of 7-8 participants (single men) led in a weekly session by two co-leaders. The results were collected by group-leader evaluations of *self-reports* by the group participants in the first of six groups that were run with this methodology.

One thing to note is the study involved single men, but this involved men who were socially isolated in a more robust sense, single in the traditional sense, and others who were dating or married, but who did not want to bring partners to therapy (or whose partners did not want to come).

Key Results: Two-thirds of the participants felt they had "completely achieved" their goals. Since the main issues were ejaculatory control and erectile dysfunction, one presumes that the goals involved were related.

A huge majority of the remaining third felt they were having more success with erections and with ejaculations.

A very small minority (two or three men) were not having sex with their partners and so, even though they expressed optimism about using what they had learned in therapy, it was hard to evaluate how grounded their optimism was.

Big Picture: This study was conducted under the assumption that though sexual surrogacy can be effective in treating partnerless men with sexual issues, there were cost and feasibility issues that make exploration of group therapy worthwhile. Group therapy was found to be effective at resolving certain sexual issues in partnerless men. There may even be advantages of group therapy over individual treatment.

Additional Notes:

Some of the techniques in *Progress group and family therapy*. Edited by Clifford J. Sager and Helen Singer Kaplan.

Masters and Johnson are cited as an example of successful surrogacy.

The main techniques used in the group therapy sessions were controlled masturbation, self-disclosure, assertiveness training, and relaxation training,

References

Aloni, R. and Katz, S. (2003). *Sexual Difficulties after Traumatic Brain Injury and Ways to Deal with It.* Springfield, IL: Charles C. Thomas.

Aloni, R., Keren, O., and Katz, S. (2007). Sex Therapy Surrogate Partners for Individuals with Very Limited Functional Ability Following Traumatic Brain Injury. *Sexual Disability,* (25), 125-134.

Apfelbaum, B. (1984). The Ego-Analytic Approach to Individual Body-Work Sex Therapy: Five Case Examples. *The Journal of Sex Research, 20*(1), 44-70.

Benton, K. and Cotter, S. (2007). It's in the Touch: … Tantratouch Therapy … to Assist an Anorgasmic Middle-Aged Male. *Presentation at the 18th World Association of Sexual Health.* Sydney, Australia.

Ben-Zion, I., Rothschild, S., Chudakov, B., and Aloni, R. (2007). Surrogate versus Couple Therapy in Vaginismus. *Journal of Sexual Medicine, 4*(3), 728-733.

Cole, M. (1985). Surrogate Sex Therapy. In W. Dryden (Eds.), *Marital Therapy in Britain* (Ch. 5). London: Harper and Row.

Cole, M. (1988). Sex Therapy for Individuals. In M. Cole, and W. Dryden (Eds.), *Sex Therapy in Britain* (Ch. 16). Open University Press.

Dauw, D. (1988). Evaluating the Effectiveness of the SECS' Surrogate-Assisted Sex Therapy Model. *The Journal of Sex Research, 21*(1), 269-275.

Johnston, D. R. (1978). *Some Current Practices in Sex Therapy with Surrogates.* (Unpublished Doctoral Dissertation). California School of Professional Psychology, Los Angeles.

Kaye, S. (2000). *Surrogate Treatment: A Case Study of 151 Male Clients and Surrogacy Coaching.* (Unpublished Doctoral Dissertation), The Institute for Advanced Study of Human Sexuality, San Francisco.

Malamuth, N., Wanderer, Z.W., Sayner, R. B., and Durrell, D. (1976). Utilization of Surrogate Partners: A Survey of Health Professionals. *Journal of Behavior Therapy and Experimental Psychiatry, 7*(2) 149-150.

Roberts, B. (1978). Utilization of a Surrogate Couple in the Treatment of a Sexually Dysfunctional Couple. *Presentation at the Society for the Scientific Study of Sex, Western Region – Sixth Conference, June 9, 10, 11.* Santa Barbara, California.

Sommers, F. (1978). Treatment of Male Sexual Dysfunction in a Psychiatric Practice Integrating the Sexual Therapy Practitioner. *Presentation at the 3rd International Congress of Sexology, October 25, 1978.* Rome, Italy.

Zilbergeld, B. (1975). Group Treatment of Sexual Dysfunction in Men Without Partners. *Journal of Sex & Marital Therapy, 1*(3): 204-214.

Appendix B: Portrayals of Surrogates in the Media

The Sessions

Therapy at Its Most Touching

'The Sessions,' With John Hawkes and Helen Hunt

By Stephen Holden

Published: October 18, 2012

At the risk of sounding hyperbolic, I would like to nominate John Hawkes and Helen Hunt in "The Sessions" as the movie couple of the year. Their extraordinary connection while re-enacting the true story of a disabled, virginal 38-year-old writer and his sexual surrogate infuses the movie, written and directed by Ben Lewin, with a piercing depth of humanity and no small amount of humor.

Mr. Hawkes, the brilliant, chameleonic actor lauded for his sinister portrayals of a backwoods meth dealer in "Winter's Bone" and of a Charles Manson-like cult leader in "Martha Marcy May Marlene," plays Mark O'Brien, a poet, writer and journalist who died in 1999 at 49. Ms. Hunt portrays Cheryl Cohen Greene, the sex therapist he hires to guide him toward his first experience of intercourse.

Arriving in a culture steeped in titillation, prurience and pornographic imagery, "The Sessions" is a pleasant shock: a touching, profoundly sex-positive film that equates sex with intimacy, tenderness and emotional connection instead of performance, competition and conquest. There are moments between the client and his surrogate that are so intensely personal that your first instinct may be to avert your eyes. But the actors' lighthearted rapport allows you to rejoice unashamedly in their characters' pleasure.

That is not to imply that "The Sessions" is visually more explicit than it need be. During much of the therapy, Ms. Hunt is nude. But the camera angles avoid showing genitalia. At the same time, when penetration is achieved, the body language and clinical dialogue clarify exactly what is happening and what is being experienced.

Mr. O'Brien has already been the subject of an Oscar-winning documentary short, "Breathing Lessons: The Life and Work of Mark O'Brien" (1996), directed by Jessica Yu. This new film is largely adapted from Mr. O'Brien's article "On Seeing a Sex Surrogate," published in 1990 in the literary magazine The Sun.

The back story: At 6, he contracted polio and lost most of his mobility and muscle coordination, but not his sensation, below the neck. He was forced to rely on artificial respiration for all but a few hours a week. His parents, instead of sending him to a nursing home, cared for him, and he attended the University of California, Berkeley, transporting himself by an electric gurney between the campus and his apartment, where his iron lung was located.

Mr. O'Brien, who was 4 feet 7 inches tall and weighed only 60 pounds (Mr. Hawkes is 5-foot-10), wrote his poems and articles by holding a stick between his teeth to tap words on a computer and to make telephone calls.

The story is set in Berkeley in 1988. A Roman Catholic, Mark consults with Father Brendan (William H. Macy), a supportive, open-minded priest, before proceeding with therapy. "I know in my heart that God will give you a free pass on this one—go for it," Father Brendan reassures him.

Mark, who is understandably sardonic about his faith, says: "I believe in a God with a sense of humor. I would find it absolutely intolerable not to be to able blame someone for all this."

From the moment Ms. Hunt appears, "The Sessions" becomes a different movie on a much higher plane. Cheryl has never worked with someone like Mark, who must remain on his back, his thin, fragile body painfully contorted. This married woman is exploring uncharted territory every bit as much as Mark, and the therapy is a dual journey in discovery. Inevitably, she makes mistakes.

Her ground rules are strict—the maximum number of sessions is six—and she voices them with the firmness of an elementary schoolteacher addressing a class and setting boundaries. But once their sessions begin, she applies herself with intense dedication, asking how this or that feels.

Mark, who has never been touched this way before, experiences waves of sensation that to his humiliation cause him to ejaculate uncontrollably. Each time Mark disappoints himself, Cheryl remains a reassuring, encouraging coach, and they make progress.

Mr. Hawkes is entirely convincing in his portrayal of a man who is by turns vulnerable, wittily self-lacerating, charming and erudite. You can feel how increasingly difficult it is for both partners to follow the rules once they have reached a certain level of intimacy.

The other aspects of the movie, though well executed, are little more than tasteful décor around which the main drama revolves. You won't forget it.

"The Sessions" is Rated R

Nudity, Sexual Situations and Clinical Sexual Terminology

http://www.nytimes.com/2012/10/19/movies/the-sessions-with-john-hawkes-and-helen-hunt.html

Private Practices

Private Practices: The Story of a Sex Surrogate (1985)

By Walter Goodman

Published: September 26, 1986

The first thing to be said about "Private Practices" is that it treats in remarkably straightforward fashion a subject that has a way of bringing out clinical pretentiousness or juvenile snickers. Kirby Dick's documentary, which opens today at the Bleecker Street Cinema after having been shown at the Margaret Mead Film Festival at the American Museum of Natural History, is subtitled "The Story of a Sex Surrogate."

The surrogate in question is a Los Angeles woman, probably in her early thirties, who when the documentary was made, in 1982, was serving 10 clients a week, referred to her by their own therapists. We meet two of them, a 25-year-old called Kipper, who can't bring himself to make an approach to a woman, and a 45-year-old called John, whose marriage and a subsequent relationship broke up, he believes, because of his sexual inadequacies.

The movie begins with the men's somewhat nervous arrival at the home of the surrogate, Maureen Sullivan, who is attractive and inviting enough to defeat most male inhibitions. In addition to sitting in on parts of their subsequent sessions, we also meet both the men's and Miss Sullivan's psychotherapists and relatives.

In the months leading up to the men's final, reluctant farewells, we witness the techniques (too formal a word perhaps for Miss Sullivan's natural manner) by which she encourages sexual self-regard. With her alluring body and soft ways, she is the incarnation of common male fantasies: "I want you to take pleasure doing anything you want to do using my body." She assures her clients of their attractiveness and of the pleasure they are giving her. When she compliments Kipper—"This is as good as it ever gets"—you may suspect she tells that to all the men. Still, you'll have no trouble believing that her ministrations can help a fellow gain confidence or that when the time comes, Kipper and John should be downcast about breaking off from so forthcoming a therapist.

The camera of Christine Burrill and Catherine Coulson manages to be at once explicit and discreet. We see a lot, but not everything. Several of the scenes are highly sensual, with not a hint of prurience. There are a few mentions along the way of the documentary team's cameras and lights, but from all appearances, the participants soon got used to them.

Why is Miss Sullivan in this line of work? Nobody mentions money; we don't learn how much she charges. But there seems to be something more. Her responses to an off-screen interviewer, a session with her own therapist and an affecting conversation with her father and brother reveal that despite appearances, she is no model of sexual health. By working on others, she is somehow working on herself. "I have so much to learn," she jokes, "that I have to practice 10 times a week." (A postscript reports that two years after the movie was filmed, she had found a boyfriend and was taking fewer clients.) No discussion of sex surrogates can avoid a certain amount of silly-sounding stuff. (Miss Sullivan talks about "sharing," and John says earnestly, "It's been a rewarding experience.") But witnessing Miss Sullivan in action allays skepticism. Whatever her training—another matter we are not informed about—she appears to have a natural sympathy for the worries of her clients, what she calls Kipper's "super uptightness" and John's shame about his tendency to premature ejaculation. No doubt her performance is practiced, the apparent spontaneity professionally controlled, but she knows how to use her feelings as well as her body to give her clients a boost to the ego and to the id as well.

Her method involves a lot of touching, and when the time arrives for separation, you may be touched, too, by this sympathetic account of a sort of human frailty that is not easy to talk about, much less make a movie about.

Sex Surrogate – Private Practices, directed and produced by Kirby Dick; camera, Christine Burrill and Catherine Coulson; edited by Lois Freeman and Mr. Dick; released by the Kino International Corporation. At the Bleecker Street Cinema 1, 144 Bleecker Street, at La Guardia Place.

Running time: 75 minutes.

This film has no rating.

Sex Is the Least of It

Interviewers…Catherine Coulson and Kirby Dick;

Narration…Noreen Hennesey

Review from *The New York Times*:

http://www.nytimes.com/movie/review?res=9A0DEFD71630F935A1575AC0A960948260

The Surrogate
(An Israeli film 2008)

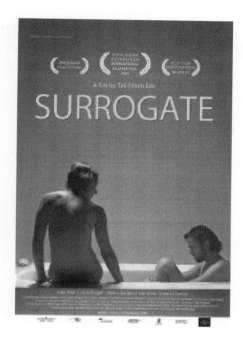

A film by Tali Shalom Ezer

Winner of Best Film Award in the International Women's Film Festival Israel.

Official selection Edinburgh International Film Festival 2009 - Jerusalem Film Festival

A story about a man who turns to sexual therapy with a surrogate.

Eli is a 32 year old man who has problems with relationships with women. Hagar is a surrogate, an alternative partner for practical, sexual therapy.

They meet once a week and practice a relationship and intimacy in laboratory conditions. The fictitious relationship between them exposes them both physically and emotionally and brings to surface repressed fears from the real world.

The changes Eli goes through during the therapy, along with the secrets revealed, not only shake his own life, but also the life of his family.

Website: http://www.surrogatethemovie.com/english.php

IMDB page - http://www.imdb.com/title/tt1407081/

Movie Trailer - https://www.youtube.com/watch?v=m04UEFbcqhM

Sex Is the Least of It

Television Series Episodes

Barney Miller

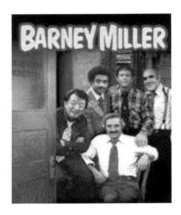

Barney investigates a sex clinic that more closely resembles a brothel. Harris investigates a rash of crimes apparently committed by a juvenile. Weary of waiting for a promotion, Levitt announces that he's quitting the force.

http://www.hulu.com/watch/47963

LA Law

Rollins feels exploited when he's asked to assist on the Chisholm case; a surprise witness testifies in Rosalind's suit; Brackman considers breaking off with sex surrogate Marilyn after one of her clients dies.

www.youtube.com/watch?v=B9nKhBTGbkk

At approximately 25 minutes he ends his relationship with a sex surrogate

Mary Hartman, Mary Hartman

In an episode, Mary invites Mona, her sex therapist, over to the house and invents a reason to rush out, leaving Tom and Mona alone together; Mary and Charlie bond over their mutual hatred of Muriel; Cathy and Dennis have their date; and Mona reveals to Tom that she is a sexual surrogate whom Mary has hired to help him with his performance anxiety. Commercials deleted.

Sex Is the Least of It

Franklin and Bash (TNT)

Season 3 Episode 3 - https://www.youtube.com/watch?v=Q5njZsY-Dak#t=0

Jane Seymour continues her limited story arc on TNT's "Franklin & Bash" Wednesday night, where she needs the title characters to get her acquitted of a prostitution charge. Seymour plays Coleen Bash, the mother of Peter (Mark-Paul Gosselaar), who happens to be a sex surrogate.

So really the episode is about how they tried to defend [Coleen] and understand what it is she actually did and is doing … It's very funny and needless to say the two guys banter with one another, and Peter is completely teased by his partner for having a mother who is a sex surrogate.

Masters of Sex (Showtime)

Masters of Sex is a one hour drama starring Emmy and BAFTA Award nominee Michael Sheen and acclaimed actress Lizzy Caplan, who portray the real-life pioneers of the science of human sexuality, William Masters and Virginia Johnson. The series chronicles the unusual lives, romance and pop culture trajectory of Masters and Johnson. Their research touched off the sexual revolution and took them from a Midwestern teaching hospital in St Louis to the cover of Time magazine and nearly a dozen appearances on Johnny Carson's couch. (http://www.sho.com/sho/masters-of-sex/home)

Preview - http://www.youtube.com/watch?v=JqwahKjI2bg

Strange Sex on TLC

What Is a Sex Surrogate? - What is a sex surrogate and what do they really do? Learn what a sex surrogate is, how common they are, and how they can help those with sexual issues.

http://www.discoveryfitandhealth.com/tv-shows/my-sex-surrogate/what-is-a-sex-surrogate-.htm

Strange Sex (Season 2): Sexual Surrogate (Video) - After 15 years of marriage, Monique and Nate can no longer live with their sexual issues. To enhance their sex life, they've enlisted the help of a sex surrogate.

http://www.discoveryfitandhealth.com/tv-shows/specials/videos/strange-sex-season-2-sexual-surrogate.htm

My Sex Surrogate {Repackage}: Clive & Cheryl (Video) - Clive (45) and Rosie (29) are both virgins - but not by choice. Follow their journeys as they embark on a radical course of sex therapy in the hopes of getting

http://www.discoveryfitandhealth.com/tv-shows/my-sex-surrogate/videos/rosie.htm

Strange Sex (Season 2): Thumbs Up (Video) - Rafe is a quadriplegic who has recently discovered his "surrogate penis." Tonight, he has a date.

www.discoveryfitandhealth.com/tv-shows/specials/videos/strange-sex-season-2-thumbs-up.htm

Sex Is the Least of It

National Geographic TV

Experts believe the use of sex surrogates in sex education began in the 1960s when Masters and Johnson used sex surrogates in their research into body function during arousal. The success rate of treating sexual problems with sexual counseling and surrogacy is believed to be near 90 percent. There used to be about 200 surrogates in the U.S. Now there are about 50. This decrease occurred in the mid-1980s with the increase in AIDS incidences.

Cheryl Cohen Greene begins at approximately 20 min

http://ohnotheydidnt.livejournal.com/60391257.html

About Tova Feder

Dr. Feder received her undergraduate degree in psychology from Ohio University. She worked as a social worker and community organizer for one of the largest family mental health agencies in Los Angeles. In pursuit of an advanced degree on the graduate level, she studied psychology at Antioch University at its Marina Del Rey campus in Los Angeles, California.

Dr. Feder then completed her studies at the Institute for the Advanced Study of Human Sexuality where she received her Ph.D. She is also a credentialed Sex Educator and Clinical Sexologist. She has continued post-graduate studies in psychology and human sexuality at UCLA. She maintains a private practice in West Los Angeles.

She is a nationally recognized expert in human sexuality, particularly sexual dysfunction. She works primarily with the behavioral "sensate focus" approach pioneered by sex researchers Masters and Johnson. Her practice includes couples, singles, men, and women. She is also a certified dating coach, which enables her to work with shy clients to help them develop their social skills.

She is a member of the American College of Sexologists. She is the author of eight books.

Books by Dr. Tova Feder

When Pleasure Becomes Pressure - http://www.amazon.com/dp/B005DSDB5A

Tantra: The Mystic Sensual Journey - http://www.amazon.com/dp/B00B4FCVCA

Building Better Erections: Get Hard, Stay Hard - http://www.amazon.com/dp/B005DRWMSS

The Body Sensual: 5 Senses That Arouse Your Passions -
http://www.amazon.com/dp/B005EH5RE8

Measuring Up - http://www.amazon.com/dp/B005DOMU0Q

Lasting Longer: Everyman's Guide to Prolonging Sex -
http://www.amazon.com/dp/B005DRWNLE

Why Don't You Understand What I'm Saying? A Communication Guide for Men and Women -
http://www.amazon.com/dp/B005DSD85S

Sex Is the Least of It - *http://www.amazon.com/Sex-Least-Surrogate-Partners-Intimacy-ebook/dp/B00LH5WJLK/* *(digital and paperback available)*

Sexual Intimacy and Healing for Couples: (est. 2015)

Printed in Great Britain
by Amazon.co.uk, Ltd.,
Marston Gate.